COLOR

for Philosophers

C. L. Hardin

L O R

for Philosophers

Unweaving the Rainbow

Hackett Publishing Company
Indianapolis/Cambridge

Winner of the 1986 Johnsonian Prize in Philosophy

The paper in this book meets the guidelines for permanence and durability established by the Committee on Production Guidelines for Book Longevity of the Council on Library Resources.

Designed by Mark E. Van Halsema

For further information, please address
Hackett Publishing Company
P.O. Box 44937
Indianapolis, Indiana 46204

Library of Congress Cataloging-in-Publication Data

Hardin, C. L., 1932–
Color for philosophers.

Bibliography: p.
Includes index.
1. Color (Philosophy) I. Title.
B105.C455H37 1987   535.6′01   87-15160
ISBN 0-87220-040-X
ISBN 0-87220-039-6 (pbk.)

9-8-89
at

To Eva,
who brought color into my life

C O N T E N T S

Foreword by Arthur Danto   ix
Preface   xv
Introduction   xix

I   Color Perception and Science

   The physical causes of color   1
   The camera and the eye   7
   Perceiving lightness and darkness   19
   Chromatic vision   26
   Chromatic response   36
   The structure of phenomenal hues   40
   Object metamerism, adaptation, and contrast   45
   Some mechanisms of chromatic perception   52

II   The Ontology of Color

   Objectivism   59
   Standard conditions   67
   Normal observers   76
   Constancy and crudity   82
   Chromatic democracy   91
   Sense data as color bearers   96
   Materialist reduction and the illusion of color   109

III   Phenomenology and Physiology

   THE RELATIONS OF COLORS TO EACH OTHER   113
   The resemblances of colors   113
   The incompatibilities of colors   121
   Deeper problems   127

   OTHER MINDS   134
   Spectral inversions and asymmetries   134

Internalism and externalism 142
Other colors, other minds 145

COLOR LANGUAGE 155
Foci 155
The evolution of color categories 165
Boundaries and indeterminacy 169
Establishing boundaries 182

Color Plates *following page 88*
Appendix: Land's Retinex Theory of Color Vision 187
Notes 195
Glossary of Technical Terms 209
Further Reading 216
Bibliography 217
Acknowledgments 234
Indexes 237

FOREWORD

Very few today still believe that philosophy is a disease of language and that its deliverances, due to disturbances of the grammatical unconscious, are neither true nor false but nonsense. But the fact remains that, very often, philosophical theory stands to positive knowledge roughly in the relationship in which hysteria is said to stand to anatomical truth. Freud said, famously, that hysteria appears to have no knowledge of physiology, for its paralyses and tics, its incapacities and pains, are located by the sufferer where there is no objective possibility of their occurring. Philosophers erase entities in defiance of common sense and postulate entities of which there is not the slightest possibility of scientific confirmation. Parsimonious with one hand and profligate with the other, philosophers behave not only as though they had no knowledge of scientific truth but as if philosophy had its own authority, and not only did not need but could not use information from science. "Oh?" I have heard philosophers sneer when a bit of positive knowledge seemed to bear upon something they said or worried about, "I didn't think one had to *know* anything in order to do philosophy."

My own etiology of this supercilious attitude takes us back to the *Tractatus Logico-Philosophicus* as its ultimate pathogen. On the one hand there is the celebrated dismissal of philosophical propositions as not really propositions at all, but symptoms of grammatical disorder. On the other hand there is the claim that "Philosophy is not one of the natural sciences," together with its parenthetical gloss that "The word 'philosophy' must mean something that stands above or below, but not beside the natural sciences." It must be such remarks as these that encouraged the view that no natural science need be known by the philosopher in order to do philosophy. And this view remained when the other claims about philosophy-as-nonsense abated as the Verificationist Criterion of Meaningfulness itself slowly unraveled, leaving philosophers free to pursue their ontological adventures without regard to the cautions recommended by Verificationism, which is what Wittgenstein's bold diagnosis of philosophical language became in coarser minds than his. Free and independent of empirical constraints, philosophy began to establish a kingdom "above or below" the sciences and hence, with no real geographical relationship to the real world, which the natural sciences have it as their prerogative to represent and explain.

In truth, I believe, the borders of philosophy remain vague and tentative, and more often than not philosophers believe themselves to be operating within their own domain when they have instead encroached upon the territories of positive knowledge and display analyses as their own which in fact collide with empirical truth. If philosophy indeed is autonomous to the point that it can be practiced in indifference to the actual world, then it plainly follows that if an analysis, presented as philosophical, in fact goes shipwreck against empirical truth, it was not philosophy to begin with. It was instead pre-emptive science hidden as such from its practitioners by a bad theory of philosophy and disguised as something higher or lower than natural science, when it was finally *just* bad science. The symptomatology of neurosis remains, even though all the warriors of therapeutic Positivism have died and their pennants lie trampled in the dust. The disease so much of philosophy consists of is the belief that it *is* philosophy when in fact it is something else.

The topic of color provides a marvelous case study for the psychotherapy of philosophy, for there is a rich—or at least copious—literature devoted to it which has no value except as a symptom of something having gone wrong: its authors thought they were elucidating conceptual structures—"the logic of our language"—when their problems had to do not with concepts or logic or language, but with the way the world is given to us. That something could not be at once all-over red and all-over green was widely accepted by philosophers as true, but they saw it as their task to analyze the "could not" in the claim and hence the status of the proposition with which it was expressed. Was it analytic and hence a matter of meaning? Or synthetic but necessary and hence a matter of something far less well understood? It certainly did not appear to be the sort of logical incompatibility involved in "Something could not at once be all-over red and not all-over red." For that would suggest that something could not at once be all-over blue and all-over red, when in fact there are reddish blues and bluish reds. But there are not—and it seemed could not be—reddish greens and greenish reds.

David Pears wrote an article deemed sufficiently important to publish in an anthology, *Logic and Language* (both volumes of which were canonical reading in the 1950s), on the topic of color incompatibilities. According to Pears, the puzzling sentence seemed both *a priori* and true. So it was dismissed *a priori*, we might say, as *a posteriori*. If it were *a posteriori* and contingent, one could look for exceptions. But—and the riposte typifies the official philosophical attitude of the era—"Anyone who began to look for exceptions would betray that he did not really understand the sentence." Since Pears saw no way in which there could coherently be exceptions, and no way either in which it could rest on a matter of meaning or of logic, he found the "could not" baffling and almost incomprehensible.

Pears might have found some help had he considered some further color relationships in his discussion. It would be curious, for example, that 'red' and 'green' should be incompatible as terms when 'red' was not incompatible with 'yellow.' Or that red and green could not co-occupy the same area when red and yellow were as chummy as coffee and cream. Convinced as he was that the problem was essentially philosophical and that philosophy analyzes language, he turned at right angles from where the truth was to be found, and addressed himself, with characteristic—if, in this instance misdirected—ingenuity, to rules of designation: semantical epicycles, as it were, inserted to preserve the autonomy of philosophy.

Of course the information he needed, to turn aside from the problem as not philosophical at all, was not widely available at the time. *Logic and Language: Series II* was published in 1953. The crucial paper of Hurvich and Jameson, "An Opponent-process Theory of Color Vision" came out in the *Psychological Review* in 1957, though preliminary studies appeared as early as 1955. The red-green incompatibility had to do neither with language nor with colors, considered in abstraction from optical physiology. It had to do rather with how we are made, with how color is processed behind the retina, and with this discovery an entire philosophical literature shivered into disuetude. The problem never had been philosophical. The philosophers who dealt with it were doing anticipatory science badly. Their thought was as obsolete as astrology. "I am not the outcome or meeting point of numerous causal agencies which determine my bodily or psychological make-up," Merleau-Ponty wrote, wrongly, rejecting as not to the point for self-understanding exactly what was to the point. How we see is what we are.

In the September 9, 1983, issue of *Science,* I read a paper with a title that ought to have been evidence that its authors did not understand their language, had Pears been right: "On Seeing Reddish Green and Yellowish Blue." From the perspective of conceptual analysis, this would have been like coming across an article called "On Squaring the Circle and Duplicating the Cube." One ought to have known, *a priori,* that the paper, if not merely jocular or arch, must be incoherent or false. Instead, the article in *Science* was informative and true, its title descriptively accurate, and it reported certain exceptions to the misclassified statement regarding red-green incompatibility, now seen to be *a posteriori* and admitting of exceptions. Its "Abstract" read as follows:

> Some dyadic color names (such as reddish green and bluish yellow) describe colors that are not normally realizable. By stabilizing the retinal image of the boundary between a pair of red and green stripes (or a pair of yellow and blue stripes), but not their outer edges, however, the entire region can be perceived simultaneously as both red and green (or blue and yellow).

Under laboratory conditions specified in the body of the paper, observers reported that, among other alternatives, "the entire field appears to be a single unitary color composed of both red and green." And against the background assumptions of philosophical analysis, this would be like inducing an experience of a single unitary plane figure composed of a circle and a square.

I clipped this striking report by H. D. Crane and T. P. Piantanida, and used it to mark the place in my copy of *Logic and Language: Second Series* which tells its earnest readers that such results are impossible. And I have often read them to my seminar students in philosophical psychology, as a salutary warning that, although Wittgenstein may be absolutely correct that psychology is no closer to philosophy than is any of the other natural sciences, the implication may well be that we were not really doing philosophy in the seminar. But perhaps neither are the legions who are writing today about minds and machines, propositional attitudes and Eliminative Materialism, what it's like to be a bat and neurophilosophy, linguistic competence and image rotation.

Consider, just for instance, the extremely popular concept of Functionalism. Functionalism is an attractive idea to philosophers these days, just because it exempts them from having to know something in order to do the philosophy of mind. Thus they need know nothing about the actual brain, the jocular point being made that it does not matter *what* the skull is stuffed with as long as we have similarity of input and output. And the thought is that the structures of interest to philosophers of mind might be realized in any number of different systems, the brain being only one. It is an approach encouraged by a perhaps premature assumption that we and the high-speed digital computer are ontological peers. But suppose we are not? Suppose it can be shown, as John Searle, surely too precipitously, has contended in his famous paper on artificial intelligence, that only the brain can realize intentionality? Suppose we are alone in the universe, or at least unique, by virtue of possessing brains, and that the issues are only irresponsibly thought to be open to philosophical fantasies and metaphysical imagination! The nature of philosophy, the scope and limitations of philosophical knowledge, is the great unsolved philosophical problem to this very day.

No better place can be found for beginning to rethink the limitations on our capability as philosophers than Larry Hardin's wise and beautiful book about color. It is not just that he gives us the knowledge we had not thought it necessary to have in order to do philosophy. He demonstrates, irresistibly and irrefutably, how barren philosophical discussion of color is without this knowledge. Philosophical questions about color fall to the ground, as if infected by an unknown virus, as Hardin's deft, elegant, and informed arguments proceed, and the landscape is strewn with dead and dying philosophy by the time the book ends. The virus in question is truth, and its bearer is something philosophers thought themselves immune to, namely science.

There is a wonderful and moving passage in one of Bertrand Russell's autobiographical writings, in which he recalls the intoxication he and G. E. Moore felt when they decided Idealism was wrong. They suddenly walked about in the real world after having long believed that it was all somehow in their minds. There is a comparable intoxication in discovering that certain phenomena are real rather than artifacts of language, to be dealt with through the methods of science rather than the analysis of words. How sweet it after all is to be in touch with truth! How profoundly refreshing to leave behind rules of designation, appeals to imaginary cases, or the cat's cradle of possible world semantics and to learn that the complexities are not in our language but in ourselves and in the world.

As an editor of *The Journal of Philosophy*, I was thrilled that my colleagues agreed that this book should receive the Johnsonian Prize for 1986. But as a philosopher, I was even more profoundly gratified that the *Journal* had helped bring into print a book of the widest significance, one that no one, even if his or her sole concern with color is to epistemologize over "Red patch now!" or to test whether good is simple and unanalyzable like yellow, can afford to neglect.

Arthur C. Danto
New York, 1987

P R E F A C E

It is said that philosophy begins in wonder. The piece of philosophy you are now holding in your hand certainly did. For years I had thought intermittently about the nature of phenomenal color and found it to be utterly opaque to my intellect. Then one day I read a passing comment in Sydney Shoemaker's "The Inverted Spectrum" concerning Bernard Harrison's claim that there are empirical grounds for supposing a spectral inversion to be impossible. This elicited from me a Hobbesian "By God, this cannot be!" and I hurried off to the library to see what scientists were saying these days about asymmetries in color perception. I did not expect much. Earlier pronouncements about the relevance of perceptual psychology to philosophical questions had proved to be mostly hot air, and nothing that I had heretofore encountered about the mechanisms of color vision had advanced my philosophical thinking about colors by as much as half a step.

A query to a colleague in psychophysics, Joe Sturr, put me on the track of Leo M. Hurvich's *Color Vision,* and it was with the reading of this book that the wonder began. The reason for the incompatibility of red with green, which had puzzled me from my first days in graduate school many years ago, suddenly became clear. Slowly but steadily, many other perplexities about color began to yield, and my wonder grew.

The present volume is an attempt to share with others the outcome of the ensuing odyssey through some of the literature on color vision. Although it is directed to my fellow philosophers and couched in their mode of discourse, I hope that it will be of some interest to other people who have been curious about the place and role of color in the world. I have had several objectives in writing it. One of them is to make philosophers aware of the rich grist for philosophic mills that has been produced by visual scientists since the mid-1950s. To do this I have written, in Chapter I, a somewhat skewed introduction to color vision. It is my hope that this will lead the reader to more thorough, systematic, and authoritative introductions such as those mentioned in the "Suggestions for Further Reading" at the end of this book.

Another of my aims has been to try to extract some of the philosophical juice from visual science and serve it to the reader. In so doing, I have not hesitated to mix in some speculations and conjectures of my own. I have tried to make clear where straightforward exposition of the science leaves off and my own contentious contributions begin, but I may not have been altogether successful in doing so. *Caveat emptor.*

Finally, I have wanted to encourage and provoke other philosophers to come to grips with the relevant scientific material, and to promulgate within the philosophical community the opinion that, henceforth, discussions about color proceeding in ignorance of visual science are intellectually irresponsible. If this book should help to effect such a change in attitude, I shall think of it as a great success, even if the other philosophical theses it contains should be consigned to the flames as sophistry and illusion.

Few books make it to the press without having the benefit of the thought and labor of many people beside the author. This one is no exception. First and foremost, I owe an enormous debt to all my philosophical colleagues at Syracuse for their years of encouragement and criticism and for making our department such a stimulating place in which to be. My special thanks go to Jonathan Bennett, Bill Alston, and Tom McKay for their very extensive and helpful comments and to José Benardete and Peter van Inwagen for pressing me to face the consequences of some of my lines of inquiry. Other philosophers have been equally helpful. Jonathan Westphal and Austen Clark both commented on the manuscript at great length and have given me the benefit of substantial and enlightening correspondence and conversation. I also want to thank Sydney Shoemaker, Ed Averill, and Jim McGilvray for their assistance and encouragement.

I could not have done the book at all without the patient tutelage of several visual scientists. A long correspondence with Leo M. Hurvich kept me from straying too far off the path during the early phases of the project, and the voluminous, detailed comments and corrections of the manuscript by Davida Teller kept me relatively honest during its later stages. I have also profited from discussions with John McCann, Peter Lennie, Dennis Pelli and Joe Sturr. None of these good and helpful people should be held responsible for the errors of fact or doctrine which are likely to have crept into these pages under cover of darkness.

There are several others whose contributions have made a great difference to me. They include the editors of the *Journal of Philosophy,* Rolf Ziemer, whose skilled hand redrew the line drawings, Frank Goodnow, who prepared the simultaneous chromatic contrast illustration, and Sue McDougall and the other members of the philosophy department's secretarial staff, who did the countless small things which collectively amount to a Very Big Thing.

I have tried to come to grips with problems about color in several previous articles; they are listed in the bibliography. In most cases, I have modified or reworked those views in the present essay, and little of the earlier texts remains. But I have used portions of previously published articles in certain sections of the present work. In particular, Chapter II, section 6 draws on Hardin 1985b, which originally appeared in *The Australasian Journal of Philosophy*. Chapter III, section 1 and Chapter I, section 6 use bits of text from Hardin 1985a, published in *Philosophical Studies*, and Chapter III section 9 is an adaptation of Hardin (forthcoming), scheduled to appear in *Noûs*. Let me express my appreciation to the editors and publishers of those journals for permission to employ these materials here.

I first encountered the delicious selection from Keats in Rossotti 1983.

Finally, I am most grateful to Syracuse University for two leaves of absence, a summer grant, and a subvention for illustration costs; and to the National Endowment for the Humanities for underwriting the leave during which the book was completed.

INTRODUCTION

What has science to say to philosophy? Opinions vary, but few would dispute the importance of special and general relativity to philosophical doctrines about space and time and the nature of a priori knowledge. Nor would there be much argument about quantum mechanics' pertinence to our views about causality and what it is to be material, though the exact character of the inferences to be drawn from that theory remain in dispute more than half a century later. And vitalism, a once-respectable philosophical theory, has not dared to show its face since the advent of molecular biology.

In things human, matters are less clear. In part, this reflects the fact that those portions of psychology and the social sciences which speak to larger themes have been short on rigor, and those portions which generate more reliable knowledge—such as physiological psychology and psychophysics—have, at least in the past, seemed to lack much theoretical import. But the latter situation seems to be changing. Although promise still outruns fulfillment, clinical and behavioral studies on the one hand and "wetware" investigations on the other have begun to bear fruit of the greatest potential importance for our understanding of language, self-identity, and mental functioning.

The problem of qualia, however, has seemed to many philosophers to be peculiarly resistant to scientific investigation. Visual and sybaritic creatures that we are, the qualitative characteristics that most seem to attract our attention are those connected with colors and pains. Let us make the more agreeable choice and elect colors as our subject of inquiry in the following pages, for there is pain enough in the effort to understand them.

What is it about colors that seems to obstruct our understanding? They are given to visual experience along with shapes, yet we have no similar difficulties with shapes. A crucial difference seems to be that the essential character of shapes is amenable to mathematical representation, but the essential nature of colors resists it; the one appears quantitative, the other qualitative. Shapes are given to more than one sense, and we are much inclined to suppose that the only sort of characteristics that can be accessible to more than one sensory mode are those which bear a *structure*. The study of structures is, of course, the special province of that form of discursive thinking *par excellence*, mathematics. And, it goes without saying, everything mathematizable is a proper object of scientific study.

Colors, on the other hand, have a brute factuality about them. From Locke and Hume to Moore and Russell, they have been taken to be the paradigmatic instances of simple unanalyzable qualities. But the supposed unanalyzability of colors, obvious though it has seemed to many reflective people, does not coexist comfortably with the equally apparent "internal relatedness" of colors, whereby they exclude—yet intimately involve—each other. There is no variation of magnitude, intensive or extensive, that connects every color with every other color. And yet colors are as systematically related to each other as are lengths or degrees of temperature. Red bears on its face no reference to the character of green. Yet red categorically excludes green while at the very same time resembling it in an incommensurably closer fashion than the resemblance of either red or green to any shape or sound. Furthermore, we can always find a place among the hues for a Humean "missing shade of blue"; but could there also be a place there for a quality that is neither bluish, nor reddish, nor greenish, nor yellowish, but resembles blue, red, green, and yellow as much as they resemble one another? We may reply that there cannot, since the hue circle is closed; there is no "logical space" for a radically novel hue. But how, given the simple unanalyzable character of each of the determinate hues, can we proceed to justify such an answer?

One way of getting clearer about the nature of colors and the relations they bear to each other would be to show that color, like heat, could be subsumed under some wider set of phenomena through which it might be explicated. Because we understand heat to be random kinetic energy, we can liberate it from conceptual bondage to our feelings of warmth and coolness, find new ways to measure it, explain the thermal behavior of bodies by appealing to their microstructure, and appreciate the role of heat in physical, chemical, and biological processes far removed from the domain of human sensation. And so, if color proves to be some complex set of physical properties that underlie the dispositions of bodies to reflect visible light in such and such a way, we shall be able to study color independently of the idiosyncrasies of our visual systems. Our limited epistemic access to colors would not then betoken an ontological isolation of colors from the general order of physical processes. According to this view, once colors can be properly identified with, or nomically related to, some congeries of material properties, those properties should give us the clue to the nature of the relations colors bear to each other as well as provide us with additional means of making epistemic contact with them. We might suppose that the advocates of such a chromatic materialism would appeal to the best scientific work to spell out the locus of colors in the material world and how we perceive them and would then go on to explicate the network of chromatic "internal relations" by means of an appropriate set of material relations. But this expectation has been largely disappointed. Materialists' writing about colors has been more often directed to polemic or program or pronouncing oaths of fealty to a scientific world view than to delivering the actual scientific goods and putting them to philosophical work.

Those who are unpersuaded by chromatic materialism accept the conceptual insularity of the domain of colors. Colors, they say, are proprietary to sight alone; the quality of a color is, by the nature of the case, inconceivable to even the most sensitive and intellectually gifted of the congenitally blind. So the only way to understand colors is to examine in detail how the members of the chromatic family relate to one another and to study the empirical conditions under which colored objects appear to the senses. This mode of investigating the problem is suitable to phenomenalists and epiphenomenalists alike, and one might have expected that at least some of them, along with those who label themselves phenomenologists, would have engaged in a thorough inquiry into the phenomenology of color, or at least have attended to the writings of the scientists and artists who do. All the more surprising, then, to find that there seems to be so little concern in these quarters for patiently uncovering and spelling out the detailed phenomenal facts of chromatic structure. For instance, a recent writer (McGinn, 1980) finds objectivist accounts of color wanting, insists that the explanation for some puzzling chromatic relationships is that they depend upon "a rich system of phenomenal laws," and then neglects to tell us what those laws are.

So those who urge the phenomenal nature of colors don't do much of the phenomenology, and the "scientific" materialists don't pay much attention to the science. Conceptual analysis and ingenious argument carry the freight, and the data base is pretty nearly that which was available to John Locke. The result is not only that the issue of the ontological status of colors is about where it was in the eighteenth century, but that questions about the resemblances and exclusions of colors are at a dead end. Beyond that, the general understanding of how color experience relates to color language is mired in confusion.

What does science have to say to philosophy about colors? In fact, a great deal. But philosophers have not supposed so, perhaps in part for reasons of simple cultural lag: the science they have looked at is twenty-five years out of date. In the eyes of the scientifically literate public, color science has never had the panache of theoretical physics or molecular biology, and few scientists outside the field realize that it underwent a theoretical revolution more than a generation ago, when the *opponent-process theory* became established. Opponent-process theory is to the study of color vision what the theory of continental drift is to geology. In both fields, a great deal of solid and lasting work was done before those theories became established, and, in both fields, disputes continue about the exact form and scope that the theory should have, and just what mechanisms underlie it. But, in each case, after the theory became established, research problems and methodology moved in fresh directions, novel phenomena were uncovered and old phenomena newly understood, and the entire discipline took on a unity and focus it had hitherto lacked. It is not unreasonable to expect that, when we turn a theoretically informed eye to the rag-bag collection of philosophical problems about color, they too will prove to be connected in a manner that had previously eluded our gaze.

In the pages that follow we shall sketch some of the scientific facts about the color-relevant properties of physical objects and processes which lie outside the organism. It will quickly become apparent that the classification of objects by color depends quite as much on the operating characteristics of visual systems as on the physical properties of objects; so we shall proceed to scrutinize those operating characteristics. In so doing, we shall find that visual science has delineated much of the phenomenology of colors and, with the assistance of neurophysiology, has explained a good deal of that phenomenology while showing real promise of explaining more. This will not only help us to ascertain the place of color in the natural order, but will also open new avenues for understanding how and why colors both resemble and exclude each other, as well as how it is that they form a closed family and how it is that they need not do so. We will be able to suggest some conditions under which it would be reasonable to claim that the qualitative character of color experience is reducible to neural processes, and what to say about color sensing in other animals. Finally, we shall see how, contrary to what the Wittgensteinians seem to have supposed, the semantics of ordinary color terms is powerfully constrained by the physiology of the human visual system. At every turn we shall discover that color science is able to cast new light into corners that have long been in shadow.

Do not all charms fly
At the mere touch of cold philosophy?
There was an awful rainbow once in heaven:
We know her woof, her texture: she is given
In the dull catalogue of common things.
Philosophy will clip an Angel's wings.
Conquer all mysteries by rule and line,
Empty the haunted air, and gnomèd mine—
Unweave a rainbow.

Keats, *Lamia*, II, 229

I

Color Perception and Science

The physical causes of color

The origins of the colors of objects largely reside in the interactions of light with electrons. Most such interactions take place within a relatively narrow band of energies.[1] Radiation of higher energy tends to ionize atoms and damage molecules, whereas lower-energy radiation will result chiefly in thermal agitation of atoms and molecules. Now it happens that this energy band coincides with the middle range of the radiation spectrum of the sun as that is measured on the earth, so the energy of sunlight is "well tuned to the electronic structure of matter."[2] It is the electronic structure of a chunk of matter, particularly the configuration of its atoms' outer electronic shells, which is responsible for its chemical properties. Reflected, refracted, and transmitted sunlight thus carries a great deal of differential information about the chemical condition of material bodies, and it is not surprising that animals should have evolved mechanisms for detecting and exploiting this information.[3] There is nothing in the nature of things which demands that the energy spectrum of the light that reaches the surface of a particular planet from its central star should be tuned to the electronic structure of matter; so color vision, like complex life itself, depends upon a fortuitous combination of circumstances.

In the middle of this "happy band" of electromagnetic energy is the range of human color vision. Students of vision measure it not as physicists usually do, in frequencies or electron volts, but in wavelengths. The unit is the *nanometer* (formerly the millimicron), abbreviated 'nm', which is a billionth of a meter. 700 nm marks the beginning of the infrared spectrum and 400 nm the start of the ultraviolet (figure I-1 and plate 1). Some individuals under some conditions can see light outside these limits. Most insects detect light of shorter wavelength—bees see down to 300 nm—but no known species visually detects light much beyond 700 nm. Later on, we shall pay considerable attention to the ways in which we and some other organisms detect, decode, and represent light stimuli. But, first, we must take a look at the different ways in which those stimuli are generated.

The number and variety of the physical properties of objects which influence their perceived color are surprisingly large. Kurt Nassau has shown that, even if we confine our attention for the time being to what we might think of as the "standard" causes of the colors we experience, thus ignoring such things as direct electrical stimulation of the brain, we can distinguish at least fifteen such causes, which he categorizes as follows (Nassau 1983, 23):

Vibrations and Simple Excitations

1. *Incandescence:* Flames, lamps, carbon arc, limelight
2. *Gas excitations:* Vapor lamps, lightning, auroras, some lasers
3. *Vibrations and rotations:* Water, ice, iodine, blue gas flame

Transitions Involving Ligand Field Effects

4. *Transition Metal Compounds:* Turquoise, many pigments, some fluorescence, lasers, and phosphors
5. *Transition Metal Impurities:* Ruby, emerald, red iron ore, some fluorescence and lasers

Transitions between Molecular Orbitals

6. *Organic Compounds:* Most dyes, most biological colorations, some fluorescence and lasers
7. *Charge Transfer:* Blue sapphire, magnetite, lapis lazuli, many pigments

Transitions Involving Energy Bands

8. *Metals:* Copper, silver, gold, iron, brass, "ruby" glass
9. *Pure Semiconductors:* Silicon, galena, cinnabar, diamond
10. *Doped or Activated Semiconductors:* Blue and yellow diamond, light-emitting diodes, some lasers and phosphors
11. *Color Centers:* Amethyst, smoky quartz, desert "amethyst" glass, some fluoresence and lasers

Geometrical and Physical Optics

12. *Dispersive Refraction, Polarization, etc:* Rainbow, halos, sun dogs, green flash of sun, "fire" in gemstones

13. *Scattering:* Blue sky, red sunset, blue moon, moonstone, Raman scattering, blue eyes and some other biological colors
14. *Interference:* Oil slick on water, soap bubbles, coating on camera lenses, some biological colors
15. *Diffraction:* Aureole, glory, diffraction gratings, opal, some biological colors, most liquid crystals.

Our purposes do not require that we attend to the full detail in this list, but simply that we take careful note of its variety. That variety

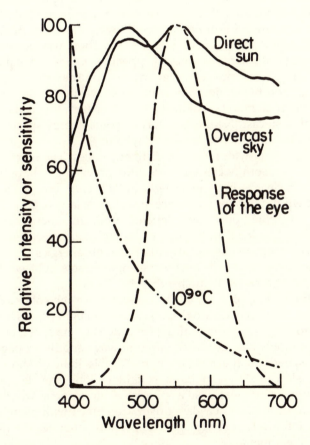

Fig. I-1. *Visible light distribution of the direct sun as seen on the surface of the earth and the overcast sky, compared with the sensitivity curve of the eye under daylight conditions. Also shown is the radiation curve for a blackbody at 10^9 degrees Celsius, which would be the spectrum for a star much hotter than the sun.*

suggests it would be in vain to suppose that objects sharing a common color resemble one another in physical structure. We may see this more clearly by attending to a diverse set of objects, all of which look blue to "normal" human observers under "normal" conditions. Our sketch will be brief: the interested reader should refer to Nassau 1983 for details.

The blue of the sky results from the differential scattering of sunlight from the atmosphere. The intensity with which light of a particular wavelength is scattered depends upon the size of the particles that scatter it. The gas molecules of the atmosphere preferentially scatter short wavelength light, whereas the larger particles of volcanic ash or various pollutants scatter the longer wavelengths. London enjoyed brilliant red sunsets for a year after the great Krakatoa explosion, and Los Angeles is often "favored" by a yellow sky. But at most other places and times, small particles and short wavelengths give the aerial regions their stereotypical appearance. One consequence of this scattering is that direct sunlight as seen on the earth's surface is deficient in shortwave light and thus looks yellowish, whereas the north daylight favored by painters (in the northern hemisphere!) has a slightly bluish cast. Neither one has an equal-energy spectrum, but both are commonly denominated "daylight."

The blueness of water has two distinct sources. The first is that, if its surface is smooth, water will reflect the prevailing light of the sky. If the day is clear, a body of water will look blue, but, if the sky is cloudy or wind roughens its surface, it will seem largely gray. Water's residual light blue appearance depends upon the characteristic energy of the vibrational transitions of its molecular electrons, which occur much more readily at low than at high energies, so infrared light is strongly absorbed, long-wavelength visible light weakly absorbed, and shortwave light absorbed hardly at all.[4]

The blue-looking portion of the rainbow, like the colors of all its other parts, is entirely due to dispersion. When light passes from one medium to another medium of different density, its speed of propagation commonly changes, with different wavelengths propagated at different speeds in the new medium. Visible light of short wavelength is slowed down more than light of long wavelength as it passes from air into water, so a spherical water droplet will disperse the light in the manner of a glass prism. Combined with a single internal reflection for each ray of light, dispersion generates the range of rainbow phenomena.

The wave nature of light plays the central role in other occurrences of blue. The iridescent blue that some beetles display when illuminated by a light source (as opposed to diffuse lighting) is a consequence of evenly spaced fine ridges on their shells which serve as a diffraction grating, rather like the grooves on a phonograph record. At a particular angle of incidence between light source, beetle shell, and eye, some wavelengths of light interfere in phase and thus become intensified, while other wavelengths interfere out of phase and consequently cancel one another. The color that is seen depends critically upon the angle of view; small shifts in angle result in noticeable shifts of color—hence the iridescent effect. The iridescent blue of a housefly's wing is also due to interference, but here the mechanism is somewhat different, involving an interaction between light waves reflected from different layers of the transparent wing material; the situation is closely analogous to the interference colors of oil films. (However, most blue coloration in animals is the result of scattering. Blue eyes are examples.)

The blue of sapphire and the blue of lapis lazuli have causes that are different from each other and from any we have considered so far; they lie in a variety of phenomena that fall under the quantum-mechanical theory of the solid state. Sapphire is blue because of the transference of ions from iron to titanium, but lapis lazuli is blue because of the vibrational-energy characteristics of conjugated bonds. The blue of both of these minerals results from charge transfers in a crystal field; so the causes are to that degree similar, but equally similar charge-transfer mechanisms in other minerals issue in a black or brown appearance. Closeness in physical structure thus need not imply closeness in color appearance. Emerald and ruby are paradigmatic of green and red, yet their chemical composition and crystal structures are very much alike; indeed, both minerals owe their color to the very same impurity, chromium. The difference in color appearance is entirely due to a slight weakening of the crystal field strength in emerald as compared with ruby.

Not all blue things rely on imported light to manifest themselves. The star Sirius is an incandescent object and thus derives its blue appearance from the average temperature of its atoms and ions. On the other hand, a phosphoric dot on the picture tube of a color television set owes its blue glow to being a doped semiconductor which undergoes stimulated light emission (another typically quantum-mechanical phenomenon) in consequence of being bombarded by a stream of electrons. And finally, there is that most curious case of blueness, the color of electrons! One may see "blue" electrons by looking into an electron storage ring, in which electrons moving at high speed are contained by a magnetic field which bends them into

5

a circular path. Because their trajectories are bent, the electrons are accelerated. When charged particles are accelerated they radiate, in this case at the shortwave end of the visible spectrum.

It should thus be clear that, if blue things have any physical feature in common at all, it will reside not in the physical microstructure of those things, but rather in their disposition to radiate light of a particular character from their surfaces. Why not, then, lump together as having the same color all those objects which yield the same spectra, regardless of similarities and differences in the micromechanisms which generate those spectra? Such a proposal seems plausible, but it involves more complexities than one might have supposed, as well as some real difficulties of principle.

To begin with a cursory survey of the complexities: Two objects may reflect a particular wavelength of light in just the same way, but transmit it differently, because the one absorbs light incident upon it to which the other permits relatively free passage. The spectrum of the reflected or transmitted light will, furthermore, quite commonly depend upon the angle between the incident light, the surface of the object, and the detecting instrument. A glossy surface may have the same average spectral reflectance, wavelength for wavelength, as a matte surface, when one integrates over all source-viewing angles, but differ very much from the matte surface in the character of the light that it reflects at any particular angle. And obviously, phenomena that depend essentially on diffraction, interference, and the like will frequently be strongly angle-dependent; rainbows exist only at very well-defined angles. The orientation of the surface is often crucial too, as in the case of dichroic materials whose transmission spectrum is a function of the angle of rotation of their surfaces. Such materials are often used in thin sheets as filters whose color-rendering properties change as they are turned. And then, the reflection spectra of two material samples may be identical when they are exposed to light that is confined to the visible region, but differ when the light includes a significant ultraviolet component which the one sample may simply absorb while the other reradiates it in the visible band. This is the situation that obtains with fluorescent materials, such as are included in "fabric brighteners." (How else could a shirt come out of the laundry "whiter than white"?)

So the assignment of colors to objects (or to pseudo objects, such as rainbows) on the basis of their physical light-transforming properties proves to be a very complicated matter. An object turns out to have a transmission color, a reflection color, an interference color, etc., no two necessarily the same, and each color is a function of detection angle as well as of the spectrum of the incident light. We must of course except incandescence, phosphorescence, and the like, when the immediately incident light is obviously of no relevance, though the input of other energy of other types or at other times may very well be relevant.

There is nothing particularly perturbing in the fact that ascriptions of colors to objects on the basis of their relevant physical properties should be substantially more complicated than we first thought, that our common-sense notion that objects have color *simpliciter* cannot withstand scientific scrutiny. But the real difficulty with the present proposal for assigning colors to objects comes when we try to link the colors of objects thus understood with the colors we perceive them as having. Objects with identical spectra will, to be sure, look to be the same color, but indefinitely large numbers of objects that are spectrally different will also look to be the same color; it is unlikely that any two things chosen at random which look to have the same blue color under normal conditions will have identical reflection spectra, let alone identical spectra of the other sorts. If an account of the nature of color is to be satisfactory, it must include a set of principles whereby one can understand the resemblances and differences that colors bear to one another. We need to understand, for instance, what it is about blue things as a group which puts them in a class different from yellow things. How do we generalize from the class of spectrally identical objects to the very much larger class of chromatically identical objects, and to the still larger class of chromatically similar objects? Is there any way of doing this if we must confine our attention to the physical properties of the objects that are seen or the patterns of light which enable us to see them? We shall come to understand that there is no such way; for the resemblances and differences of the colors are grounded not just in the physical properties of objects but even more in the biological makeup of the animal that perceives them. In order to get clearer about this, let us now take a closer look at our own visual systems and those of our cousins, the old-world monkeys.

The camera and the eye

The eye has frequently been likened to a camera. This metaphor is apt to deceive, for it represents the eye as a passive conveyer of images to some other more active organ which views them and uses them to glean information about the world. Such a picture of perceptual acquaintance was well-nigh irresistible to many thinkers of the seventeenth century (Yolton, 1984, chapter 7), and even now the retinal image is surely the implicit prototype of the sense datum.

To be sure, the optical system of the eye is very cameralike. The pupil expands and contracts, adjusting depth of field and governing the amount of light to reach the retina. By changing its thickness and shape, the lens, in collaboration with the cornea, varies its focal length to optimize the images of objects which are at varying distances from the eye. The result is an image of fine detail projected onto the retina—or so we seem to be informed by viewing the image formed in an excised eye.

The retinal image must of course contain the information needed for seeing. But it need not therefore closely match the properties of what we actually discover in our visual fields. How close is the correspondence in fact? We must first note that, from a purely optical standpoint, the resolution of the retina is limited by the packing density of its receptors; in terms of the camera analogy, by the grain of the film. Now the diameter of a cone in the center of the *fovea*—the retinal region of the most acute daytime seeing—is about one-half of a minute (30 seconds) of arc. But we can recognize a lateral displacement of two abutting line segments, or a misalignment of three dots, which is only one-third of that amount. Beyond that, the mosaic of receptors shows no particular geometrical orientation, but horizontal and vertical gratings are better resolved by human visual systems than are oblique gratings (Westheimer 1972, 177). What we see is thus a reorganization of the retinal image. Second, as we can see in figure I-2, the densities of the numbers of receptors in the fovea—which is located close to the eye's visual axis—and an equal-sized retina area 20 degrees away from the fovea are approximately equal (figure I-2), but the resolution that is achieved in the corresponding regions of the visual field is drastically different, as the most casual observation will show. Third, as figure I-2 indicates, there is an area, the *optic disk*, or blind spot, of 6 degrees in diameter which lies about 16 degrees from the fovea. (As an intuitive reference for visual angle, an American quarter held at arms' length subtends 2 degrees; the sun and the full moon each subtend half a degree.) The optic disk is the exit point for nerves which leave the retina for other brain areas and contains no receptors at all. It thus corresponds to an area of the visual field with zero information—an area that is a dozen full moons across— and yet there is no corresponding phenomenal discontinuity in the visual field. Fourth, the image cast onto the retina has been blurred within the eye by scattering of the light and by chromatic aberration, as well as being traversed by shadows cast by retinal blood vessels. Yet we see neither shadows, nor colored fringes, nor fuzzy contours.

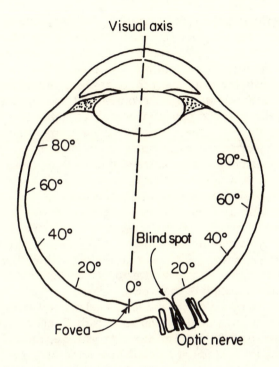

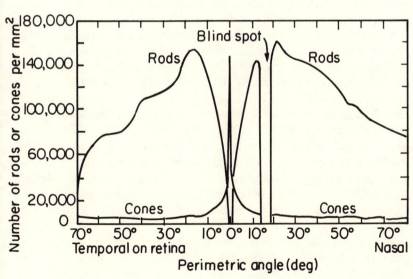

Fig. I-2. *Rod and cone density as a function of retinal location.*

Finally, and perhaps most importantly, the living eye is in constant motion. It quivers at a frequency of 30 to 80 times a second with an amplitude of 10 to 30 seconds of arc, it slowly drifts with an amplitude of up to 6 minutes of arc, and it makes rapid corrective movements at intervals ranging from .03 seconds to 5 seconds with amplitudes of from 1 to 20 minutes of arc (Von Fieandt and Moustgaard 1977, 100). Thus there is in practice no well-defined stationary retinal image at all, but only a vibrating blur. Yet we are aware of neither motion nor blur. Indeed, if an image is stabilized with respect to the retina so that there is no motional blurring, it fades from view within a few seconds!

Unlike a passive camera, the eye begins from the moment its receptors absorb light to transform and reorganize the optical information that comes to it from the world. The retina is, in fact, a bit of extruded brain, and by examining those first steps of visual processing which it executes we may hope to gain an inkling of how the brain constructs those chromatic experiences which constitute a portion of its sensory representation of the world.

Let us begin by looking at the receptoral network itself. The retina comprises some 120 million rods and nearly 7 million cones (Haber and Hershenson 1980, 19). The *rods* are specialized for seeing at night, whereas the three kinds of *cones* operate under daytime light levels. Stimulation of the rods alone yields only achromatic (black, white, and gray) perceptions, whereas stimulation of the cones produces both achromatic and chromatic perceptions. Cone vision is typically discriminative and of high acuity; rod vision is normally summative (for maximum detection under circumstances of impoverished lighting) and, hence, of low acuity (if several receptors pool their signals, their outputs cannot be distinguished). For the most part, then, the rods and cones form two distinct visual systems which overlap only under twilight conditions. There is, however, substantial evidence of rod-cone interactions under special circumstances and, in particular, evidence that the rods and middle-wavelength cones can collaborate to produce perceptions of chromatic color (see, for instance, McCann and Benton 1969). So it is not strictly correct to describe the rods as "color blind," if by this we mean that they are totally excluded from the processes of color vision.

A duplex visual system is of obvious benefit to its owner, because it permits around-the-clock operation. Chickens, who have only cones, must go to bed early, while owls, who have only rods, are useless during the day. Our visual systems, in contrast, are capable of operating over an enormous luminance range, about 10^{13} to 1 (Haber and

Hershenson 1980, 10). At the low end, the human eye can success-fully detect as few as 100 quanta of light striking the cornea, which translates to about 10 quanta being absorbed by the rods, while the brightest (safely) perceivable light for human eyes is about 100 trillion quanta.

Rods and cones are differently distributed in our retinas, with 50,000 cones squeezed into the fovea, a 2-degree retinal sector which is depressed relative to the rest of the retina and which contains no rods. The fovea lies close to the eye's optical axis (figure I-2). In this one square millimeter of neural tissue our most detailed seeing and our most detailed chromatic perception have their start. As figure I-2 shows, cone density drops rapidly outside the fovea, and rod density increases. One might expect that the most acute nighttime vision would be had a few degrees from the center of the visual field, and this is indeed the case; amateur astronomers well know that the best way to view a planet or a star is to look a bit to one side of it. But, for most purposes, we notice those events which transpire in the cen-ter of the visual field where the fovea provides us with the best res-olution of both detail and color. Although both sorts of resolution deteriorate as the angular distance from the center of vision increases, the periphery proves to be very sensitive to motion; so changes at the edge of vision capture our attention and immediately induce us either to duck or to turn our field of view to scrutinize the intruder.

We must here mention one structure in the central retina which is normally invisible, but is capable of engendering significant variation in visual color matching. It is the macula lutea, or *macula*, an irregu-larly shaped pigmented region of 4 or 5 degrees visual diameter which overlays the fovea. The macular pigment is essentially a yellow filter which reduces the amount of shortwave light reaching the fo-veal receptors, substantially understimulating those shortwave cones which are centrally located (Judd and Wyszecki 1975, 14–15). Nor-mally this pigmented region is not noticed because the receptors un-derneath it adapt to it, just as the rod-cone systems adapt to the dark, or as the cone system adapts to the spectral changes involved in going from sunlight to incandescent light so that objects maintain an ap-proximately constant color appearance. For the same reason that we do not usually see the image of the macular pigment (called the *Max-well spot*), we also do not see the blood vessels that crisscross our retinas. But, in both cases, a sudden change in the intensity or spec-tral constitution of incident light can upset the adaptation balance, and these features—or their afterimages—may be glimpsed for a sec-ond or two before readaptation occurs.[5] Shifting one's glance from one colored region to another of similar appearance but different spectral composition will have the same effect, generating chromatic inhomogeneities in largish (10-degree) color fields. Adaptation is an important part of our story, and we shall have more to say about it shortly.

Let us now turn our attention to the microstructure of the retina and the connections among its components. Figure I-3 is a schematic diagram of a retinal section. Notice that the light comes in from the bottom of the figure and that the receptors are at the top; the mammalian retina is turned inside out! One might suppose that the neural structures (and the blood vessels, not shown in figure I-3) would scatter a great deal of the light. Actually, the effect is less than might be supposed, since those structures are transparent, but there is nevertheless some degrading effect on the image. It is interesting to notice that the nerves and blood vessels are displaced away from the fovea, thus maximizing foveal acuity; this is why the fovea is depressed with respect to the rest of the retina. The plump receptors at the top of the diagram are the cones; the skinny ones are the rods. As the figure shows, rods and cones are connected with one another and with higher-level cells by means of horizontal, bipolar, and amacrine cells. The latter three types of cells can either enhance or inhibit the response of the cells to which they are connected—a fact of the greatest importance for vision in general and for color vision in particular. At the far end of the retina's information-processing chain are the *ganglion cells*, whose output is sent up the optic nerve to the brain. The net result of these complicated interconnections is that, first, a receptor's output can alter the effects of the outputs of its neighboring receptors; second, every receptor is connected to several ganglion cells; and, third, every ganglion cell is connected to several receptors. This would lead us to expect that what goes on in one ganglion cell will depend upon what happens in an extended region of the retinal image, and that is just what happens.

Let us introduce some terminology. The region of the retina over which lights affect the activity of a particular neuron is known as the *receptive field* for that neuron. The receptive field of a ganglion cell is the region of the retinal surface and, hence, the set of neighboring receptors to which it is connected. Together the ganglion cell and its associated receptors form a *neural unit*. If we examine the functional arrangement of a ganglion cell's receptive field (figure I-4), we often find that it is constituted by a central group of receptors whose outputs excite the next cells in the sequence and that this central group is surrounded by a population of cells whose outputs inhibit the next cells in the sequence. In a situation in which a neural unit's whole receptive field is uniformly stimulated, its ganglion cell will fire at a statistically regular spontaneous rate, its *base rate*. The base rate is to a small extent a function of the level of background illumination, but the cell is never silent, always sustaining its discharge even in total darkness. The base rate represents a neutral balance between the inputs to the cell's light-loving center and its light-hating surround. This sort of neural unit is an *on-center, off-surround* unit. Such cells also have transient responses—they tend to respond to changes in

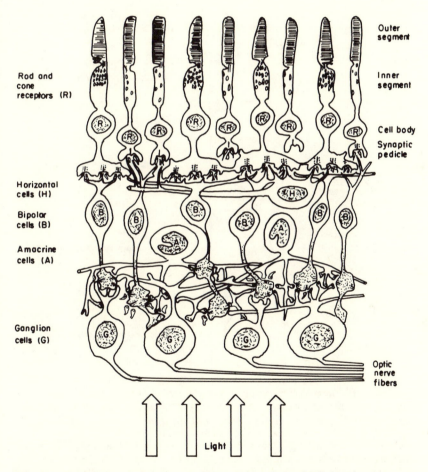

Fig. I-3. *Crosssection of the primate retina. Notice the multiplicity of crossconnections between the receptors and the ganglion cells as well as the direction from which the light comes.*

the level of illumination, but tend to be excited much less vigorously by continued stimulation than by stimulus onset or offset. Many other neural units are of opposite polarity—off-center, on-surround. Either way, the form of receptive field organization in which center and surround are antagonistically related is typical of ganglion cells. Let us look at the behavior of a prototypical on-center unit.[6]

Shine a light on the center but not the surround of such a unit (figure I-4). The center will be excited, but the surround will not be;

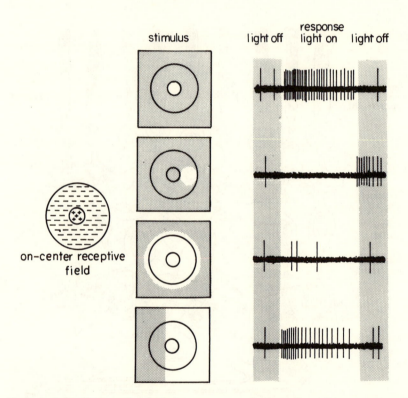

Fig. I-4. Left: *The receptive field of an on-center retinal ganglion cell in a cat, plotted on a screen in front of the eyes. The plus signs show areas of on-responses, the minus signs areas of off-responses.* Right: *Demonstrations of these responses when a spot or edge of light is flashed on the receptive field and then turned off 5 seconds later. Every vertical deflection in the oscilloscope recordings is an impulse from the ganglion cell. First, a small spot is centered in the on area, then the same spot falls on the off area. A large spot then covers the whole receptive field, causing very little response, and finally, a correctly positioned edge leaves much of the inhibitory surround unstimulated and so produces a vigorous response.*

Fig. I-5. *A series of graduated lightness steps. Each step is of uniform light intensity, but at each edge there is a lightening of the lighter side and a darkening of the darker side. This is the* Mach band *effect.*

so the unit will fire faster. Move the light spot off of the center and onto the surround. Now the center is undisturbed, but the surround is perturbed, and the unit's firing rate therefore decreases. Spotlight half the center and half the surround; the excitations and inhibitions balance each other, and the unit fires at its base rate. But light all of the center and shadow part of the surround, and the balance between center and surround will be shifted so that the cell will respond almost as vigorously as when only the center was lit. This mode of response of our prototypical ganglion cell is an instance of *lateral inhibition,* a tendency that sensory systems have of inhibiting activity in one region when an adjoining region is stimulated. For instance, lateral inhibition in hearing makes possible sharper auditory tuning in the basilar membrane of the cochlea. In touch, it is responsible for the momentary reduction in itching that is produced when one scratches in the neighborhood of the itchy spot. The general effect of lateral inhibition mechanisms is to encode contrast. Our prototypical ganglion cell encodes local light-dark contrast but relatively little information about the absolute illumination level. Since higher-level visual cells can "know" only what the lower-level cells "tell" them, this selective emphasis on contrast at such an early level of visual processing is bound to have a powerful effect on what we see.

It is a long inferential leap from data about the pattern of activity of a single cell or small groups of ganglion cells to the explanation of a perceptual phenomenon which is presumably related to the firing pattern of an assembly of more centrally-located cells. To make the leap requires, among other things, that one establish that several such peripheral cells of similar characteristics cooperate appropriately to produce a pattern of activity which is transmitted in a relatively unscathed manner through several intermediate links. That work has not so far been done, and so the textbook explanation we are about to present must be regarded by the cautious as simply a highly suggestive analogy between ganglion-cell activity and a perceptual pattern of light and dark bands (Teller 1984). The perceptual phenomenon in question is the appearance of *Mach bands,* named after Ernst Mach, who first discussed them. Figure I-5 is a series of graduated lightness steps. Each step is a gray box that is physically uniform, but, if you look at the junction of two boxes, you will notice that the lighter side of the boundary looks even lighter, and the dark side looks even darker. It is tempting to see the appearance of Mach bands as an instance of the edge-enchancing activities of a population of prototypical ganglion cells. The account would go as follows:

Let us suppose that a homogeneous population of our on-center units is arrayed beneath a fuzzy shadow. In figure I-6, (a) and (d) have centers and surrounds equally illuminated or shaded, as the

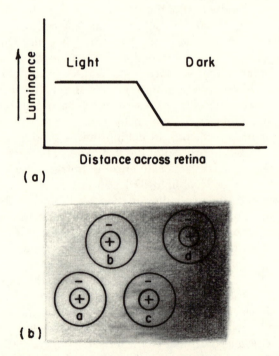

Fig. I-6. *This illustrates how antagonist center-surround receptive fields might account for Mach bands. Top: A luminance profile is shown as imaged over part of the retina. Bottom: The antagonistic areas of fields (a) and (d) are equally illuminated and there is a minimal response. In fields (b) and (c), the antagonistic areas are unequally illuminated, so that (b) should give a greater positive response than (a), and (c) a greater negative response than (d).*

case may be. Unit (b) has part of its surround—the part in shadow—excited rather than inhibited, while its center, bathed in light, remains excited, so the unit receives a net stimulation, but neural unit (c) has its center inhibited by the shadow, and the left-hand part of its surround inhibited by the light, so the cell is, on balance, inhibited. Consequently, (b) is firing faster than (a), and (c) is firing slower than (d), with the result that contrast across the border is enhanced. Think of base rate as zero, excitation as positive, and inhibition as negative. Then (a) is zero, (b) is positive, (c) is negative, and (d) is zero. The left-hand side has a net positive response, the right side a net negative response, with the border regions showing a sharpened contrast. In an equivalent way, we could haul a dark edge across a single unit, getting a sharp decrease in firing, followed by a sharp increase before the unit's activity reverts to its base rate. Figure I-7 portrays the output of the cell.

In a similar fashion, the effects of the antagonist center-surround organization of the retina *might* be making themselves felt in the Hermann grid illusion (figure I-8). A textbook explanation sketch of the appearance of the gray dots that appear at the white intersections of the grid would ask you to suppose that the white areas fall on the receptive fields of on-center prototypical ganglion cells. Now consider two such ganglion cells whose receptive field centers fall directly beneath the white bars, one at the intersection, the other not. The latter will have its center illuminated and most of its inhibitory surround in darkness. In consequence, it will fire vigorously. The cell at the intersection, on the other hand, will have twice as much of its inhibitory surround stimulated, so it will fire correspondingly less vigorously than the cell that is away from the intersection. So the brain will get two messages, the one telling it that the white bar is bright, the other telling it that the cross is not so bright.

When you look at the Hermann grid you will notice that the gray dots do not appear as markedly at intersections that are directly in the center of vision. In the terms of the preceding explanatory scheme, this is because the receptive fields of neural units in your fovea are small, permitting foveal viewing to be of high resolution. When the image of an intersection is projected onto such a unit, both its center and its surround will be illuminated, and the surrounding black areas will have no effect. If, however, you move the grid pattern farther away from your eye, the grid image will be reduced in size at the fovea, and gray dots will appear at an intersection in your center of vision. You will also notice that as you continue to look at the grid, the center of the white bars will look grayer. This is the Mach-band

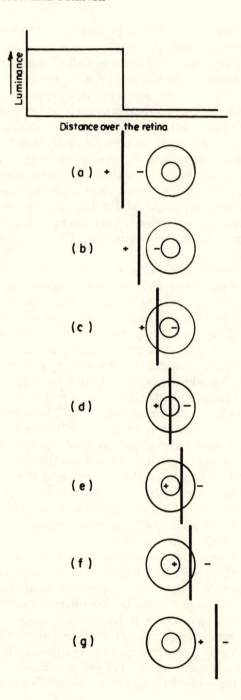

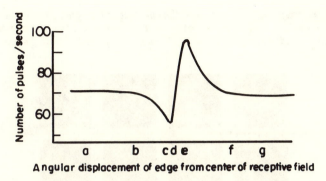

Fig. I-7. Facing page: *Seven successive alignments of a square luminance profile (top) as it moves from left to right across an on-center, off-surround receptive field. In (a), the edge is still entirely to the left of the field, while by (c) the intense side of the edge covers part of the off-surround. In (d) the edge is centered on the field, by (e) the intense side of the edge covers mainly the on-center of the field, and by (g) the intense side of the edge completely covers the field. Above: Measurements of the static response of an on-center ganglion cell to the movement of an edge across it. The edge is as in the figure on the left, and the positions indicated by the letters a-g refer to the successive frames of the left figure.*

effect once more; the black regions are inducing additional brightness in the immediately adjoining white areas. The central regions, however, are unenhanced, and thus seem, by comparison, grayer.

Perceiving lightness and darkness

We have emphasized the tendency of neural units to react most vigorously to spatial and temporal changes in the intensity of the light that falls on them, with much less response to sustained stimulation and to homogeneous fields of light. As we might expect, retinal cells differ from one another in these respects, but preference for transients is widespread. At first blush this seems surprising. Are we not able to distinguish a brightly lit scene from a dimly lit one? And can we not, in the same scene, see the difference between a homogeneously bright region and a homogeneously dark region without having to rely on luminance changes at their boundaries? We can, and this shows that there must be ganglion cells that differ somewhat in their mode of function from the ''prototypical'' cells we have been describing. But the prototypical cells tend to dominate our perception, as we shall now illustrate.

Look at figure I-9. The top picture and the bottom picture seem to be very much alike, with a light area at the left adjoining a dark area

Fig. I-8. Below: *The Hermann grid illusion. Notice that gray spots appear at the intersections of the white bars except at the center of your gaze. The two ganglion cell receptive fields have been drawn in to suggest a possible neural ground for the effect.*

at the right. But if we look more carefully, we see that the bottom picture is a fake: all the contrast is in the border between the two areas. Obscure that border with a pencil, and the two sides prove to be of equal lightness. Our brains docilely follow edge information and fill in perceived darkness and lightness correspondingly. Since there are other borders to the bottom figure, a second look will tell us that it is different from the top one. But even then, it remains difficult to avoid seeing the two bottom squares as having different overall lightnesses and difficult to judge the comparative lightnesses of the left upper rectangle and left lower rectangle, separated as they are by a sequence of alternating dark and light boundaries. So we encode

Fig. I-9. Facing page: *The upper and lower patterns look very similar, with a light rectangle on the left and a dark rectangle on the right. But the light distributions drawn beneath each pattern tell us that they are physically quite different. The discontinuity of the light distribution in the lower pattern dominates our perception of the relative lightnesses of the rectangles on each side of it. Try covering up the discontinuity with a pencil.*

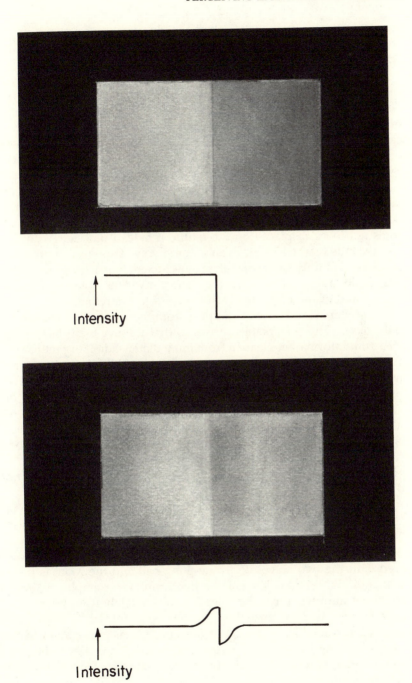

Intensity

Intensity

abrupt changes much better than we do absolute levels or slow changes in space or time. The neural recoding in the retina suggests why this might be so.

The importance of edge information can be strikingly shown, though not, alas, on the printed page, by stabilizing an image on a person's retina with an image-bearing contact lens that moves with his eyeball. We have previously called attention to the constant, intricate, and involuntary motions of our eyes which incessantly move dark and light edges across our retinas. Were the neural units of the retina primarily responsive to sustained information, the effect would simply be to blur the image and grossly interfere with seeing. But, in fact, the movement of luminance edges refreshes our visual awareness of contours and renders seeing possible. If an image is stabilized so as not to be displaced on the retina, it fades from view within a few seconds (Yarbus 1967). Even voluntary eye fixation will produce substantial fading; try staring at an object fixedly for 15 to 30 seconds. This rapid fading accounts for the normal invisibility of retinal blood vessels and of the macula, which are fixed to the retina.

But if stabilized images disappear from view, what do we see in their place? The remarkable answer is that the eye-brain *fills in* the area with information gleaned from immediately adjoining retinal regions. Consider the receptorless optic disk, or "blind spot," formed where the bundle of optic fibers leaves the retina for the brain. We recall that this area is only 16 degrees removed from the center of vision. It covers an area with a 6 degree visual diameter, enough to hold the images of ten full moons placed end to end, and yet there is no hole in the corresponding region of the visual field. This is because the eye-brain fills in with whatever is seen in the adjoining regions. If that is blue, it fills in blue; if it is plaid, we are aware of no discontinuity in the expanse of plaid.

Stabilized images are only one demonstration of the dominance of change over uniformity in the visual field. That dominance may also be seen in the so-called *ganzfeld* phenomenon, in which the visual field is made perfectly uniform, as it is when a subject's eyes are covered with the two halves of a ping-pong ball and the room is filled with a diffuse, shadowless colored light, pink for example. Within a couple of minutes' time, the color fades completely from view; subjects frequently claim that the light has been turned off. What replaces the color? There is no surrounding visual information to be used for filling in, since the visual field is so arranged as to be perfectly homogeneous. What the brain must settle for from the prototypical ganglion cells is the state of zero information, the sensation

Fig. I-10. *Simultaneous lightness contrast. The two center squares have equal reflect-ances. This will become apparent if you use a piece of paper to cover the regions immediately surrounding them.*

that corresponds to base-rate firing of the visual neural units. This is the visual sensation one has in a totally dark environment, after the eyes have completely adapted to the dark. Is it the experience of black? We are at first tempted to say "yes," but a more reflective response must be "no." What one sees is in fact a gray, in German called "eigengrau" or "characteristic gray," and known to English-speaking psychologists as *brain gray*. Think once more about a proto-typical neural unit with an on-center, off-surround receptive field. It signals an increment of light with an increase in firing rate, which, it is reasonable to suppose, the higher visual centers read as brightening, and signals a decrement of light by a decrease in firing rate which the higher centers read as darkening. So it must be possible to experience something darker than what is represented by base-rate firing, darker than brain gray. This is the experience of black, and we thus see how black can arise as a result of contrast.

Any gray can be driven toward black by increasing the lightness of the area that immediately surrounds it, and the same gray can be driven toward white by decreasing the lightness of its surround. This can be illustrated best by a pair of variable-brightness spotlights so arranged that the one projects a disk of light and the other an annulus of light around the disk. The effect can be dramatic because of the wide range of stimulus intensities. A page of a book admits of far less stimulus variation, but figure I-10 will nevertheless serve our purpose well enough because it more nearly typifies the simultaneous contrast situations of everyday life. The two grays are identical in reflectance, but they are driven in opposite directions by their surroundings. The equality of their reflectances may be visually appreciated by the use of a *reduction screen*, which is nothing more than a piece of neutral paper of medium darkness with a hole in it or, better, a viewing tube lined with dark gray material. The effect of a reduction screen is to remove the visual contrast between the target object, which is seen through the aperture, and its surround, the view of which is interrupted by the paper or the interior of the viewing tube. A reduction screen will prevent the effects of simultaneous contrast. Whether we are entitled to say that it enables us to see the "true" colors of things is another matter, which will be discussed in due time. For now, we may notice that, if black arises only by contrast with white, removing that contrast will deprive us of blackness as well.

The generation of black by the action of simultaneous contrast is an everyday phenomenon, but one of which we are normally unaware. For example, look at the screen of your television set under normal room illumination when the power to the set is turned off. The screen will look to be a dark gray rather than black. Now turn on the set and find a noise-free picture with a good black in it. That black will be noticeably darker than the gray of the inactivated screen. But television pictures are brought into being by *adding* light to the screen, not by *subtracting* it.

Simultaneous brightness contrast is very important in enabling us to assess the levels of the illumination of a scene. It was earlier remarked that the eye is capable of operating over a huge dynamic range of light intensities, on the order of ten trillion to one. But for any single scene with which the eye can deal, the intensity ratio of the brightest to the dimmest object rarely exceeds 200 to 1, and this is about the limit of differences that can be signaled by a visual neuron (Haber and Hershenson 1980, 50-51; Evans 1974, 195; Barlow and Mollon 1982, 102). It is therefore obvious that the visual system must continually recalibrate—adapt—itself, and as it does so it will largely preserve relative rather than absolute information about light intensities. By firelight as well as by sunlight, a piece of white paper looks white, a piece of coal black. Yet the sunlit lump of coal reflects a hundred times more light than the firelit piece of paper. So, in many ways, objects retain their appearances despite great changes in illumination.

Nevertheless, lightness constancy is certainly not perfect; we can easily distinguish firelight from sunlight and twilight from midday by appearances alone. We do this in many ways, but here are two of the more important: Noon reveals finer detail than twilight, and noon brings us greater subjective contrast, a longer distance from white to black, which is to say, more available shades of gray. At noon, not only are the whites whiter, the blacks are blacker. This expansion of the gray range can readily be seen if one carefully observes a collection of gray pieces of paper of various lightnesses by means of a lamp with a dimmer.

It is perceptually just as absurd to say that black is the absence of color as it is to say that white is the presence of all colors. When people talk this way, it is because their speech has been contaminated by science teachers who tell them that colors are particular wavelengths of light and that white light is that light which has as its constituents all wavelengths. By perception and common speech, Joseph's coat may have had many colors, but the color of the bride's dress is just one color, white. And her cocktail dress is not colorless, but black. On the other hand, it must be acknowledged that her desire for a color television set would not have been satisfied by one that displayed only black and white. So there is probably no completely univocal ordinary use of 'color.' It will therefore be helpful to introduce a bit of clarifying terminology.

We may distinguish three dimensions of perceived color: hue, brightness, and saturation. Inevitably, we must rely on instances for their specification. Thus, the *hue* of a color is its redness, or greenness, or yellowness, or blueness. White and black and the grays are the colors with zero hue; they are technically known as the *achromatic colors*. The achromatic colors are colors in a limiting sense, just as zero is a number in a limiting sense. Those colors with nonzero hue are the *chromatic colors*. It is these which we demand to see when we pay for a color television set. Colors with the same hue may differ in the strength of that hue; they may have very little hue and thus be close to gray, or they may be strongly hued. We shall say that these colors differ in *saturation*. The spectrum is the hue gamut of maximum saturation. Finally, colors seen through apertures or perceived as self-luminous will vary along a range, with very dim colors at one end of the range and very bright or dazzling colors at the other. The colors ranged in this way vary in *brightness*. Objects that are not seen through apertures or perceived to be self-luminous vary in *lightness*.

Let us take stock of what we have found out so far about the visual system in general and the achromatic colors in particular. The visual system establishes a reference level and tends to maximize differences on either side of that reference level. This emphasis on contrast is even-handed, however: a swing in one direction is accompanied by a swing in the opposite sense. The light-dark system comprises what we may call an antagonist or *opponent* pair: a blackness response and a whiteness response, working on either side of a neutral state which, in moderate illumination conditions, is always a middle gray. An opponent pair is like a spring, a distension or compression of which leads to a reaction in the opposite direction—not, however, without overshooting on occasion. Antagonist systems are a biological commonplace, serving, as they do, the organism's need to adjust to a changing environment while maintaining internal equilibrium. They are essential ingredients in homeostasis.

Chromatic vision

With this conception of opponent pairs firmly in mind, let us turn to chromatic vision and the receptors that normally initiate it, the cones. There are three types of cones, corresponding to three types of photopigments. Their collective sensitivity covers the range of the electromagnetic spectrum from a little less than 400 nm to a little more than 700 nm. Each cone type has a distinct and characteristic spectral absorption curve which represents the probability that a photon of a given wavelength will be absorbed (figure I-11). When a receptor absorbs a photon, it generates a neural signal that is independent of the wavelength of that photon. This fact is called *the principle of univariance*. An immediate consequence of the principle of univariance is that there is, at the level of each single receptor, a profound loss of information about the wavelength of light which is incident upon the eye. If the receptor absorbs 100 quanta of light of wavelength λ_1 and then 100 quanta of λ_2, its output will be just the same in both cases. Information lost at an earlier stage of a sequential process cannot be restored at a later stage. So the *only* visual remnants of wavelength differences in the stimulus will be differences in the relative outputs of the three receptor types. The common informational currency of the chromatic visual system consists entirely of output differences which are a function of three-term cone-excitation ratios. (For most stimulus intensities and over most of their operating ranges, the outputs of visual receptors are logarithmically related to their inputs. Now the ratio of two numbers is equal to the difference of their logarithms. So *differences* in receptoral outputs will correspond to *ratios* of receptoral stimulations.) From this it follows that if two or more light stimuli with physically distinct wavelength compositions produce the same ratios of stimulation among the receptor types, they will not be

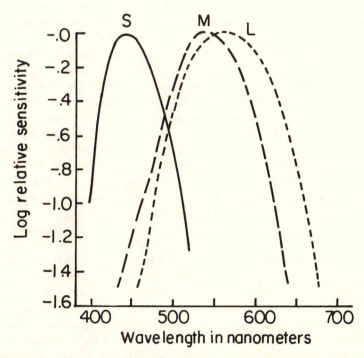

Fig. I-11. *Normalized spectral sensitivity functions for the three human and macaque monkey cone types: shortwave (S), middlewave (M), and longwave (L). The sensitivity at each wavelength is proportional to the probability that the cone type will absorb a quantum of light at that wavelength.*

distinguishable by the eye. And indeed, for indefinitely many particular light distributions, there will be indefinitely many distributions that will be indistinguishable from them in color.

Two light distributions that differ in their wavelength constituents but are indistinguishable in color for a given observer are said to be *metamers* for that observer. By extension, one can speak of objects that match in color (for a given observer) under a given illumination as matching *metamerically* (for that observer). If they match under *all* illuminations, they are said to match *isomerically*. In that case, they will reflect light wavelength for wavelength in exactly the same way. There can be degrees of object metamerism: two material samples may match under only one or two illuminants, or they may match under most illuminants. It is common practice to specify sets of metamerically matching light distributions by reference to an *average observer*, which is an internationally standardized statistical construct obtained by averaging the color matches made by a number of normal observers.[7] It is apparent that small differences in ratios of cone absorbances from one observer to the next will produce corresponding small differences in the metameric sets of the observers. Metameric matching involves indistinguishability in all three dimensions of brightness, saturation, and hue. A given observer can also match lights of different physical composition with respect to one or two of these dimensions. We shall be particularly interested in matches of hue. The members of a set of light distributions that match in hue a spectral (monochromatic) stimulus are specified in terms of the wavelength of that stimulus, which is referred to as their *dominant wavelength*. Thus, a light which, for the average observer, matches in hue a monochromatic 550 nm stimulus is said to have a dominant wavelength of 550 nm. We shall have more to say about metamerism and hue matching later on when we discuss color ontology.

The existence of three cone types with distinct spectral absorbances is responsible for the fact that three appropriately chosen spectral lights can, under a wide variety of conditions, be separately adjusted in intensity and mixed to provide a color match for any arbitrarily selected test light (the match will always be a hue match, but an achromatic desaturating light may have to be added to the test light to get a saturation—and thus a color—match). The three spectral lights must be such that none can be matched by a mixture of the other two. Indefinitely many triples of lights will qualify—there is no such thing as *the* light-mixing primaries—but, in order to maximize the range of producible hues, one member of the triple will always look mostly blue, one mostly green, and one mostly red. Once the trivariate nature of the laws of color mixture, which were given a definitive formulation in 1853 by Hermann Grassman,[8] were properly understood, it was readily seen that they could be accounted for by supposing there to be exactly three receptor types.

To nineteenth-century scientists, it also seemed natural to suppose that all color experiences were the result of the neural outputs of the three types being proportionately (additively) mixed as the three primary lights were mixed and, therefore, to label the three cone types as, respectively, the "blue," "green," and "red" cones. This usage persists among many color scientists as well as the educated public, although the assumptions on which it once rested have proved highly questionable.[9]

The chief critic of the emerging nineteenth-century consensus was Ewald Hering (1920; 1964), who pointed to many fundamental facts that went unexplained by the model, which called only for additive mixtures of the outputs of the three receptor types to be sent to the brain.[10] For instance, purple seems to have both reddish and bluish constituents in it, and is readily describable as a reddish blue or bluish red. It could thus plausibly be the result of mixing "red" cone outputs with "blue" cone outputs, by analogy with the mixture of "red" light and "blue" light to give "purple" light. But yellow, which is generated by mixing "red" light with "green" light, does not seem to be a reddish green or a greenish red. Indeed, there *are* no reddish greens. On the (then) accepted model, how could one account for the perceptually unitary character of yellow and the perceptually composite character of purple, when the model calls for them to be produced by similar processes, red-blue neural mixture on the one hand and red-green neural mixture on the other? And how could the perceptual absence of reddish greens and yellowish blues be explained?

In Hering's view, the phenomenology of color appearances suggested that there are not three but four fundamental chromatic processes and that these are arranged in opponent pairs, like muscles or a multitude of other physiological elements. (Hering was a physiologist.) The "red process" (i.e., the process giving rise to the sensation of red) is opposed to the green, so an increase in the one must be gained at the expense of the other, and the yellow process is, in a similar fashion, opposed to the blue. In addition, there is an achromatic pair, in which the black is opposed to, and produced solely by the inhibition of, the white process. The phenomenal characters of purple and yellow thus reflect their neural representations. The phenomenally complex color purple is represented by the joint occurrence of red and blue processes, and the phenomenally simple color yellow is represented by a noncomposite yellow process, the red and green processes in this case being in neutral balance. (Notice that none of this has anything to do with whether the wavelength composition of the stimulus is monochromatic or complex; a phenomenally simple yellow hue can be produced by either sort of stimulus composition.) The red and green processes are not constituents of the yellow process, any more than perceived red and green are constituents of pure yellow. There may of course be reddish yellows or greenish yellows, but no yellows that are reddish *and* greenish. There cannot be a reddish greenish appearance, because the occurrence of either the red or the green process involves the inhibition of the other. It is as if there were a two-person tug of war; a net pull to the right is red, a net pull to the left is green, and a neutral balance is achromatic.

Hering's theory was as capable of accounting for the established facts of color mixture as the accepted theory, championed by Helmholtz. We shall not go into the comparative merits of the views of Hering and Helmholtz on several related phenomena of color vision, although we shall touch on some of these phenomena later. Hering's theory was generally rejected in the first half of the twentieth century because it was supposed that he was positing the existence of four types of chromatic receptors, for which there was scant evidence, and because his theory was qualitative rather than quantitative and the arguments on its behalf phenomenal rather than behavioral.

This state of affairs changed drastically during the 1950s when Dorothea Jameson and Leo M. Hurvich performed a set of psychophysical experiments on which they based a quantitative version of the opponent theory (Jameson and Hurvich 1955 and 1956, Hurvich and Jameson 1955 and 1956). Independently of Jameson and Hurvich, Gunnar Svaetichin and others discovered, through direct electrophysiological recordings of individual visual cells, a wavelength-dependent opponency in their outputs (Svaetichin and MacNichol 1958). The general features of Hering's theory (though not, of course, many of its details) received physiological support, and psychophysical methods that rely on subjects' qualitative judgments were given a new respectability in the eyes of many investigators. In what follows we shall sketch with broad strokes the opponent theory and the evidence and methods on which it is based, and suggest some of its philosophically interesting consequences.

First, we need to look further at the absorption responses of the cones. There are, indeed, just three types; so the front end of the system is as Helmholtz and others had supposed it to be; opponency enters at the second stage, in the cross-connections among the cells to which the cones send their output. Since there are at least two stages in the color-coding process, it seems inappropriate to assign color names to the cones. And, if we look at the peak sensitivities of the cone types (figure I-11) and compare them to the hues seen at the corresponding points in the spectrum at moderate light levels (see the spectrum graph on plate 1), we must notice that the peak sensitivity of the "red" cone falls at a point—about 560 nm—which most people would see as a greenish yellow. Accordingly, the three cone types will hereafter be designated the 'S' (shortwave), 'M' (middle-wave) and 'L' (longwave) cones.

Perhaps the most striking fact about the photopigment absorption curves of the three cone types is that they overlap so much. Given this degree of overlap, if the output signals of the cone types simply added, they could not successfully differentiate wavelength information from intensity information. We can see this in figure I-12, which compares a one-photopigment system with a two-photopigment system in which the outputs are summed and with a two-photopigment system in which the outputs are differenced. Suppose, as in (A), that there is but one receptor type. The spectrum of its neural output is the image of its absorption. It cannot serve to differentiate wavelength changes from intensity changes, since any wavelength difference (between 500 nm and 550 nm, say) that would make itself known by a difference in the strength of the receptor's output could be simulated for the organism in question by a difference in intensity in the absence of a wavelength difference. Compare this with the situation depicted in (B), in which there are two receptor types with photopigments of different absorbances whose outputs are simply summed. The spectrum of its neural response is essentially the envelope of the spectrum of its absorbances. Such a system is no more capable of distinguishing wavelength differences from intensity differences than is the system in (A). But now consider (C), a visual system with the same receptor types as (B), but with the outputs of those receptors connected so that the signal from the one type is *subtracted* from the signal produced by the other type. If we consider a pair of wavelengths such as 500 nm and 550 nm, we see that no change in the intensity at the one wavelength is capable of provoking a neural response that mimics the response of the system to the other wavelength. (C) is an opponent system, and unlike the systems of (A) and (B), satisfies a necessary condition for being a wavelength differentiator. It is, however, only a necessary condition; by itself such a system can tell only whether an absorbed photon had a wavelength greater than or less than that associated with the cell's basal response. But

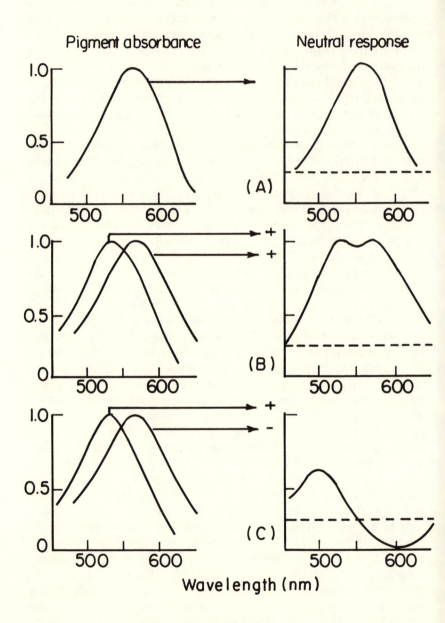

Pigment absorbance

Neutral response

Wavelength (nm)

add a second opponent system with a different neutral point and a way of comparing the differences of the outputs of the two systems, and far more wavelength information can be encoded.[11]

A differencing system for receptor outputs has a further engineering advantage: greater transmission efficiency. We recall that the retinal image is sampled by more than 120 million receptors, of which 7 million are foveal cones. Yet all of that information must be transmitted over an optic nerve that contains only 1.2 million fibers (Lennie 1984). Part of the required transmission economy is achieved by letting the achromatic system handle fine resolution: psychophysical experiments show that small spatial differences in *luminance* (light energy flow per unit area) with constant wavelength are much more easily detected than small spatial differences in wavelength with constant luminance. The other part can be achieved by exploiting the redundancy inherent in the considerable overlap of the absorption spectra of the cones. Because of this, the only chromatic information that needs to be transmitted are the *differences* of the cone outputs, a far more economical alternative than transmitting the output for each cone type separately. It is interesting to notice that when color television transmission systems were devised, and the human visual system was not as well understood as it is now, engineers were confronted with the problem of transmitting the maximum amount of chromatic information over a restricted bandwidth. They chose (a) to let the black-and-white signal handle the fine detail and (b) to convey chromatic information by a difference signal. They also decided to have the chromatic signal ride piggyback on the achromatic signal, letting the transmission and detection circuitry do double duty, and to separate the two signals at the receiver. Recent research indicates that the macaque monkey (and presumably the human) visual system adopts a similar strategy for information transmission across the optic nerve (Lennie, 1984).

Fig. I-12. Facing page: *Schematic indication of possible relationships between photopigment absorbance properties (left) and the responses of neural elements receiving inputs from these photopigments (right). (A) The response of an element receiving input from a single photopigment class mirrors the spectral response properties of the pigment. (B) The outputs from two different photopigment classes are summed to produce a neural response whose spectral properties are roughly the envelope of the two pigment curves. (C) The outputs from the two photopigment classes generate neural changes of opposite sign that are combined algebraically. The horizontal dashed lines represent the level of spontaneous activity in the neural elements.*

We have seen the design principles that seem to regulate the generation and transmission of chromatic signals to the brain. What are the details of their implementation? At this and several other points in our discussion, it is important to bear in mind that, although there is nowadays a consensus that chromatic opponency occurs, there are also many detailed and much disputed variants of mathematical opponent theories.[12] Here we can aspire only to locate and sketch what appears to be the middle road, and hope that we shall not wander too deeply into error.

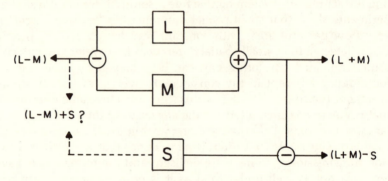

Fig. I-13. *A schematic representation of a quantitative opponent theory.*

A representative simple version of a quantitative mathematical opponent theory is shown in figure I-13. The outputs of **L** and **M** are summed to give an achromatic channel, and differenced to generate a red-green opponent channel. (Bear in mind that the neural counterpart of differencing is inhibition. "Channel" is to be understood as a functional notion. It is quite commonly psychophysically defined, and its neural realization, which may be physically complex, is subsequently looked for, and with a little luck, found.) In addition to providing an achromatic signal, the summed output of **L** and **M** is differenced with the **S** output to yield a yellow-blue channel. Whether the **S** cone makes a contribution to the achromatic channel is a matter of dispute, though it seems likely that, if such a contribution exists, it is very small under most conditions (Boynton 1979, 325-327). It has not been indicated in the figure. The input of the **S** cone to the red-green channel is also a matter of controversy. The contribution is, once again, most probably small, but there is good evidence that it does play some role (Ingling 1977). It has been noted in the figure by means of a broken line, but will not be included in our specification of the neural code.

Letting '0' represent the base rate of neural activity, we may spell out this version of the neural code as follows:

(L + M) is the achromatic signal.
    (L + M) > 0 codes whiteness;
    (L + M) < 0 codes blackness;
    (L + M) = 0 codes for "brain gray", as do all '0' values.
(L − M) is the red-green signal.
    (L − M) > 0 codes redness;
    (L − M) < 0 codes greenness.
(L + M) − S is the yellow-blue signal.
    (L + M) − S > 0 codes yellowness;
    (L + M) − S < 0 codes blueness.

Saturation at a wavelength is coded by the ratio of the response for both chromatic channels at that wavelength to the sum of chromatic and whiteness response at that wavelength.

Some further comments should be made about this representation of opponent theory. First, in its present form it is too simple, since there is evidence that some of the interactions, particularly those involving the yellow-blue channel, are nonlinear (Werner and Wooten 1979; Hunt 1982). Second, the choice of sign (e.g., greenness as negative, redness as positive) is, at the present state of knowledge, merely conventional. That greenness and redness should be given *opposite* signs is, of course, essential to the theory. Third, the formulae need to be assigned coefficients that reflect the weighting to be given to each cone type. The values of the coefficients will depend upon such factors as the relative efficiency with which the cone transforms radiant energy into neural energy, the proportions of each cone type at a particular retinal region, etc. Although these matters are of obvious importance to visual science, the particulars need not detain our inquiry further. Finally, there is the question of how far up the visual-processing line this particular form of coding goes. Something like it is probably right for the stretch from retina to cortex, but whether recoding occurs and whether this invariably has an opponent character is something we are not, at this stage, able to decide. The phenomenology, which presumably reflects the upshot of the total process, bears the earmarks of opponency, but this does not of itself enable us to decide whether opponent coding is maintained at every stage subsequent to the retina or whether or later, nonopponent coding conveys a signal that has been shaped by earlier opponent stages (Teller 1984). If the latter is the case, it might under some circumstances be possible to gain alternative access to such a later stage or stages and generate color experiences not generable by opponent processing. We shall subsequently return to—but not answer—this question.

Chromatic response

Once coefficients have been assigned to the neural-code formulae, they could be used, along with data about the relative amplitude of absorption for each wavelength for each receptor type, to generate a set of predicted *chromatic-response* curves.[13] In fact, the inference works the other way: chromatic-response curves are empirically determined by psychophysical measurements, the procedures for which we shall examine shortly. The measurements are then used with the absorbance data (which have recently become quite reliable, having been obtained by a variety of converging procedures) to make inferences about the form and coefficients of the neural code. The chromatic-response curves sum up a great deal of important perceptual information in a theoretically perspicuous form. Let us look at a representative set, checking their numerical values against a calibrated color picture of the spectrum (Plate 1).

Figure I-14 is really a set of three curves, representing on a common set of coordinates the responses of the three opponent systems. The data on the basis of which the curves were drawn are the responses of a human subject viewing mixtures of spectral lights. The achromatic curve is therefore always positive, since blackness (negative values) can be produced only by contrast, which does not occur in viewing isolated light spots. It may thus be construed as a whiteness response. Notice the whiteness response rising to a maximum in the region in which the yellowness response is large, but becoming small at the red and blue ends. This would lead us to expect that yellows would be typically brighter but less saturated than reds and particularly less saturated than blues. Saturation, we recall, is taken to be the ratio of the chromatic response to the sum of the chromatic and whiteness responses. Since that ratio is much higher for spectral blue than for spectral yellow, yellow will, at its most colorful, be less colorful than blue. (Each spectral color, because it is evoked by monochromatic light, always involves the minimum possible whiteness response and is, therefore, the maximally saturated version of that hue.) Yellows will typically be brighter than blues because, for light of moderate intensity, they are seen at that region in the spectrum for which the eye is most sensitive.

Now notice that, at several spectral loci, one or the other of the opponent curves crosses the zero line. This means that the corresponding opponent system is in neutral balance at that point. From left to right, the first of these neutral balance points occurs where the red-green curve crosses the axis at 475 nm. At 475 nm, the yellow-

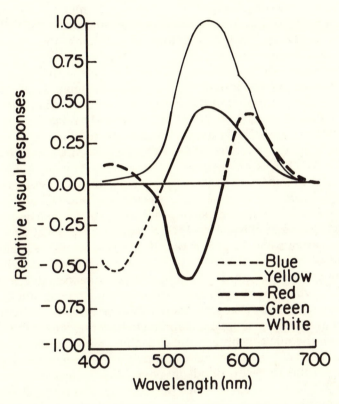

Fig. I-14. *Chromatic and achromatic responses for an equal-energy spectrum and a single observer.*

blue system is negative and, hence, signals blue. So here redness, greenness, and yellowness are all zero. What the subject sees is a blue without any other chromatic component—a *unique* blue, as it is called in the trade. Unique blue is an instance of the phenomenally simple hues to which Hering called attention. The next axis crossing is at 500 nm, where the yellow-blue system is in neutral balance, but the red-green system is in a negative state. This is the locus of the subject's unique green. At 577 nm, the red-green system is in balance once more, and the yellow-blue system is in a positive state. This is the locus of unique yellow. What about unique red? We can see that, on the longwave end of the spectrum, the yellow-blue curve remains slightly positive until the end, so every spectral red comes with a small yellow addendum (at moderately high light levels). There is thus no unique red on a spectrum of moderate intensity. Unique red must be obtained by taking a spectral red and adding a dollop of short-wavelength ("blue") light to it, so as to make the yellow-blue curve take a zero value.

If we return to the far shortwave end of the spectrum, we notice that the redness response makes a surprising, though small, return. This is because this end of the spectrum is, in fact, violet (a reddish blue) rather than just blue. Why this is so is unclear, but there is some reason to suppose that **S** cones may provide an inhibitory contribution to **M** cones, thus altering the balance between **L** and **M** outputs (Ingling 1977). This was represented in figure I-13 by the broken line.

Almost as important as the zero crossings of the curves are those points at which the chromatic curves cross each other. For instance, around 590 nm, both curves are positive—thus both yellow and red are signaled—and of equal strength. 590 nm is the point at which this subject sees a balanced yellow-red, that is to say, orange. Similarly, turquoise and cyan make their appearance between unique blue at 475 nm and unique green at 500 nm. One might expect that, at those points at which the chromatic response curves are steep and the hue constituents rapidly changing, there would be better hue discrimination than at those points corresponding to flatter regions of the curves in which the hue constituents are changing relatively slowly. An example of this effect is to be found around 550 nm, where hue discrimination for this subject is decidedly poorer than at 590 nm.

We might make many other observations about the chromatic-response curves, such as how they represent the banded appearance of the spectrum and the relative widths of the bands. But let us be content with one further remark. It is that, since the neutral point of an opponent pair is achromatic, any stimulus that will put both chromatic opponent systems in balance will yield an achromatic perception, the degree of lightness or whiteness of which will depend on the activity in the achromatic channel. Speaking loosely (i.e., assigning color names to stimuli), if we are given a yellowish green light, we can render the appearance of this stimulus achromatic by adding enough blue to offset the yellow and enough red to balance the green. Far from its being the case that whiteness is identical to an assemblage of all wavelengths, whiteness may be generated by as few as two wavelengths and in an indefinitely large number of ways. Pairs of chromatic lights that can be added together to give an achromatic appearance are said to be (additive) *complements*.

This cancellation of chromatic stimuli is, in fact, at the root of the experimental procedure originally used to generate the opponent curves. This chromatic cancellation procedure, due to Hurvich and Jameson, is carried out in the following way: A subject is seated before a device, a dual monochromator, which can select single wavelengths from anywhere in the spectrum or combine any two such wavelengths. The wavelength and energy of each wavelength can be adjusted at the subject's pleasure. She first establishes her unique hues, looking through the spectrum for a blue that is neither reddish nor greenish, a green that is neither yellowish nor bluish, and a yellow that is neither reddish nor greenish. Notice that these instructions for finding unique hues could not be translated into instructions for finding composite, or as we shall call them, *binary* hues. There is no such thing as, for instance, an orange that is neither reddish nor yellowish. On the contrary, *every* orange is to some degree reddish and also to some degree yellowish. A *balanced* orange is one in which the red component and the yellow component are of equal perceived chromatic strength; such an orange is no more reddish than it is yellowish. Furthermore we can see that it makes perfectly good sense to describe an orange as a reddish yellow or a yellowish red, but it makes no sense at all to describe a red as a purplish orange or an orangish purple.

For each unique hue there will be a precise setting on the instrument, calibrated in nanometers. For any individual subject, the unique hue settings will be stable and reliable, even for sessions some weeks apart. There will, however, be differences in unique hue settings from one subject to another. For moderate intensities, as we have previously noted, there will be no unique red hue on the spectrum. Nevertheless, the wavelengths from 650 to 700 nm are virtually indistinguishable and are perceived as containing only a small amount of yellowness, so 650 nm can serve as a unique-red setting for the cancellation experiments with only a small error.

Once the unique hue settings are established, a set of wavelengths spanning the spectrum at 10 nm intervals is specified, and they are dialed up on the instrument in turn. Suppose that one of these is 600 nm. For normal observers at moderate light intensities, this will be perceived as a reddish orange, which, in unique-hue terms, is a yellowish red. When the energy of the 600 nm light is recorded, the subject proceeds to cancel the yellowness in the light by mixing in a spectral light which, when the subject sees it in isolation, looks unique blue, until a point is reached at which all the yellowness disappears without there being any appearance of blueness. (The light will look reddish.) The energy of the canceling blue is recorded, the blue is turned off, and the subject proceeds to cancel the redness in the 600 nm stimulus with unique green. The energy of the green setting is then recorded. When the cancellation is complete, the blue equivalent of the yellowness at 600 nm will be established along with the green equivalent of the redness. Proceeding in this way through the spectrum at 10 nm intervals, the greenness and redness responses are calibrated relative to each other, as are the yellowness and blueness responses. Other procedures involving the location of balanced binary hues are used to fit the one opponent pair to the other, so that a consistent and useful set of curves results.

The structure of phenomenal hues

If you feel uncomfortable with the appeals to subjective quality assessments in this procedure, you will be sharing the sentiments and scruples of the majority of psychophysicists before about 1960. They felt comfortable with what G. S. Brindley dubbed "Class A" experiments, in which subjects are asked to report the presence or absence of something or to say whether or not two stimuli match, but tended to shy away from "Class B" experiments in which, in Brindley's words, "the subject must describe the quality or intensity of his sensations, or abstract from two different sensations some aspect in which they are alike" (Brindley 1960, 145; quoted and discussed in Teller 1984 and in Teller and Pugh 1983). The Hurvich-Jameson experiments are plainly Class B. Brindley expressed the doubts of many about the security of inferences from phenomenal descriptions to underlying visual mechanisms, and the general acceptance of opponent process theory had to await confirmation from physiological inquiries and Class A psychophysical experiments. But one result of that confirmation was to give well-conceived Class B experiments a new authority and to make well-drawn inferences from phenomenal descriptions more respectable. The distinction between unique and binary hues in the Hering theory proves not to rest on some accident of description or parochial feature of European languages, but rather to pick out a fundamental functional feature of the visual system which is reflected quite generally in color-classifying behavior and linguistic practices. The relationship between the functional configuration and color language will receive detailed attention later. Let us now look at some of the behavioral evidence that shows the natural primacy of the unique hues.

(1) Those who study infants commonly make the plausible supposition that a baby will exhibit its division of objects into resemblance classes by the amount of time that it spends looking at them. Suppose, for instance, that a young child is presented sequentially with stimuli A and B. She is shown A until she "habituates" and stops looking, then she is shown B. If the child sees B as different from A, she will "dishabituate," and start looking at B, but if she sees B as similar or identical to A, she will not dishabituate. A group of four-month-old experimental subjects were presented with randomized sequences of colored lights. The population of lights from which the sequences were drawn had characteristic (dominant) wavelengths 30 nm apart. For example, the infant was habituated to a 480 nm light, then shown a light of 450 nm or a light of 510 nm. Most adults would see the 480 nm light as more like the 450 nm light than like the 510 nm light. Does the infants' eye-fixation time partition the stimuli in the same way? The experimenters tell us that it does, and it thus appears that infant hue space is neatly divided into four similarity classes centered upon the four unique hues.[14]

(2) The Dani people of New Guinea have no abstract words for the chromatic colors, though they do have equivalents of our 'light' and 'dark'. E. H. Rosch selected some Dani youths who had shown an aptitude for formal learning and divided them into two groups. To the one group she showed samples of (nearly) unique hues and assigned to them Dani kinship names. To the other group she showed samples of binary hues and assigned to them the same kinship names. She then presented the members of each group with assorted color samples and asked them to pick out the paradigmatic examples. The members of the first group required significantly less time to complete the task correctly (Rosch 1973; Heider 1972 (Heider = Rosch)).

(3) Adult subjects were shown, two at a time, fourteen colors, differing primarily in hue. They were asked to rate the "qualitative similarity" of each color pair on a five step scale. The results were subjected to a mathematical technique known as *analysis of proximities*. If distances between American cities were replaced by their rank orderings, a proximity analysis of these could generate a two-dimensional Euclidean representation that would come close to replicating the original distance relations. In the experiment at hand, when the method was applied to the "qualitative similarity" ratings

of the colors, the resulting two-dimensional map was figure I-15. The numbers are the dominant wavelengths of the color samples, and the dotted line represents the nonspectral purples, which were not included among the samples (Ekman 1954; Shepard 1962).

Notice particularly that the unique hues, whose spectral positions are approximately indicated by the words 'RED', 'YELLOW', etc., are spaced about 90 degrees apart, which is the spacing that the opponent theory would have led one to expect. Were there just three psychologically basic hues, such as the "additive primaries" red, green, and blue, or the "subtractive primaries"[15] red, yellow, and blue, one would have expected these hues to be spaced about 120 degrees apart. Proximity analysis applied to quite distinct color-ordering techniques, such as color naming (see below) and a technique based on the formation of minimally distinct borders, have yielded very similar results (Boynton 1975). In all instances, the ordering is based upon the phenomenal characteristics of colors.

(4) In the procedure known as *color naming*, subjects are shown randomized sequences of, for example, 25 perceptually distinct monochromatic lights and asked to describe their hues by using a restricted set of names. In one version of the procedure, the "subjects are told to treat the light they are viewing as consisting of a color sensation equal to a value of 100 per cent. They are asked to assign percentages to each of the color names allowed in a given session that represent the amount of each of these colors *perceived* in this light. The subjects are told that the total need not add to 100 per cent if the color names permitted for a particular session are not adequate for a complete description." There are two notable outcomes of such experiments. First, it was discovered that subjects could completely describe all the spectral lights as well as the purples by using just the unique-hue names, but that they were unable to give a complete description if the names to which they were restricted lacked one of the unique-hue names. Second, the hue-percentage estimates the subjects gave were compared with their monochromator settings in hue-cancellation procedures. Figure I-16 shows the averages of the hue-naming percentage estimates by the three subjects of one experiment compared with the averages of their hue-cancellation settings. These were, by the way, theoretically naive subjects (Werner and Wooten 1979. Cf. Boynton 1979, 210-211).

Such results should be examined against that long philosophical tradition exemplified by David Hume and G. E. Moore which has held phenomenal colors to be paradigmatic of simple, unanalyzable qualities. But since people can with rather high reliability and precision analyze colors, we had better conclude that colors are, after all, analyzable. Why then has the hoary prejudice to the contrary persisted so long in philosophical circles? There may be two reasons. In the first place, there seems to have been a tendency to think that if colors are analyzable they are analyzable into *parts*, whereas we might better think of them as being, like vectoral quantities in physics, an-

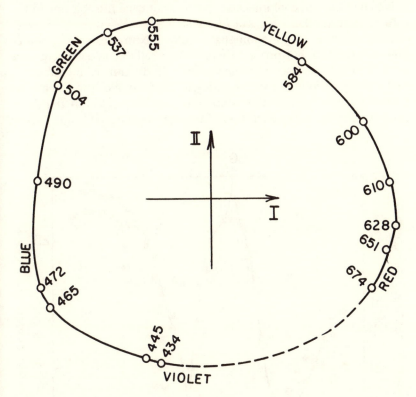

Fig. I-15. *Proximity analysis of the ratings of the "qualitative similarity" of fourteen colors by adult subjects.*

alyzable into *components*. A component of a vector is not part of a vector. A second source of the persistence of the belief may be a reaction to the rather confused lore about colors which we have absorbed in school. The art teacher (speaking of pigment mixing) told us that blue and yellow make green. But we could easily see that green doesn't *look* as if it were made up of blue and yellow. The physics teacher (speaking of light mixing) informed us that red and green make yellow. But of course yellow doesn't *look* as if it had red and green constituents. One's natural reaction to all of this is to regard all talk about color constituents as talk about how physical things get put together to provide stimuli for color perception and, thus, not to expect that they be perceptually manifest in the product. We don't, after all, expect table salt to be green and poisonous just because it has chlorine in it. (The greater phenomenological wisdom, however, was to be found in cooking class: you cannot taste the chlorine in the salt, but you *can* taste the salt in the stew.)

Let us look at the phenomena of color mixture from the point of view of the opponent-process theory. We recall that as a consequence of the fact that all discriminable wavelength differences must be represented by differences in the ratios of excitations of the three cone types, any two stimuli that stimulate the three types in the same ratios will be seen as matching in hue. For instance, a unique yellow

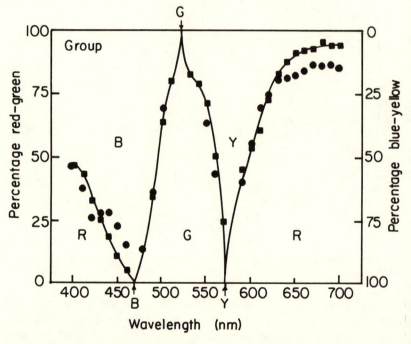

Fig. I-16. *Average hue-naming data (squares) and average hue-naming predicted from the opponent cancellation functions (circles) for three observers. Red-green is plotted from 0% to 100% according to the left vertical axis and yellow-blue is plotted from 100% to 0% according to the right vertical axis. The smooth line was drawn by eye through the obtained hue-naming data, ignoring the predicted hue-naming points. The arrows indicate the average unique-hue loci.*

may be evoked in a particular observer by stimulating the eye with monochromatic light of 580 nm. But it may equally be evoked at that light level by a suitable mixture of 540 nm and 670 nm. Seen separately, 540 nm is a yellowish green and 670 nm a slightly yellowish red. The mixture has 580 nm as its dominant wavelength, even though it has no 580 nm constituent. Any light with a wavelength between 520 and 580 nm can be made to look uniquely yellow if the proper amount of red can be injected to cancel the greenness, and any light from 580 nm up to the longwave end of the visible spectrum can similarly be made to look uniquely yellow by canceling the redness with an appropriate amount of green.

Once a match between two light spots is effected, it remains a match over a wide range of intensity levels. Except for the unique hues, however, the hue appearance of both spots will commonly change with changes of intensity; they will continue to match each other, but their hues will not match the hues of spots of the same wavelength composition at other levels. Color samples will look more reddish or greenish at lower light levels, and more yellowish or bluish at higher light levels. This phenomenon is known as the *Bezold-Brücke hue shift* (figure II-1). It is usually explained by supposing that the red-green system is more active than the yellow-blue system at low light levels, but that activity of the yellow-blue system increases proportionately more with increases in light level than the activity of the red-green system. We shall have more to say about the hue shift later.

One must also bear in mind that, although monochromatic spots of light may be matched in hue by polychromatic spots of properly chosen composition, the latter will generally be less saturated. Non-monochromatic light will excite the whiteness response at more than one locus, and the excitations will add, in most—though by no means all—cases giving a color more desaturated than the spectral hue of the same dominant wavelength. This is because each additional wavelength will evoke its own achromatic response, and these achromatic responses will add. So a hue match of a polychromatic to a monochromatic stimulus will often not be a metameric color match unless "white" desaturating light is added to the monochromatic spot. But, like a hue match, a metameric color match remains a match with changes of stimulus intensity.

Object metamerism, adaptation, and contrast

Experiments based on the careful comparison of light spots are very useful for probing the color-processing capabilities of the visual system in a precise, well controlled and relatively simple way, but they do not tell us all we would like to know about the color perceptions of natural scenes. These mostly involve assemblages of reflecting objects illuminated in a particular manner. The same physiological mechanisms involved in the perception of *aperture colors*—the colors of isolated lights or illuminated samples viewed through a reduction screen—are, of course, also involved in the perceptions of *surface colors*—the colors of illuminated surfaces seen under conditions in which it is possible for the organism to distinguish, at least to some extent, the spectral characteristics of the surfaces from the spectral characteristics of the ambient light. But additional factors are at work in the case of surface colors, factors which substantially modify the resulting perception. We shall consider two of them, which we have already encountered in connection with the achromatic system: adaptation and contrast.

In the perception of aperture colors, the proportionate number of quanta absorbed by each cone type will depend upon two factors: the spectrum of the light, and the wavelength-by-wavelength sensitivity of the cones. In perceiving surface colors, the spectrum of the light that reaches the eye is a product of the spectrum of the illuminant and the selectivity—normally reflectivity—of the surface. When either of these factors changes, the composition of the light that reaches the eye is also likely to change. This might be expected to result in constant shifts of the perceived surface color with the constant changes in the character of the illuminant which occur as one passes from sunlight to shadow to artificial lights of various sorts. In fact, the perceived colors of surfaces show a remarkable (though by no means perfect) constancy over a wide range of illuminance changes. The explanation of this approximate constancy is one of the major—and only partly solved—problems of visual science.

But color constancy is only approximate; so, just as there are metameric matches of colored lights, there are metameric matches of colored surfaces. These surfaces will match under some, but not all, illuminations. Consider, for example, the surfaces whose reflectances are graphed in figure I-17. In daylight, which has a relatively constant intensity for all points in the spectrum, both surfaces look green. The surface whose spectrum is represented by the dashed line reflects 500 nm very strongly, with a secondary peak at about 650 nm. Because of the resulting cone-excitation ratios, blueness and yellowness responses will be evoked weakly and approximately equally, and the greenness response will outweigh the redness response, not only because of higher reflectance in the appropriate region, but because the eye's sensitivity at 650 nm and up is less than its sensitivity around 500 nm. The solid curve shows a reflectance much larger in the spectral region that normally evokes a green response than in the region that normally evokes a red response. Incandescent light has an energy spectrum weak in short wavelengths and strong in long wavelengths, so its curve slopes upward to the right. This changes the relative proportions of the wavelengths around 500 nm leaving the surface and those around 650 nm, and so tips the balance toward net evocation of redness response. The equilibrium between the blueness and yellowness excitations will also be disturbed in favor of the latter. The net effect will be a darkened orange (brown) appearance in incandescent light. The surface whose spectrum is represented by the solid curve is one whose reflectance in the 500 nm to 580 nm range sufficiently exceeds its reflectance in any other region for it to withstand a substantial tilt in the illumination spectrum and still retain its green appearance. This single example shows the implausibility of the supposition that daylight appearance suffices to reveal the "true" colors

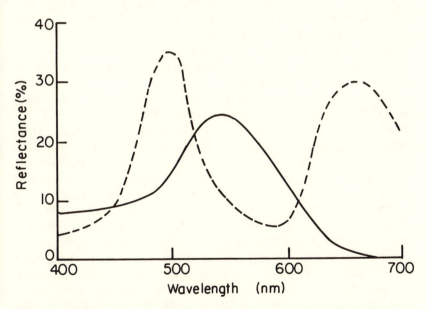

Fig. I-17. *Reflectance as a function of wavelength for two objects that both appear green and are metamers in daylight. In tungsten light, the object with the dashed reflectance curve looks brown, while the object with the solid reflectance curve still looks green. So, in tungsten illumination, the objects are not metamers.*

of objects. It is indeed a commonplace that objects that seem to match under one "white" illuminant may fail to match under a different one. The jacket and trousers that look so well together in the light of the clothing store may disappoint on the street, and makeup applied beneath a fluorescent tube in the bathroom may not have its intended effect at a candlelit dinner table.[16]

Fortunately for those who make their living with color, the eye is for the most part forgiving of changes in color balance with changes in illumination. This is in large measure due to the fact that our eyes adapt to changes in the chromaticity of the illumination much as they adapt to changes in its intensity. Amateur photographers who use outdoor color film for artificially lit subjects discover to their sorrow that their pictures are yellowish, just as those who use tungsten film for outdoor scenes discover that everything has a bluish tinge. Although we are, if we think about it, aware that incandescent light imparts a "warm," yellowish cast to things, the magnitude of the difference as revealed by the camera startles us. We are once again reminded of the gulf that separates eye and camera. But the eye looks at the picture; so why does it not adapt and help us out with the picture? The answer is that it is the general illumination of the space in which we see the picture which largely determines the adaptation of the eye, and, indeed, if the picture can be made into a slide and so, in its mode of projection, made to play a larger role in determining the general illumination of the environment, a larger portion of the yellowishness will "adapt out."

Several mechanisms at different levels of visual processing seem to underlie chromatic adaptation. One of the chief of these is a shift in relative sensitivity of the different cone types under repeated stimulation. Close one eye and put a piece of transparent green (say) celluloid in front of the other for a minute or two. Then, keeping the one eye closed, remove the celluloid and notice that things have taken on a reddish cast. If you now open the closed eye, the magnitude of the change will be very striking. We can readily interpret what has happened as a desensitization of the M cones relative to the other two cone types. This shifts the inputs to the red-green opponent system in favor of redness response, with the effect of canceling out a fair amount of greenness in the scene; in fact, as you continue looking through the green filter, you will, if you pay careful attention, notice that things soon come to look less greenish. When the celluloid filter is removed, the net redness persists briefly, then quickly fades as the system readapts. We are usually unaware of these constant, though normally smaller, changes in chromatic calibration, in part, at least, because our color memories are usually poor and short-lived; were they not, opening the other eye would not have so striking an effect.

A large part of chromatic adaptation is doubtless due to changes in the receptors themselves. The psychophysical effects of these receptoral alterations in sensitivity have been understood since the pioneering investigations of Johannes von Kries in the early part of the present century. The time course of such changes in light-adapted cones is much faster than that of adaptation to darkness; physiological studies of the response of turtle cones suggest that there is substantial adaptation in as short a time as 50 milliseconds (Lamb 1985). Nevertheless, studies of color adaptation in human beings show that at least a portion of the adaptation is of neural origin (Jameson and Hurvich 1972), and other experimental data suggest that some of it must lie in the visual cortex rather than in the retina.[17] Current visual science's understanding of the mechanisms of this rapid adaptation and its contribution to approximate color constancy is, at best, incomplete, although there has been substantial recent work in the area. There is considerable controversy about the relative importance of retinal as opposed to cortical sites for chromatic adaptation, although it is clear that both play a role.[18]

Perceived differences of surface colors in the face of illumination changes are maintained by *simultaneous contrast*, which we have already encountered in connection with the achromatic system. Simultaneous chromatic contrast is not usually so strong an effect as simultaneous brightness contrast, though it is very definite, as plate 2 makes plain. The small blue-green squares are cut from the same piece of colored paper. But see the shift in hue as the green of the upper right rectangle cancels some of the green in its inserted square, making it look more blue than green, whereas the blue lower left rectangle cancels much of its insert's blueness, making it appear more green than blue. Here we see the opponent systems tending to maximize visual differences while at the same time working toward an overall net chromatic balance. It is worth while, when examining this and other examples of simultaneous contrast, to use a reduction screen to view the colored areas separately and thus undo the contrast. But it is important to choose a dark gray for the paper of which the screen is made, or else new contrast effects will be introduced.

Delacroix once said, "Give me mud, let me surround it as I think fit, and it shall be the radiant flesh of Venus." Decorum forbids this being a dirty book, so we shall not see in its pages mud, or for that matter, the naked flesh of Venus, but we can see other examples of simultaneous contrast. For instance, plate 2 shows how a patch of color can take on very different characteristics according to the color context in which it is placed. You will find it instructive to see to what extent the opponent relations enable you to predict the hue induced in the test patch by the hue of the inducing surround.

One form of simultaneous contrast which came strongly into the consciousness of painters in the last half of the nineteenth century was the phenomenon of colored shadows. You may observe colored shadows for yourself as J. W. Goethe did (Goethe 1840; 1970, Pt. I sec. 6). You will need two sources of light with somewhat different spectra, such as candlelight and daylight, or candlelight and incandescent light. Arrange things so that an object intercepts each light from a different direction, casting two shadows. The shadows will be of contrasting colors, usually magenta (a bluish red) and bluish green. (The extra bluish component in both shadows will depend on the extent to which the light sources are yellowish rather than chromatically neutral.) An even more striking demonstration can be had with two slide projectors, configured so that the image projected by one coincides with the image projected by the other. In one projector, insert a slide made up of a piece of transparent green celluloid with a piece of opaque tape covering part of the celluloid, arranged so that what is projected on the screen is a black shape (a cross, say) on a green field. In the other projector, insert an empty slide frame, so that the image consists of a rectangular patch of projector light. Now turn on both projectors so that the image from one is superimposed on the image cast by the other. What the laws of color mixture tell us is that the slightly yellowish light from the second projector should desaturate the green field just a bit, and tinge it with yellow. The black cross, illuminated with the projector light, should become a slightly yellowish gray. And, indeed, a spectrophotometer measuring the wavelengths of light coming from the superimposed images would not give us any reason to expect to see anything but a grayish cross on a greenish field. What we actually see, however, is a bright *pink* cross on a greenish field. The pink color is entirely the product of the chromatic opponent system, and a carefully used reduction tube aimed at just the cross will make the pinkness disappear in favor of the color predicted by the color-mixture laws. With ingenuity and photographic skill, the effect can be tricked up to be far more impressive, and this seems to be exactly what happened with Edwin Land's celebrated two-projector demonstrations (Land 1959).

The French impressionist painters drew colored shadows to the attention of the general public, contravening the prevailing convention that shadows were to be represented by darkening and desaturating the local color. In nature, colored shadows are most readily noticed on snow, when the yellow rays of the sun are interrupted by obstacles which are then seen to cast blue shadows, as in Monet's "Haystack in Winter" of 1891 (plate 3). It is, however, a tricky matter to catch the actual manifestation of simultaneous contrast, since another effect works in the same direction. The sky is blue because light of short wavelength is preferentially scattered by the molecules of the atmosphere. Snow reflects this blue light, which, in the absence of shadows, is canceled in its perceptual effect by the yellowness of sunlight. But, in shadows, the yellow sunlight is blocked and the blue reflection remains. So the proper effect of simultaneous contrast is unambiguously noticed when a large cloud is directly overhead, filtering the skylight but not completely obstructing the sun, whose cast shadows are true blue contrast (Walls 1960). This effect may be seen in Monet's "Haystacks, Foggy Morning" of 1891. Blue shadows are there in the summertime too, though harder to notice against chromatic surfaces. For instance, in Monet's "Haystack in Field" of 1893, the haystack's blue shadow mixes with the yellowish green of the grass to give an intense green.

The impressionists not only painted colored shadows, but exaggerated them. Why did they exaggerate these and other chromatic effects of light and shade? We can understand this at least in part by appreciating the impressionist landscape painter's problem, which was to duplicate a natural light intensity ratio that is typically 40 to 1 with a set of pigments that have an intensity ratio of perhaps 4 to 1 (Evans 1974, 205). His dodge was to substitute chromatic range, which he had in abundance, for the deficiency in intensity range to which his subtractive palette condemned him. We see sunlight as yellowish; so he represented increases in its intensity by increases in its yellowness. This he balanced by stronger bluing of the shadows, thus effectively replacing brightness contrast by chromatic contrast, just as recording engineers introduce a degree of stereo localization never heard in the concert hall to replace the visual localization of instruments necessarily missing on records and tapes.

Simultaneous contrast is opponency across space. There is opponency across time, too. This is *successive contrast*, better known as *afterimaging*. Afterimage demonstrations are very familiar, and what we have said so far about differential desensitization of cones in connection with adaptation will make it clear what basic mechanisms are at work (Hurvich 1981, ch. 14, and Brown 1965). But there is an afterimage demonstration which has a particular charm. Under a bright light, stare at the fixation dot in plate 4 for about thirty seconds, try-ing to keep your eye movements at a minimum. As you stare, notice the extent to which the image begins to fade and how markedly the yellow is desaturated. Before you stare, think about what afterimage colors you expect to see when you subsequently avert your gaze to the adjoining white area. It will be more fun if you pause to perform the experiment before reading further.

The surprising effect you experience is due to simultaneous contrast, which was quietly doing its work as you were staring, turning the white background violet. Successive and simultaneous contrast can work together in rather intricate ways. In this case, you have seen the negative afterimage of an induced color.

Some mechanisms of chromatic perception

In the past several pages we have discussed the pervasive and fundamentally important phenomena of adaptation and contrast. It is clear that these fit comfortably into the general conceptual scheme of opponent theory, but a great deal more must be said about the underlying mechanisms of chromatic vision before we can claim to have a full and proper understanding of these phenomena. In fact, visual scientists have come part of the way toward that larger understanding. At the same time that the hue-cancellation technique was being established, it became technically feasible to make direct recordings of the outputs of individual visual cells while animals were being visually stimulated. Large numbers of chromatically opponent cells were found at various stages in the visual-processing chain (Hurvich 1981, ch. 12, and DeValois and DeValois 1975). To call these cells "chromatically opponent" is to say that their output increases over their base rate when their receptive fields are stimulated with light of certain wavelengths, but falls below base rate when they are stimulated by light at other wavelengths.

We recall from our discussion of the achromatic system that neural units show spatial opponency, in that a light that excites or inhibits the center of their receptive fields will have the reverse effect on the surround. Such units play a central role in enhancing the edge contrasts which are so important to seeing. Quite a few of the chromatically opponent higher-level cells prove to be spatially opponent as well; so, for example, their receptive field centers are preferentially excited by red, and their receptive field surrounds preferentially inhibited by green. Furthermore, some of these are double-opponent cells with, for instance, a center excited by red and inhibited by green and a surround excited by green and inhibited by red. (One must here, as always, take this use of hue names for stimuli as a *façon de parler* for certain roughly specified wavelength classes. When animal data are in question, this sort of talk can be seriously misleading, since we are not entitled to suppose, without further ado, that the animal makes the same hue classifications that we do.) It seems attractive to suppose that neural units with a double-opponent structure play a significant role in simultaneous contrast. It is not, however, sufficient to draw on the analogies between these double-opponent cells and the units that are usually supposed to form the neural substrate of Mach bands. Mach bands are an example of short-range edge contrast. But simultaneous contrast, both chromatic and achromatic, works across relatively large regions of the visual field; chromatic contrast is little facilitated by sharpness of edge gradients; and there is no persuasive evidence of hue Mach bands, i.e., enhancement of hue effects at boundaries. (What might casually appear to be such enhancement is in fact the combined effect of eye movement and afterimage formation. The colored fringes one notices on a red-green border take a few seconds to develop, unlike simultaneous contrast effects.) Visual scientists often refer to the neural processes that underlie short-range edge enhancement and long-range simultaneous contrast as "Mach-type" and "Hering-type" lateral inhibition respectively. Undoubtedly there is a lateral-inhibition story involving double-opponent cells which underlies chromatic simultaneous contrast, but it cannot simply be a rerun of the explanation of Mach bands. We do know, on the other hand, that there are extensive interconnections across the neural representations of the visual field. Moreover, there are extensive psychophysical data which suggest that seeing involves some sort of *distributed representation* in which information about each region in the input pattern is located over the entire representation of the pattern rather than restricted to a small region in the representation. Or, to put it in mathematical terms, the eye-brain performs something very much like a spatial Fourier analysis of the visual field (see the chapters by Robson, Graham, and Weisstein and Harris, in Harris 1980, or Levine and Sheffner 1981, ch. 9). So long-range Hering-type lateral inhibition is probably embedded in the most basic mechanisms of seeing.

As one moves up the visual-processing chain, the nervous system continues and extends the analysis of the pattern of retinal excitation that the retina itself began. When the optic nerve leaves the retina, it divides at the *optic chiasma*, which sends the signals corresponding to the left half of the visual fields of both eyes to the right side of the visual cortex, and the signals corresponding to the right half of both visual fields to the left side of the visual cortex. En route, the signal goes to a part of the thalamus known as the *lateral geniculate nucleus* (LGN). The LGN interdigitates the outputs from the two eyes in alternate layers. LGN cells seem to have most of the same characteristics as ganglion cells, with the same range of types of concentric receptive field organization. They divide into two classes, fast-conducting achromatic ones (about 20 per cent) and slow-conducting ones, most of which are chromatically responsive but probably carry a great deal of achromatic information as well (Lennie 1984). The chromatic and achromatic systems are thus to a considerable extent functionally rather than anatomically distinct. Some of the chromatically responsive cells show opponent-response patterns that fit the psychophysically inferred chromatic-response patterns beautifully (figure I-18). However, the picture on the individual cell level is not nearly so neat as these selected examples might suggest, and statistical analyses have not "nailed down" a quantitative picture to general satisfaction. For instance, one statistical analysis of LGN cell responses to habituating chromatic stimuli does show chromatic equilibrium points that cluster tightly around the psychophysically determined equilibrium lines for red-green and yellow-blue habituation. The trouble is that, although one of these habituation lines corresponds to the red-green unique-hue axis, the other is rotated somewhat with respect to the yellow-blue unique-hue axis.[19] Up to this point in the processing chain, the opponent scheme may be said to be physiologically confirmed in rough outline, but not in detail.

Everything becomes more complicated at the level of the visual cortex, where a great deal of further analysis of the visual signal occurs and cells therefore become more specialized. We shall content ourselves with a perfunctory sketch of the principal features as they are currently understood. The famous work of David Hubel and Thorsten Wiesel[20] showed that the primary, or striate, visual cortex (area 17) is arranged in approximately 1 mm × 2 mm blocks, each of which represents a particular area of the visual field. The blocks consist of vertical columns, each of which cuts through all six layers of the cortex. The middle layer of each block is made up of cells with a

Fig. I-18. Facing page: *Average spectral-response curves for six types of cells recorded from the LGN of a macaque monkey. The top four panels represent four classes of spectrally opponent cells; the bottom two curves show spectrally nonopponent cells. The horizontal dashed line in each graph represents the average spontaneous discharge rate. In each instance the response was recorded for a brief flash of monochromatic light that covered a large portion of the receptive field of the cell.*

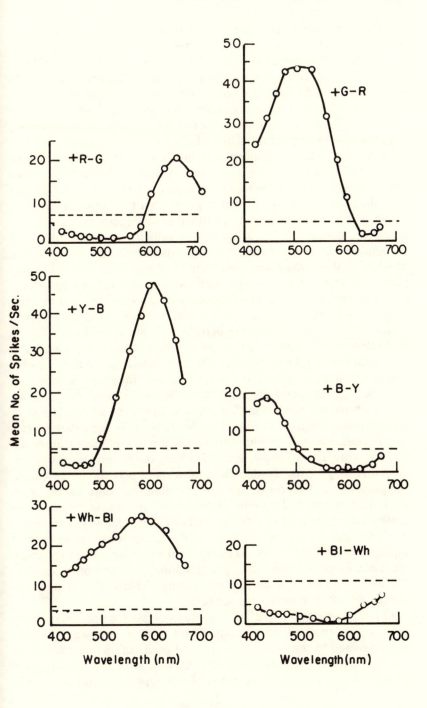

concentric receptive field configuration, and it is these cells which receive inputs from the LGN. The other cells in the column respond selectively to the orientation and width of bar-shaped stimuli in their receptive fields. These are the so-called *simple* cells. The *complex* cells show preferential response to particular directions of motion of stimuli as well. Cells with the same orientation preference are in the same column. Neighboring columns have similar but different preferences, with the constituent columns of a block spanning the entire range of orientations. Columns displaying right-eye dominance alternate with columns displaying left-eye dominance. Visual hemifield inputs from the left and right eyes are routed to adjacent layers of the LGN, but they do not synapse to a common point until they reach the cortex. There, the left-eye and right-eye maps of analogous visual field regions interconnect and overlap so that cells in a given column will respond to stimulation of that column's visual field region, regardless of whether the stimulation comes from one eye or the other, but will prefer the input from one eye, while an adjacent column may have the opposite preference. The blocks are of uniform size, but more of them are allocated to regions in the center of the visual field than to regions of the same size in the periphery of the visual field.

At this point, caution obliges us to forbear describing the cortical cells with preferred responses as "feature detectors" of the stimulus characteristic in question. We must also ask, for example, whether the cell might respond just as well, or better, to some characteristic for which we did not test and, if so, how the visual system is able to disambiguate the two stimuli (cf. Teller 1984). It is likely that ensembles of cells, rather than individual cells, are the ultimate feature detectors. Nonetheless, the cells of the visual cortex tend to be specialists, involved in the systematic analysis of such things as edges, orientations, and motions. We can see here the continuation of an overall organizational scheme of the visual system, in which many lower-order cells feed into fewer higher-order cells which compare, analyze, and abstract information which is, in turn, fed to cells of higher order still. (The flow is by no means one way: there are many feedback loops, so talk of a unidirectional information-processing "chain" will sooner or later be misleading.[21]) Now what happens to chromatic information in this scheme?

Our knowledge of this is, alas, considerably more fragmentary than it is in the case of orientation and motion. Less attention has been devoted to color cells, and spectral information is harder to obtain, since many cortical cells, unlike retinal and LGN cells, are quiescent until stimulated. Three types of chromatically responsive cells have been found in the cortexes of monkeys.[22] The first type is spectrally opponent, like ganglion and LGN cells, and some cells of this type show a double-opponent organization. The second type responds only to wavelengths of a very restricted range. Such sharply tuned chromatic cells are also found outside the striate cortex in visual area V4, where their peak sensitivities are widely distributed across the spectrum. Since their bandwidths are much narrower than those of cone responses, these cells would seem to be receiving inputs from spectrally opponent cells. Furthermore,

> This visual area V4 appears to be organized into color columns. Zeki finds that the cells in a given column will all respond to the same color, e.g. red, but have different demands as to the shape of the red object. For some cells, any red light in the appropriate visual location suffices; others require a red object of a particular shape, or a red border of a particular orientation before they will fire. The cells in a neighboring column might be similarly diverse in their shape requirements but all demand that the objects be blue.[23]

If this second type of cell generalizes across form information to specify color more sharply, the third type does just the reverse. This third sort of cell does not favor any particular wavelength, but responds to figures that differ from their backgrounds in hue, regardless of the pair of hues involved and regardless of variations in luminance.

> Our conclusion, then, is that color information in the cortex must go two ways: into color-specific paths, which maintain and even increase the color specificity seen at the LGN, and into multiple color cells, which use color (and luminance) information to detect form but do not care what colors are involved. (DeValois and DeValois 1975, 139)

It thus appears that the brain is engaging in a variety of chromatic as well as spatial and temporal classificatory operations. The emphasis throughout seems to be on the analysis of differences and boundaries.

When one considers the problem of the perception of color in complex scenes, one quickly becomes aware that there exists no biological model of, for example, the process by which our visual systems can estimate the reflectances of objects, which is at all comparable to the opponent-process scheme for the analysis of the appearance of colors in simple stimulus situations. The best we can hope for at present are computational models with processes that may turn out to have no organic counterparts, though they should not of course be incompatible with anything we have good reason to suppose is true. Much more is known about the mechanisms of the retina and LGN than about the visual cortex, and more about the striate cortex than about subsequent visually important areas. In general, the closer we are to the receptors, the more reliable our neurophysiological understanding. It is fortunate, then, that so many of the important processes of color vision are shaped at the early stages and that so much of that early information is preserved at later stages. This makes it frequently possible, *caeteris paribus* and to a reasonable degree of approximation, to characterize a sensory experience, such as of a green patch in one's visual field, in terms of an early-stage coding process, such as a cone or opponent-system response difference. One is then, in principle at least, able to speak in a contentful way about chromatic color sensing without having to be bound to stimulus terms on the one hand or to talk about sense data on the other. For it is the biological perspective which is the *via media* between the way that would place colors in the extradermal physical world and the way that would have it that colors are properties of sense data. To show that these two are indeed the ways of error will be our next task.

II

The Ontology of Color

Objectivism

"By convention color exists, by convention bitter, by convention sweet but in reality atoms and void." Thus spake Democritus. But even the friends of atoms and void have been slow to acknowledge that color exists by convention. Unwilling to provide a Cartesian home for dispossessed colors and tastes, most contemporary materialists seem equally resistant to following Democritus in his renunciation of the testimony of the senses. For what could be plainer than that rubies are red and that grass is green? Endeavoring to find a home for colors among the objects that appear to bear them, some materialists hold that colors are constituents of the physical world, quite independent of human or other sentient beings. These are the *objectivists*. Others hold that although colors are indeed features of material objects, they are so only as dispositions of those objects to affect organisms in an appropriate sensory fashion under the proper circumstances. These are the *subjectivists*.[1] Democritus might be regarded as holding to a particularly strong version of subjectivism, whereby the ascription of colors to physical objects can be justified on practical but not theoretical grounds—or, as he might have put it, by convention rather than nature. A careful examination of objectivism and subjectivism will give us reason to think that Democritus was nearer the mark than many of his successors.

Let us begin with objectivism. The versions of objectivism with which we shall be concerned accept the essential correctness of the characterization of physical objects given by that part of physical theory which concerns the interactions between light and matter. This restriction is significant. Nobody supposes that physical theory is

59

complete, or that all portions of it are correct, or that all of it is to be construed as literal description of objects and processes. But the part that has to do with the production of light in the visible range and with the ways in which it interacts with matter is, on the whole, quite well understood. It is a part of nonrelativistic quantum theory of matter and electrodynamics, an established theory whose validity limits are known.[2] As such, it is unlikely to be dismantled or even substantially revised as a result of some future scientific revolution. In future science it is likely to have the same secure status that nineteenth-century planetary mechanics has today after two major revolutions in physics.

Our understanding of the early stages of the processing of color information in the human visual system is more recent and less secure in its details. Nonetheless, the general features of those early stages are established to the satisfaction of competent researchers in the field, and it would seem unwise in the extreme for any philosopher to advance an account of the ontology of color which bets that the consensus of opinion in visual science is wrong. Let us then take it as axiomatic in our present inquiry that any philosophical theory of color must be consistent with the best available accounts of physics, physiology and psychophysics. To accept this constraint is, of course, not the same as supposing that the account of color given by the relevant sciences is, or will ever be, a *complete* account.

The objectivist can adopt one of two strategies. The first is to suppose that physical objects (construed broadly so as to include such entities as the electromagnetic field) are, at the level relevant to scientific theories of color, what the physicist says they are and that color must therefore be a physical property or combination of physical properties or else be supervenient on some set of physical properties. This is main-line objectivism, with David Armstrong as a typical proponent (Armstrong 1961, 1968, 1969). A minority opinion, represented by James Cornman, has it that color is an objective property of physical objects over and above the properties with which the physicist endows them and that it is in no way reducible to or supervenient upon those properties (Cornman 1974 and 1975). We shall consider this minority position first, and then the more widely held one.

Cornman's view is the product of an attempt to reconcile our common-sense, difficult-to-resist inclination to take colors as qualifying the surfaces of objects with the scientific picture which seems to make no mention of them. Some philosophers have advanced arguments to show that the common-sense and scientific views are incompatible, so that acceptance of the latter requires surrender of the former. The larger part of Cornman's effort is devoted to showing that these arguments fail and that there is, in fact, no good reason for supposing that the two views exclude each other. We need not enter into this dispute here; let us, for the sake of argument, grant that the incompatibility of the two pictures has not been demonstrated. Let us even suppose, again for the sake of argument, that it *cannot* be demonstrated that some material objects do not include colors among their elementary properties.

But is there any reason to suppose that colors *are* among the elementary properties of bodies? Consider: either the colors that Cornman supposes to attach to physical objects (call them *Cornman colors* or *C-colors* for short) are causally connected to the other physical properties of those objects or else they are not so connected. Suppose that they are, and that C-colors have physical effects. Then one ought to be able to test for their presence or absence by physical means, and a physical theory that makes no reference to them would be incomplete. But Cornman makes no claim to be remedying a deficiency in existing physical theories. So it seems that we must take C-colors either to be free of causal relations to an object's physical properties or else to be epiphenomena of some of them. In neither case will C-colors play a role in determining what wavelengths of light are emitted or reflected from or transmitted through the surface of a physical object, nor will they determine which photons are absorbed by retinal photoreceptors. In other words, C-colors can make no difference in normal human color perception. How, then, could they make any difference to our beliefs about colors? If a common person supposes her skirt to be green, her belief would have to be correct either as a matter of blind luck or in consequence of some pre-established harmony. Indeed, such beliefs might be consistently false. For all we know, objects that are C-color pink might typically cause us to experience "greenly" and thus be taken by us to be green. So the practitioner of common-sense metaphysics might be globally right about the ontological status of colors, but almost always wrong in judging what colors things have. Common sense with friends like C-colors needs no enemies.

Main-line objectivism has no such causally disconnected items. Colors are identical with (or supervenient upon) certain physical features of objects, and color perception consists in the appropriate detection of this physical complex of features and its registration in the nervous system. It would seem that this complex must either comprise the mechanisms in the object which are responsible for the character of the light that leaves its surface, or else be some features of the light itself.

One of the motivations for objectivism is no doubt the hope that when people typically experience, say, yellow, there exists some aspect of the microstructure of the yellow thing which is similar to the microstructure of other yellow things, but different from the microstructure of red things. Yellow things would form one physical class, red things another. What we would then want to know would be what feature or features yellow things share with one another that they do not share with red things, so that we could construct a pair of formulae:

(1) Yellow things are. . . .

(2) Red things are. . . .

Like most hopes for conceptual neatness and unity, this one is doomed to disappointment, and for reasons we have already considered. There are just too many heterogeneous causal factors in objects which can cause them to look yellow to us in normal circumstances. It is not at all plausible to suppose that yellow things are members of a physical natural kind, and one who claims that there is such a natural kind must bear the intellectual burden of producing an actual candidate. Until that happens, there is no reason to view this version of objectivism as a viable alternative.

Perhaps there is, however, a common theme. The specifiable feature which yellow things have in common but which they do not share with red things might be their disposition to cause characteristic sorts of light to issue from their surfaces. And since it is that light which is typically the immediate physical stimulus for our perceptions of the colors of objects, let us see whether we can find some common trait among the sorts of light coming from "yellow" things. To what features of light must we look? The only relevant variables are intensity and wavelength, each of which can affect what color a spot of light is seen to have.[3] Of these, wavelength seems to be the more important. To fix our ideas, let us take a particular yellow—unique yellow[4]—and suppose that there is a standard observer who sees unique yellow when stimulated by photons with a wavelength of 575 nm. It is perhaps tempting to suppose that unique yellow things are those things which reflect (or emit, etc.) 575 nm photons.

The temptation must be resisted. Remember that the eye is a very coarse harmonic analyzer[5] because it contains only three types of color receptors, their response curves are broad and overlap markedly, and each one will generate a signal whenever it captures a photon anywhere within its response range. Once a photon is absorbed, the wavelength information that it bears is lost. All the nervous system "knows" is whether or to what degree each of the three receptor types has been excited. Any two events that produce the same response pattern will be seen the same way. We recall from our earlier discussion of color matching that any stimulus which causes the red and green opponent responses to remain in zero balance and drives the yellow-blue response in the yellowness direction will be perceived as unique yellow. There are indefinitely many such hue-matching stimuli (though not single-wavelength ones) which will have this effect on our standard observer,[6] and most of them do not include 575 nm photons.

Faced with these facts, an objectivist might reply that he will give up the requirement of a common, unitary physical property for yellow things and will settle instead for a complicated disjunction of properties. We might, at this stage, ask what is to motivate the choice of the members of this disjunction. Are they to be selected because, and only because, of how they affect normal human perceivers, or is there to be some more physically natural basis for the choice? Let us consider the latter possibility first. Once again, wishing for an appropriate physical candidate is one thing, producing it quite another. Such a candidate need not be physically basic in the way that electronic charge or electric field strength are basic. Since the physical objects that we can see typically comprise very large numbers of more elementary bodies arranged in complicated ways, the objectivist ought to expect color to be a higher-level or even supervenient property like temperature or elasticity, very complicated looking from the standpoint of elementary physical properties. On the other hand, temperature and elasticity are, once we choose the proper level of physical complexity,

(1) readily expressible in a vocabulary appropriate to their physical level of application;

(2) characterizable independently of the relations they might bear to organisms;

(3) related through a system of laws to other physically significant magnitudes.

There are properties of objects which meet these three criteria and which are highly relevant to color perception. They are the *relative spectral energy* of light sources, the *relative reflectance* of opaque bodies, and the *relative transmittance* of transparent or translucent bodies. The light-energy distribution per unit area (radiance) for each wavelength that reaches an observer's eye will depend upon the spectral energy (irradiance) of the sources for that wavelength, multiplied by the relative reflectance for that wavelength of a body illuminated by those sources, multiplied by the relative transmittance for that wavelength of the intervening media. It is the radiance at each wavelength for each portion of the field of view that is the physical, extrabiological determinant of the perceived color of a spot of light. If a LaPlacean demon were to know the radiance pattern for each wavelength at the cornea, he would be able to calculate just what color would be perceived—provided, of course, that he also knew the transmission properties of the ocular media, the cone action spectra, the opponent response function of the particular eye at the moment in question for the retinal size and location and duration of the spot of light, and the nature of the composition of the rest of the field of view.[7] Spectral energy, reflectance and transmittance are quite obviously physically specifiable and significant. They are causally central to color perception and play a fundamental role in all parts of color science. They are doubtless the characteristics of the physical world which are in some fashion picked out by perceived color; if any physical properties deserve to be identified with color, it is they.

Unfortunately, however, they can't fill that role—basically because of the phenomena of metamerism. We recall that colored lights are metameric (for an observer) if they are indistinguishable (for that observer) and yet differ in spectral composition. Reflective objects are metameric under a given illumination if they match under that illumination and yet have different relative spectral reflectances. But because their relative spectral reflectances are different, there will be some illuminant for which they will not match. There is, perhaps, a tendency to suppose that daylight is the ultimate arbiter of metamerism, but we have already considered (figure I-17) a case in which two surfaces match in daylight but not in incandescent light. There is, in fact, no single illuminant that will suffice to distinguish the members of every metameric pair. We shall attend to the consequences of this situation a bit later. For now, we need only observe that there is little *physical* justification for putting the material whose reflectance is represented by the dotted line of figure I-17 into the same color class with that represented by the solid line. Assimilating these to each other could, it appears, be motivated only by the similar effect they have upon organisms constructed like ourselves.

As physical candidates for identification with the colors, we have so far considered: detailed physical mechanisms, such as those mentioned in Chapter I; higher-level properties of matter, such as reflectance; and the basic characteristics of light, particularly wavelength. All of these are causally important to the perception of color, but none of them can serve as a basis for sorting visible objects into the color classes that we and like creatures employ. We may, of course, decide to settle for such properties as relative spectral reflectance, illuminance, etc. as constituting "physical color," and drop the requirement that objects that match metamerically over a wide range of illuminants are to be denominated as having the same color.[8] However attractive this strategy may seem on other grounds, one must realize that the concept of "color" it yields is one in which two matching yellow spots will usually not have the same color. If one wants an account of the ontological locus of red, green, yellow, and blue—what features they share, and in what ways they differ—one must look elsewhere. And it may fairly be said that it is these questions which have excited the attention of philosophers.

We must now examine the position of those who look for no physically natural candidate for yellowness. We might think of them as falling into two classes. The members of the first class see colors as perfectly good properties of physical objects, properties which not only exist independently of human beings, but which could in principle have been specified independently of human beings. They are, however, anthropocentric properties which, although of interest to us, are of no great importance in the formulation of the laws of nature. We human beings are apt detectors of these properties, and are thus useful in singling them out, but our relation to such properties is only accidental. These properties would constitute the colors in a possible world in which they did not bear the causal relationships to human perceptual systems that they bear in the actual world. Those who take this point of view are thus, in our present sense of the term, *objectivists.*[9]

The members of the second class also hold that colors are, after a fashion, properties of bodies, but only insofar as they form the occurrent basis of dispositions to put human beings into certain sensory states. It is not merely that human senses provide us with convenient ways of picking out the properties in question, but that those properties are to be thought of as colors only because they bear the proper causal relations to our sensory states. There need be no physically characterizable resemblance, no matter how tenuous, which connects instances of, say, red things, save their ability to affect us in the appropriate fashion. Our relations to color properties are essential, not only to their discovery, but to their being. Adherents of this view are, by our lights, *subjectivists.*[10] We shall examine their position shortly.

Suppose that someone, using the human visual system as a stalking-horse, picks out a very complicated, gerrymandered property *F* which characterizes the state that a physical object has just in case it looks yellow to a normal observer under standard conditions.

Is that person entitled to say that *F* is identical with yellow? To answer this question, we must have some sufficiently contentful notion of yellow, and this we have in the first instance only by having sensory experiences of yellow. The hues are qualities with which we are acquainted. One can succeed in the task of identifying the hues with some physical structure only if that structure captures the *essential* features of the hues as these are displayed to us in experience. The physical structure can have properties in addition to those discernible in perception, and we may even allow it to fail to have certain properties of the hues that we regard as accidental; for instance, we might not require *F* to occur in afterimages. This we may grant for the sake of the argument. But hues do have certain characteristics necessarily. This is a central truth, no less true for having been so frequently overlooked. If we reflect upon what it is to be red, we readily see that it is *possible* for there to be a red that is unique, i.e., neither yellowish nor bluish. It is equally apparent that it is *impossible* for there to be a unique orange, one that is neither reddish nor yellowish. Since there are necessary properties of hues, nothing can be a hue without having the appropriate properties necessarily. If yellow is identical with **G**, and orange is identical with **H**, it must be possible for there to be a unique **G** but impossible for there to be a unique **H**. If hues are physical complexes, those physical complexes must admit of a division into unique and binary complexes. No matter how gerrymandered the physical complex that is to be identical with the hues, it must have this fourfold structure, and, if objectivism is to be sustained, once the complex is identified, it must be possible to characterize that structure on the basis of physical predicates alone.

How might this be done in terms of the physics of bodies? We have no clue, not because we are ignorant of the properties of bodies which are causally relevant to color perceiving, though they are many, but because those properties do not appear to contain any remotely plausible candidates that satisfy the constraints. Once again, the objectivist has the burden of producing something specific or leaving the game. What about the physics of light? Here we may survey the field more easily, since there are so few causally relevant variables. They are wavelength, intensity, and phase. As before, wavelength seems to be the crucial variable. Could we not just identify monochromatic light with unique hues and light of mixed wavelength with binary hues? No, and for reasons that have already been made clear. One who sees unique yellow when stimulated by 575 nm light will also see it when the stimulus is a mixture of 550 nm and 650 nm light.

And a monochromatic 490 nm stimulus will be seen as turquoise—a green-blue binary.

Standard conditions

At this point the reader is likely to be restless; so much about the colors—particularly the division between unique and binary hues—is manifestly bound up with the peculiar characteristics of the human visual system that it seems a vain pursuit indeed to search for a parallel set of structures in the general order of nature. One might as well set about earnestly constructing improved Ptolemaic epicycles. Instead, it seems sensible simply to choose a normal observer O, specify a set of standard conditions S, and decree that all objects that look color K to that observer under those conditions be K, no matter how ragtag a lot they may be under other physical descriptions. The *only* thing that K-colored things need have in common is that they look K to O under S. Then, unique hues are the hues that look unique to O under S and binary hues are the hues that look binary to O under S. K-looking things are physical things or configurations (we need to allow for such things as rainbows and sky) and are thus objective, despite the fact that their principle of collection into color classes depends only upon their relations to particular sorts of organisms.

Although this doctrine has here been called "subjectivism" in order to call attention to the conceptually central role that the perceptual states of human subjects play in it, many of its adherents might, with some justice, object that the term 'subjectivism' connotes more idiosyncrasy and less determination by the physical world than they are prepared to accept when it comes to colors. In the pages that follow, the notions of "standard conditions" and "normal observer" will come in for close examination, and from that examination an argument will be advanced for subjectivism in a stronger, more Democritean sense.

Standard conditions are chosen by color scientists with three considerations in mind: (1) the nature of the object or property to be observed or measured, (2) the capabilities and limitation of the observer or measuring instrument, and (3) the purposes for which the observation or measurement is to be taken. As one or another of these considerations changes, the prescribed conditions may be expected to change as well. There are many descriptions of standard conditions in color science (American Society for Testing and Materials 1968, Judd and Wyszecki 1963, Kelly and Judd 1976, Wyszecki and Stiles

1967), but no prescription for fixing *the* color of an object *simpliciter.*[11] Instead one has procedures for determining such things as the reflectance or transmittance or dominant wavelength for a variety of bodies and circumstances, and ways of associating these with perceptual variables like lightness and hue. Color scientists are concerned with such matters as degrees of metamerism, the extent to which perceived color shifts with angular subtense at the eye, and methods of specifying the colors of glossy and fluorescent materials. How it is that one problem—establishing a set of standard conditions for determining *the* color of an object—comes to be replaced by a multitude of problems can be appreciated by considering a simple case.

The instructions that come with the set of color chips in the *Munsell Book of Color* tell us that the samples should be placed against a dark achromatic background and "colors should be arranged under North Daylight or scientific daylight having a color temperature of from 6500 degrees to 7500 degrees Kelvin. Colors should be illuminated at 90 degrees and viewed at 45 degrees, or the exact opposite of these conditions." This is a good basic procedure for assigning a color to many reflecting objects by visual match to a standard, and is fully adequate to its intended task. But are the colors of stars and neon tubes to be determined with the use of "North Daylight"? What about the

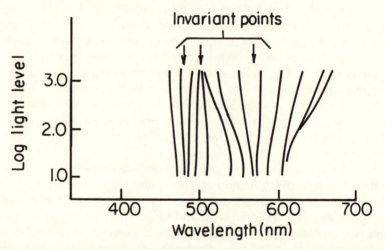

Fig. II-1. *The Bezold-Brücke hue shift. As the light intensity is increased, the hue associated with a particular wavelength will change. The only exceptions (for a condition of neutral adaptation) are the wavelengths associated with unique blue, unique green and unique yellow—the "invariant points." The curved lines connect wavelength-intensity combinations that have the same hue.*

moon? (Do some objects have their own special "standard conditions" for viewing?) How about bioluminescent fish? A rainbow *cannot* be "illuminated at 90 degrees and viewed at 45 degrees," and many reflective materials are directionally reflective; i.e., their perceived color is a function of the angle between light source, surface, and observer (Austin 1962, 66). The use of a material also governs its color: gold used as a filter is greenish, but it reflects reddishly. Dichroic filters transmit the complement of the color they reflect, with the added complication that the color they reflect is also directionally dependent. In some cases, such as the measurement of translucent materials, variations in the conditions of measurement (or, if you will, observation) produce such wide variations in outcome as to make it not worthwhile to establish standard conditions at all. In Judd and Wyszecki's authoritative text on color measurements we read:

> It becomes clear that the losses of radiant flux due to scattering on the surface of the specimen, and within the specimen, must be largely affected by the size of the aperture of the integrating sphere holding the specimen and the cross-section of the incident beam at the surface of the specimen. In reflectance measurements the backing (black or white) applied to the specimen also becomes of great importance. There are no standard conditions for measuring spectral transmittances or reflectances of translucent materials, and it is left to the investigator to decide which conditions are most realistic to the particular situation at hand. (Judd and Wyszecki 1963, 103)

Here, in a particularly plain way, the measurement conditions are a matter of *choice* and depend upon one's purposes.

One tactic we can employ to cope with this welter of cases is relativization. Bodies and regions of bodies are first divided by type: those with opaque surfaces, those with transparent volumes, those with self-luminous areas. A color is then assigned to each by a standard procedure (involving standard conditions) for each type. Furthermore, colors may be relativized by direction: X is a reddish purple on surface Y at an angle of Z degrees from the standard light source. Indeed, these sorts of relativizing classifications are used in color science. But often the matter becomes very complicated, as in the case of dichroic materials or translucent objects. The relevant information can be presented only graphically, the relationships between that information and color appearance are not always clear, and the practice of assigning a color to the object seems increasingly pointless.

A chief concern of *visual colorimetry* is to establish conditions under which it can be determined whether or not given samples will match in color. We recall that a match once made will continue to be a match regardless of luminance level (within broad limits). But the appearance of the samples does not remain constant with changes in luminance. Except for the three spectral unique-hue loci (unique red is to be found on the spectrum only at low luminances), the hue seen at any particular point in the spectrum will be yellower or bluer at higher luminances and redder or greener at lower luminances (figure II-1). This effect, the Bezold-Brücke hue shift, can be accounted for by supposing that the red-green and yellow-blue opponent systems differ in sensitivity, the yellow-blue system being less sensitive at low levels, but increasing in sensitivity with increasing luminance levels at a higher rate than the red-green system.[12] For small spots, short exposures, or dim light, the "drop-out" of the yellow-blue system is marked. A yellow life raft contrasts well with the sea if the search plane is flying low, but it disappears for spotters in high-flying aircraft, who can still make out a reddish spot of the same visual size. On the other end of things, a landscape yellows at midday, a fact often noted by artists. The upshot of this for colorimetry is that the determination of the dominant wavelength of a sample will tell one what the sample will match in hue, but not what hue the sample will have.

The peculiarities of the human observer enter in other ways as well. As we know, the perceived color of a region will be a function of the color of its surround, because of contrast. We may eliminate contrast by viewing the region of interest through a dark tube of small aperture. But there are tradeoffs: to use a viewing tube is to eliminate those perceived colors, such as black and brown, which depend upon contrast essentially. (This is why there are no brown lights; more about the peculiarities of brown later.) And to use a viewing tube is to eliminate clues to illumination which enable us to distinguish the brightness and chromatic character of the incident light from those of the object and so to rob the object of the relative color and lightness constancy that are its hallmark in normal perceptual circumstances. In such cases, we are reminded that *standard* conditions of observation may differ substantially from *typical* conditions.

The angular size of the viewing tube is important too. The 1931 standard of the Commission Internationale de l'Éclairage (C.I.E.) calls for a 2 degree angular subtense of the specimen at the eye. This is a very small spot, and it makes precise matching difficult. Judd and Wyszecki remark, "By increasing the field from 2 to 10 degrees, we may increase the precision by a factor of 2.5 or more. A further increase in field size does not increase the precision very much." So why not adopt a 10-degree standard? Judd and Wyszecki continue,

Large-field color matching may, however, present a problem of a special kind. If the two adjacent specimens we wish to compare are of a similar color, but of very different spectral compositions, we may find it difficult to make an accurate color comparison. The projection of the macular pigment will show up plainly. We might find the two specimens to color-match near the fixation point, but fail to match elsewhere. Or, if the two specimens match in general, the center of the visual field will fail to match. (Judd and Wyszecki 1963, 140-141)

Other factors besides the projection of the macula (whose involvement in color matching we discussed in Chapter I) seem to be involved as well; the unfortunate upshot is that "a color match obtained for two specimens in a 10-degree field does not remain a color match when viewed in a 2-degree field, and vice-versa."

It seems reasonable to speak, as we did earlier, of object X having color K at source-object-subject viewing angle Z; it seems less reasonable to speak of it as having K at viewing subtense Z at the eye of observer O. The difference is that, in the former case, the variation of color with viewing angle is strongly related to a physical magnitude, directional reflectance, whereas the latter depends mostly upon accidental features of the human eye. The more plausible way to think of the angular subtense problem is that one *chooses* the 2-degree field or the 10-degree field on the basis of the problem to be solved.

Another problem concerns the resolution with which the specimen is to be viewed. This is an old issue: Locke remarks that blood looks "pellucid" under a microscope, and Berkeley asks whether mites or men ought to be the arbiters of the colors of bodies. Four-color printing and color television have meant that much of our time is spent looking at color areas that are the products of the optical fusion of colored dots. This may seem a nonproblem, since these dots are not resolvable at all, or resolvable only with difficulty, by the unaided human eye. But the issue arises in other situations too. The colors of an area of a divisionist (pointillist) painting, such as Seurat's "Les Poseuses," or of a cluster of tree leaves seen at a distance depend upon the same phenomenon. Furthermore, the effect ramifies: as an area is resolved into colored constituents, the constituents' previously perceived color may prove to be the result of groups of cones whose outputs pool the available wavelength information.

It has been suggested that the standard condition for viewing should be the point at which maximum resolution is available. The trouble with this suggestion is that since the receptive fields of the retinal neural units are of various sizes, there may be no single point of maximum resolution. For any given distance, adjacent small colored areas may be seen as distinct (because the small-receptive field neural units resolve them) and yet affect one another's perceived color (because of pooling of light among the receptors in large-field units). This is the *spreading effect* of von Bezold, and it gives rise to peculiar circumstances in which the same region of color may seem to remain constant and also seem to vary, depending upon one's point of comparison.[13] We shall return to the spreading effect later.

Analogous to the question of the eye's color-resolving power in space is its color resolution in time. The eye integrates over both spatial and temporal inhomogeneity. Color television again gives us an example. In a region of the screen which appears to us to be of constant color, each phosphor dot is glowing only one-thousandth of the time; at any one instant, most of the screen is dark. Since, to a normal observer, a given region appears to be color K, we ought to be prepared, according to the subjectivist criterion, to say that the region is K. Now consider a *Benham disk* (figure II-2). When the disk is rotated at a rate of about 6–8 Hz (cycles per second), the black-and-white pattern is perceived as a set of desaturated bands of different hues. The particular hues that are seen depend upon the rate and direction of rotation of the disk. These are the so-called Benham-Prevost-Fechner "subjective" colors, and they may be seen on rotating disks of various patterns which look achromatic when resting.[14] These strike one as anomalous cases, and the rule for excluding them seems very simple: accept as standard only those specimens which do not move with respect to the eye. There are at least three difficulties with this initially plausible restriction. First, we need not move the black-and-white stimulus at all. It is the pulsed sequence of presentations that matters. One stillborn proposal for color television derived a chromatic effect from a suitably pulsed set of black-and-white signals. The "Butterfield encoder" gave fairly good color rendition, including reasonable skin tone, but suffered from the fatal and intrinsic flaw that the colors flickered (Butterfield 1968 and 1970). One can in fact see faint, desaturated subjective colors by looking closely at the noise pattern of an unoccupied channel on a black-and-white television set (or a color set with the color control turned off). The second difficulty with the restriction is that the eye moves involuntarily and incessantly in a random series of drifts and jerks, and these are sufficient to generate "subjective" colors on a stationary black-and-white pattern (figure II-3). The third difficulty is the mate of the second: if all relative motion between target and eyeball is prevented, both the outline and the colors of the object soon disappear.[15]

Finally, we should look at an essential component of any standard

Fig. II-2. *The Benham disk. If the disk is rotated at a rate between 5 and 10 times per second and viewed under a bright tungsten light, desaturated bands of various colors will be clearly seen. Their sequence will depend upon the speed and direction of rotation of the disk.*

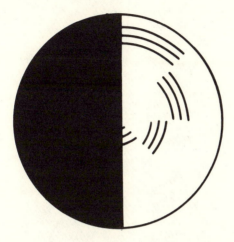

condition for determining the color of a reflective object, the choice of the illuminant. The C.I.E. specifies a series of standard illuminants with controlled spectral characteristics, such as source A (incandescent lamp), source B (near sunlight) and source C (near daylight— "North Daylight" of the Munsell specification).[16] When a subjectivist thinks of specifying a reflective color, he is likely to suppose an illuminant like source C. Two samples that are perceptually indistinguishable in color under source C will, when suitably viewed, count as having the same color according to this subjectivist. We naturally select source C rather than A, because experience tells us that objects that match in color in incandescent light sometimes fail to match in daylight, but the reverse is less likely to be the case. However, as we have already seen, source C has its metamers too: it enables us to distinguish more natural colorants than A does, as evolution leads one to expect, but artificial colorants are another matter. Judd and Wyszecki comment on the problem of distinguishing isomers (samples with physically identical spectral characteristics) from metamers:

> We have shown that metamerism of spectral-reflectance (or transmittance) functions always refers to a particular set of weighting functions, that is, a set of functions describing a source and an observer. When we change either the source or the observer, or both, the original metameric match may be destroyed. This may cause us to believe that there is a simple

Fig. II-3. *Stare at the pattern and let your eye move slowly across it. You will be able to see a variety of faint pastel hues.*

check on metamerism. To find out whether two specimens form a pair of isomeric or metameric colors, we would simply look at these specimens under another light source with a spectral-irradiance distribution different from that of the original source. If we find that under the other source the two colors do not match any more, we conclude the two specimens must have different spectral compositions, that is, they are definitely not isomeric but instead are metameric under the original source. However, if they also match under the other source, the result is inconclusive. Although in most practical cases we would be safe to conclude that the pair is isomeric, there is still the possibility that they are metameric. Figure II-4 illustrates a pair of spectral-transmittance curves which provide metameric lights for the standard observer when illuminated by source C as well as when illuminated by source A. We could go on and construct spectral-transmittance curves which would be metameric not only to two sources, such as C and A, but, at the same time, also to several other sources. It would be increasingly difficult to find such spectral-transmittance curves; but theoretically it would still be possible. The limit, of course, occurs when we try to find specimens which are metameric with respect to all possible sources; in that case we will find that these specimens must have identical spectral compositions throughout the visible spectrum, that is, they must be isomeric. (Judd and Wyszecki 1963, 151–152)

We see two specimens in daylight; they match. The first we had already decided was *K*, since it looks *K* in daylight, so we feel obliged to call the other *K* as well. But in incandescent light the first looks *K*-ish still, but the second does not look *K*-ish. Shall we continue to call it *K*? Or suppose sample 1 and sample 2 both look *K'* in illuminant C, both look alike and *K'*-ish in illuminant A, but under illuminant X

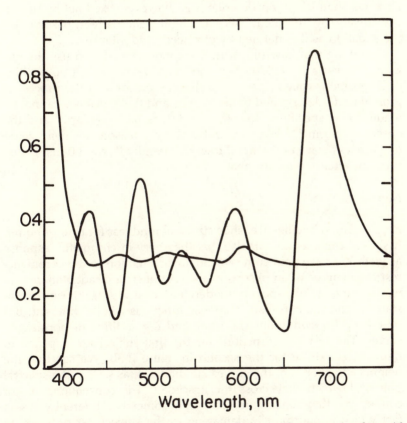

Fig. II-4. *Two spectral-transmittance curves which provide metameric colors with respect to source C and the C.I.E. average observer as well as with respect to source A and the average observer.*

75

they don't match and neither looks K'-ish. Should we regard 1 as K' and 2 as not? Or the other way around? Or are both K'? Or is neither?

The color scientist will refrain from answering such questions, but will endeavor to determine the reflectance of each sample, calculate a triple of numbers (the tristimulus values) for each illumination condition under which the samples are to be seen, and come as close as possible to a prediction of what the likely observers will see and how close that will come to what they are intended to see. Given an object, an illumination configuration whereby a spot of light of a particular size and spectral content and intensity and duration falls on a given retinal area, a fully specified visual surround and an observer in a particular adaptive state, the result of the interaction is determinate by nature though by no means readily determined by the scientist. How we shall label and describe it is, however, fixed *not* by nature but, ideally, by informed choice among the alternatives, based upon the situation as it is defined by our needs and interests.

One thing that is wrong with the notion that we can use the human observer as a stalking horse to locate a complex set of qualities or dispositions called "colors" is that the outcome of the process is grossly underdetermined by the object, and the deficiency cannot be made up by specifying that the conditions be "standard" and the observer "normal." We have in hand some reasons for being leery of a careless wave of the hand toward "standard" conditions. Let us turn our attention to "normal" observers.

Normal observers

People vary in intelligence, shoe size, and fondness for peanut butter. It should come as no surprise that they vary in chromatic response as well. We have paid some considerable attention to the chromatic-response curves of an observer in a neutral state of adaptation who was looking at light spots of moderate intensity. Alter those circumstances, and the chromatic-response functions will be different. But now keep the conditions the same and test a different normal observer. The response functions for the first subject are depicted in figure II-5A, those for the second in figure II-5B. We see that the heights and shapes of the curves are different, as well as the spectral points at which they cross the abscissa.[17] The consequence is, of course, that they see identical stimuli in somewhat different ways—a fact which is enormously damaging to the subjectivist proposal to specify the color properties of physical objects by means of their effects on "a normal observer."

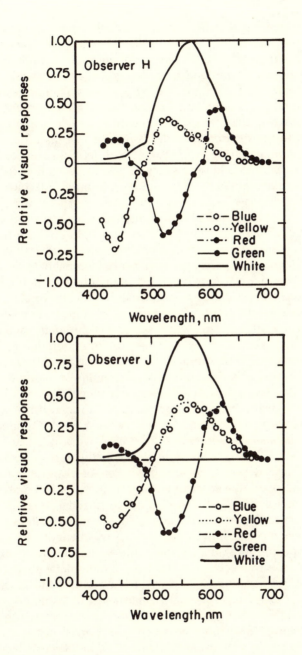

Fig. II-5A and 5B. *Chromatic and achromatic response functions for an equal-energy spectrum and two neutrally adapted normal observers.*

77

Before pursuing this further, let us look briefly at what distinguishes "normal" from "color-deficient" observers (Hurvich 1981, chs. 16–19; Hurvich 1972). Like most classifications of human capabilities, the "normal" and "deficient" categories are statistically defined and their extension distinguished by a set of screening tests which are substantially but not totally in agreement with one another. Those people classed as color deficient range from the relatively rare monochromats, to the dichromats, who comprise less than 3 per cent of the male population (the incidence of color-deficient females is much smaller), to the more loosely specified group of anomalous trichromats. An explanation of the terminology is in order. All color normals are called *trichromats* because, in a hue-matching procedure, they require exactly three lights of independent hue to match an arbitrary test light. *Dichromats* require just two such lights to be mixed for a hue match that perceptually satisfies them, and *monochromats* require only one. Most color-perception deficiencies probably involve receptors with missing or anomalous photopigments, although it is possible that some may have post-receptoral deficiencies or anomalies as well. Characterized in opponent-response terms, monochromats have only a working black-white system; dichromats have only an operating red-green or a yellow-blue system in addition to a black-white system, while trichromats have response in all three systems. Whether a system is responding to a stimulus is to some extent a matter of degree, so it is not always clear whether someone should be labeled a dichromat or an anomalous trichromat if his red-green system, say, seems to function at a very weak level. Opponent systems may be *anomalous* in either or both of two ways: one response pair may have a peak amplitude closer to the zero point than the other pair and hence be relatively weaker, or else the crossing, or equilibrium, point, the spectrum locus at which, for instance, the red-green response changes from positive to negative, may be shifted with respect to the "normal" range. The former condition will typically involve a comparative deficiency in wavelength discrimination in some spectral locations, whereas the latter will show itself by a shift in the spectral locus of at least one of the unique hues. It is only the first of these conditions that we are fully entitled to describe as a deficiency; those whose anomaly consists just in a shift of a crossing point are deficient only with respect to those tasks which require color matchings that would be acceptable to most people. Like left-handed people in a right-handed world, shifted trichromats are the victims of statistically based standardization. (The shifted anomalous are not *very* deviant either; their perceptual differences are likely to show up only in precise color tasks.)

Despite their occasionally unfortunate side effects, statistically based standardizations quite often have ample justification in practice, although their application to certain theoretical matters is certainly questionable. But let us agree to disregard the most deviant cases. How much variance is there among observers who are normal according to all the accepted screening tests? We need not answer the general question here, but a look at a particular case, the spectral locus of unique green, should prove edifying. For a start, notice that in figures II-5A and 5B, observer J's unique green is around 500 nm and observer H's is in the neighborhood of 495 nm. These are genuine individual differences, and the variance in a particular observer's instrument settings does not exceed plus or minus a nanometer or two from one trial to the next. What is the distribution of unique-green loci among a large (by psychophysical standards *very* large) population of normal observers? Figure II-6 summarizes Hurvich and Jameson's study of fifty subjects (Hurvich, Jameson and Cohen 1968). The raw numbers of nanometers are not, of course, revealing to most people. If you will cover the spectrum of plate 1, except for the range

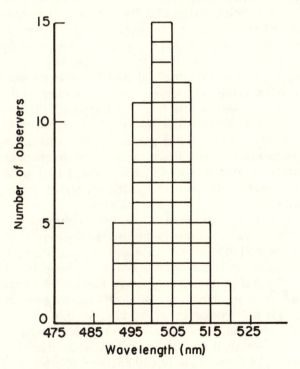

Fig. II-6. *Frequency distribution of unique-green loci for 50 observers.*

from 490 to 520 nanometers, you will get some idea of the range involved. Another way for the more ambitious to appreciate the span is by connecting the end points to a recognized color appearance standard. If you will look in the *Munsell Book of Color*,[18] which may be found in almost all university libraries, you can find medium Value, high Chroma chips in the Hue sequence from 5 Blue-Green to 2.5 Green. This is a fairly good approximation to the range of hues in question. The variation in hue from one end of this range to the other is quite marked.

Imagine that, instead of the selection of chips in the *Book of Color*, all of the (much larger number of) hue chips manufactured by the Munsell Company covering that 5 Blue-Green to 2.5 Green range were randomly spread out before you to be separately viewed on a dark gray background in North Daylight. One of them would be your considered choice for unique green. Your colleague might make a different choice. If so, which of the chips *is* unique green?[19]

If this question is to be answered at all, it can be answered only by convention. We might, for example, decree that the most frequently chosen chip is to be unique green. But we could decide otherwise, just as we could choose a chip of a different size, sit a different distance away, select a different illuminant—and get at least somewhat different results. If we must assign colors to objects according to the "standard conditions, normal observer" recipe, either arbitrariness of choice or choice based on practical interest seems unavoidable. 'Is unique green' turns out to be less like 'is water soluble' and more like 'is disgusting' than we might at first have supposed. Of course, if we make the color classification coarse enough, every normal observer will agree about its application in paradigm cases: this fire hydrant is red, that sunset is red. But if we make some circumstance coarse enough, every normal person will agree that *it* is disgusting: this plateful of maggots is disgusting . . . (delicacy forbids other paradigmatic examples).

From our preceding discussions of the assignment of colors to physical objects, we may draw two broad conclusions.

(1) There is nothing in the world as described by the physicist which corresponds to the division of colors into hues. If we suppose hues to be physical properties that are neither on the physicist's list nor derivable from anything on the list, our knowledge of object color becomes totally mysterious. If, on the other hand, we identify colors with *bona fide* physical properties such as spectral reflectance or emittance profiles, we shall indeed have object characteristics that are typically essential ingredients of explanations of why we have the

color experiences we do. Distinct reflectance profiles then become distinct colors regardless of whether they are distinguishable by any human observers, and indefinitely many objects will be taken by us to be qualified by the same hue family despite marked dissimilarities in their reflectance profiles. Colors will thus be properties of objects, but red, green, yellow and blue will not. This does not seem to be a satisfactory solution to the problem of the ontological status of colors.

(2) An appeal to the color experiences of normal observers under standard conditions will assign colors to objects only approximately and relatively to particular interest and purposes. It is not just that colors turn out to be, as J. J. C. Smart supposes (Smart 1975), disjunctive, gerrymandered physical properties when assigned according to *the* normal observer/standard condition procedure; it is, rather, that there is *no* such single, purpose-free procedure. In consequence, we are not entitled to say that physical objects have determinate colors *simpliciter*. Given a particular observer in a particular adaptational state and particular standard conditions, a color can be assigned to an object as precisely as the observer's perceptual condition warrants, but we cannot expect the assignment to remain the same when the set of conditions or the observer's adaptational state is changed. Assignments of colors to physical dispositions would thus not be just homocentric or even idiocentric, but idiocentric *and* situational.

Both of these broad conclusions are really commonplaces of visual science, but they raise a number of important issues. The first of these concerns our everyday view of the colors of objects and our knowledge of them; for colors do seem to be integral parts of objects as we see them, glued as it were to their surfaces, and not at all states of ourselves. Furthermore, objects seem to maintain their colors over wide variations in lighting conditions and seem to be seen in much the same way by different people. The subjectivist view suggests an instability and indeterminacy of colors which ordinary experience does not seem to sustain. Although, if our preceding arguments are sound, colors are not in fact qualities of physical objects, they certainly seem to be such. Just as Hume was obliged to account for the fact that we seem to experience causal connections, even though we do not actually do so, we are now obliged to give some account of the psychological underpinnings of the natural illusion of a world of colored objects. Secondly, subjectivism gives primacy to the way that colors *appear* or to color *impressions* or to color *experiences*. How are we to understand any or all of these notions? It seems natural to explain, for example, 'appears red' in terms of 'is red', or to characterize an experience of red as the visual experience undergone by a normal observer who views a red object under standard conditions. But since subjectivism seems to deprive us of redness as a property of objects, how do we proceed to elucidate the appropriate sensory predicates? This difficulty is particularly acute for materialists, who do not, of course, wish to countenance sense impressions as part of their basic ontology. Finally, if physical objects are not determinately colored, what is? Must we not acknowledge something like sense data as the ultimate bearers of colors?

Constancy and crudity

The first of the issues may be divided into two: the question of the externality of colors and the question of the stability of colors. To some extent the division is artificial, since the stability of colors in experience is a ground for taking them to be external. Both are questions of psychology. Part of the answer to the externality question is that the nervous system processes color and shape information together to a considerable extent,[20] so whatever it is that makes visual shapes seem to be outside our bodies does the same for colors. As we shall see in section 5, colors that everyone will admit to be purely subjective in origin have that same quality of externality, so this cannot be taken as persuasive evidence that colors are not in some fashion states of ourselves. Why it is that visual shapes present themselves as outside our bodies is something that will not be discussed further in these pages, largely because of a lack of useful ideas on the part of the author. The experienced stability of colors across variations in illumination conditions is, on the other hand, something about which informative things can be said, although the matter is far from being adequately understood.

The immediate physical stimulus for color perception is, of course, the spectral composition and intensity, as well as the size and duration of the light that strikes the retina. Under ordinary conditions of seeing reflecting objects, this light is the product of the spectrum of the incident illumination and the spectral reflectance of the object. One might have supposed that the wavelength composition of the light incident on the retina would control the visual experience, but the fact is that the colors we experience, over a wide variety of lighting conditions, more closely correspond to the reflectances of the objects. The eye-brain must therefore have a way of decomposing the incident light into its components: the spectral composition of the ambient light and the spectral reflectance of the illuminated object, and, as it were, of discounting the former and attending to the latter.

How is this done? Under what conditions and to what extent does this take place? Is it, as Helmholtz supposed, an unconscious inferencelike process, or is it, as Hering thought, like simultaneous contrast, a purely sensory, automatic response?[21]

This problem of approximate color constancy is the color analogue of approximate size and shape constancy, our propensity to see objects as having a much more stable size and shape than one would have expected on the basis of the characteristics of the retinal image. All these (approximate) constancies are often investigated, copiously discussed and far from properly explained. We touched on some of the purely automatic mechanisms involved in color constancy when we talked, about chromatic adaptation and simultaneous contrast. Let us now take a broader look at the problem by considering four examples.

(1) The first example we have already discussed. Photographs taken indoors with incandescent light and outdoor film are much too strong in yellows and weak in blues. For such conditions one must use a tungsten film or a filter whose transmittance is the inverse of the spectrum of incandescent light. We find the outdoor film unsatisfactory when used indoors because our visual system undergoes a spectral sensitivity change which complements the spectrum of the prevailing light—a biological tungsten filter, as it were. This sensitivity change is largely accounted for by a linear adaptation of the cones, and a smaller nonlinear neural adaptation at the post-receptoral level (Jameson and Hurvich 1972). The precise locus or loci and mechanism(s) of this latter sensitivity shift are among the central questions in current research on the constancy problem.

(2) A piece of white writing paper may have a nonselective reflectance of 80 per cent or more, whereas a lump of coal may have a nonselective reflectance of about 5 per cent. Put the coal in the sunlight, the writing paper in the shade. The coal will reflect substantially more light than the paper, yet it will continue to look black and the paper white. In this case, the two may be in the same field of view, and the effect remains constant when the eye moves from the one to the other. An understanding of this phenomenon obviously must appeal to something besides receptoral adaptation.

(3) Closely connected with the previous example is the situation in which one sees a homogeneously painted object partially illuminated, partially in shadow. The object appears to maintain its color across its surface; the darkened part seems to be just that: a portion in shadow, but not darker in color. If, however, we peer through a reduction screen at a portion of the object in which there is a sharp transition

from illumination to shadow, we will see a patch that looks inhomogeneously colored rather than homogeneously colored but shadowed. The change in appearance effected by the use of a reduction screen is here, as in other cases, dramatic. When one views an object in the "aperture mode," one's experience is dominated by the luminance pattern of what is seen, and it appears as a light spot. Seen naturally, in its full visual context, in the "surface" or "object" mode of perception, the object's reflectance predominates. To a very significant extent, phenomena of color constancy disappear in the aperture mode of viewing, as do simultaneous-contrast effects. The aperture mode emphasizes small differences, and is generally used in colorimetric work. But it is not the way we normally see things; here is a particularly clear instance in which *standard* viewing conditions are different from *normal* or *typical* viewing conditions.

(4) "White things look red when seen through red-tinted spectacles." Here we have another of those truisms which are, taken strictly, false. It is true that, if a white piece of paper is seen through a red transparency that covers a small portion of the visual scene, it can look red. But if most of a field of view is seen through such a transparency, a piece of white paper that forms part of that field will look not red, but white—indeed, it will look like a white paper in red light. The central variable here is the extent of the field seen through the filter; the analogy with the reduction screen is apparent.

Whereas example (1) is best understood as exhibiting a largely physiological response of the visual system, examples (2)-(4) seem to involve, to a greater or lesser extent, quasi-judgmental processes, in that the character of the experience—and certainly a subject's description of it—will be strongly affected by the attitude taken toward it. The difference between the aperture and surface modes of perception is, after all, a difference between conditions of lesser and greater information. A small viewing field that has a brighter half and a dimmer half is an ambiguous presentation. One could, for instance, be seeing a uniformly illuminated portion of a surface painted with two different pigments, or one could be seeing a nonuniformly illuminated portion painted with a single pigment. Enlarge the field of view, providing more clues to the position, intensity and chromaticity of the

---

Fig. II-7. Facing page: *In the picture at the bottom, the fuzzy penumbra of the shadow shown at the top has been covered by a black border. Notice that the effect of the border is to make the shadowed area appear to be a dark spot on the paper rather than a shadowed region of white paper. The presence of the border has altered the perception of lightness constancy.*

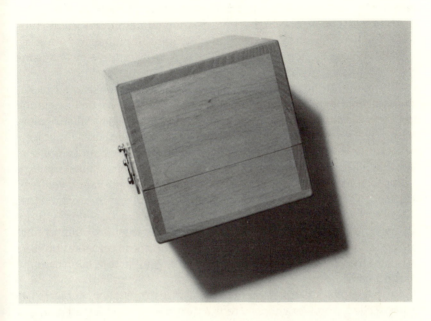

illuminant, and the ambiguity is commonly resolved—to the satisfaction of the visual system, but not necessarily correctly; such is the stuff of illusion. In the higher-information situation, sufficient clues exist for reflectance to be disentangled from illuminance with high reliability, and higher-order cognitive or quasi-cognitive mechanisms proceed to do just that.

By taking an appropriate attitudinal stance, an observer can abstract from the informational richness of the surface mode toward the poverty of the aperture mode. Skilled painters of the realist persuasion must learn to do this as a matter of course, to represent objects seen in nonuniform illuminations by a picture to be seen in uniform illumination. To represent the shadowed rock, they must, for instance, choose a low-value, bluer pigment and a high-value, yellower pigment. They select pigments according to the aperture mode so that their audiences may enjoy scenes in the surface mode.[22] On the other hand, naive artists often paint things as they take them to be, in color as well as perspective. Compare the chromatic renditions in a scene by Claude Monet with those in a comparable landscape by Grandma Moses.

In psychological experiments of lightness constancy, subjects are often called upon to choose from a set of samples viewed under a standard illuminant the achromatic paper which most nearly matches an achromatic target paper seen under a test illuminant. The subject's matches are often rated on a *Brunswik ratio scale* (Beck 1972, 57-58, Evans 1948, 162-163). The details of the scale's construction need not concern us; suffice it to say that it ranges from a perfect reflectance match with a Brunswik ratio of 1, to a perfect luminance match with a Brunswik ratio of 0. Subjects' matches rarely reach either extreme, and there is a great deal of individual variation, but there is a tendency for matches to fall into two groups, a high-value one and a low-value one, "corresponding respectively to people who tend to look at *surfaces* and [to people] who tend to look at light intensities. There is some indication that the ordinary naive observer (including children) tends to fall in the first group and the trained artist or observer in the second."[23] Monkeys, it might be added, also tend to fall in the first group. (Beck 1972, 67) A rather high degree of constancy is, in general, evolutionarily advantageous because it significantly assists the animal to reidentify objects; attention to proximal rather than distal stimuli is a sophisticated luxury. It is interesting to notice that "instruction to the observer to look for the reflectance or the luminance can in some instances change the observed ratio over a range which is much greater for some observers than for others. Some observers seem incapable of obtaining anything but the reflectance type of perception" (Evans 1948, 163–164).

All of this strongly suggests that a great deal of what is called color constancy is cognitive rather than sensory in character. So no account of color constancy such as Edwin Land's, which regards constancy as an automatic part of the color-processing machinery of the brain, can be regarded as entirely satisfactory. Constancy is in this way unlike simultaneous contrast: no amount of instruction or alteration of attitudinal set will make a gray paper square on a large black surround match in appearance a gray square cut from the same paper presented against a white surround.

Nevertheless, there are plenty of experiments to show that there is an automatic, sensory component of color constancy. In particular, whether the visual system "reads" a transition from a dark area to a light area as an edge or as a change in illumination will depend on the abruptness of the transition. Hering showed that one can make a cast shadow look like a dark surface area by drawing an outline around it (figure II-7). Here the shift in appearance is very resistant to being undone by a change in perceptual set; it is rather like the Müller-Lyer illusion in that respect. We have already seen how an abrupt luminance change at a visual edge strongly affects the perceived lightness of the whole of the area it bounds (figure I-9), and that this phenomenon seems deeply embedded in the mechanisms of achromatic vision. (Because the spatial resolution of the chromatic system is less than that of the achromatic system, the effects of abrupt wavelength changes are much weaker. This should caution one not to generalize too readily from achromatic to chromatic phenomena.)

These few remarks should suggest how tangled the issues of color constancy really are, particularly the respective roles performed by and the demarcation between what has here been termed the "cognitive" and the "sensory" components of constancy. Is it, for example, evident that the phenomenal character of a color is invariant under changes in perceptual attitude? Structural differences in individual perceptual physiology and philosophical skepticism aside, are Monet's color sensations the same as Grandma Moses'? This issue will occupy us more fully in section 6, but for now, here are two considerations to suggest that it is far from clear that one can neatly separate the sensory from the cognitive state of an observer, and likewise far from obvious that, to the extent that such a separation is effected, the cognitive state cannot alter the sensory state.

First, conscious attempts even by trained observers seldom succeed in moving the Brunswik ratio to either 0 or 1 (Evans 1948, 164).

This suggests either that it is exceedingly difficult for anyone required to perceive objects in the surface mode to make a clear differentiation between the sensory and the cognitive component of his own perception, or else that the sensory component is actually altered by the cognitive component. Second, perceptual set frequently acts in what one might call a "presentational" rather than a "judgmental" fashion. Examples are well known in other areas of visual perception, such as the gestalt switches with the Necker cube (figure II-11B). Context can push the observer almost irresistibly to seeing something as X rather than as Y, seeing, for instance, an object's surface as partly shadowed and homogeneous in color rather than as uniformly illuminated and variegated in color. A context switch may actually change the perceived color, as in the case of the lightness change in the Mach card, to be discussed in section II-5.

Regardless of how the relative contributions of sensation and cognition are factored out in the various cases of color constancy, it is clear that approximate color constancy is a phenomenon which pervades our everyday experience of physical objects, playing much the same kind of role as approximate size constancy in giving us animals a sense that these properties of objects are stable and independent of the conditions of observation. Still, objects only approximately maintain constancy of color appearance across changes in illumination, and highly chromatic illuminations will cause constancy to collapse. Even in the most straightforwardly physiological sorts of adaptation—in adaptation from dark to light, or from natural to artificial light, with plenty of time for the receptors to change sensitivity—the colors of objects do not look *exactly* the same. Furthermore, there is a certain level of precision of color matching and discrimination at which, because of lighting conditions, the perceived colors of objects are constantly changing. Add to this the inhomogeneities of color in any one object and the difficulty of matching the colors of two objects with different surface characteristics (texture, glossiness, etc.), and it becomes clear that in everyday circumstances it is simply futile to characterize the colors of objects in any but coarse ways (Evans 1974, 199).

Other factors are also at work to guarantee the crudity of everyday color categories. One frequently hears that human beings are capable of distinguishing something on the order of ten million colors. This is correct, but it can be misleading if one supposes that this kind of discrimination capability can be brought into play in any but the most severely controlled conditions. (And one must also bear in mind that under those conditions individual differences will become very

P L A T E S

Plate 1: The visible spectrum.

Plate 2: Goodnow: Simultaneous chromatic contrast.
Perceived differences of surface colors in the face of illumination changes are maintained by simultaneous contrast, which we have already encountered in connection with the achromatic system. Simultaneous chromatic contrast is not usually so strong an effect as simultaneous brightness contrast, though it is very definite, as plate 2 makes plain. The small blue-green squares are cut from the same piece of colored paper. But see the shift in hue as the green of the upper right rectangle cancels some of the green in its inserted square, making it look more blue than green, whereas the blue lower left rectangle cancels much of its insert's blueness, making it appear more green than blue. Here we see the opponent systems tending to maximize visual differences while at the same time working toward an overall net chromatic balance.

Plate 3: Monet: Haystack in winter, 1891. Reproduced courtesy of the Museum of Fine Arts, Boston, Mass.

Plate 4: Albers: Afterimage.
In a strong light, stare for thirty seconds or so at the fixation dot in the center of the figure with the yellow disks, then shift your eyes quickly to the dot in the center of the white rectangle.

Plate 5: The McCullough aftereffect.
In a strong light, look at the colored adaptation figure at your normal reading distance. Do not stare at the figure, but rather let your eyes wander across it, devoting equal looking time to the red and to the green bars. After five to ten minutes of consecutive viewing of the colored bars, look at the black-and-white test figure. Its bars will appear faintly colored, and their colors will be complementary to the colors of the similarly oriented bars in the first figure. Notice that this is not a conventional afterimage, for it will not move with your eyes, nor will the colors appear anywhere except on bars of similar width and orientation (try rotating the test figure). The strength of the effect depends directly on the amount of time you spend viewing the adaptation figure and inversely on the amount of time you devote to looking at the test figure. If you spend only a minute or two looking at the test figure now, it is likely that you will still be able to see some coloration on the bars of the figure tomorrow; in this case, nature rewards delayed gratification.

Plate 6: The Von Bezold spreading effect.
This is an anti-contrast effect. Notice the phantom contours across the colored areas.

Tec

400

500 Waveler

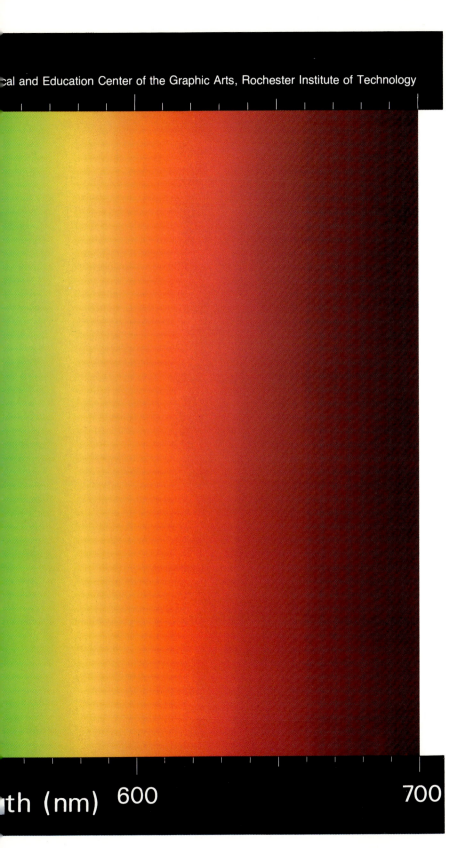

th (nm)   600   700

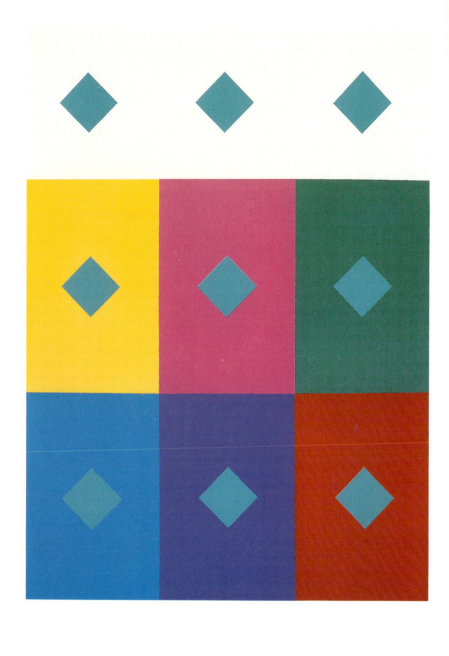

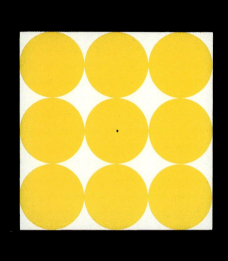

marked.) If the task is to identify a color in the absence of a reference standard, the case is very different: "Even for fairly good observers, positive identification of a color without a comparison is of the order of thirty colors, and for the naive it may be more nearly eight to ten."[24] And if it is a matter of reliable identification on demand, in a life-and-death situation, as in railway signal lights, the number is reduced to a maximum of six (Terstiege 1983). This limited identification capability is reflected in the small number of color terms in common use. For example, a survey of seventeen best sellers revealed that 87 per cent of the occurrences of color words were tokens of just ten types (Evans 1948, 230). (We shall take an extended look at color language later.)

Given our generally strong ability and inclination to distinguish reflectance from illumination, our propensity to overlook the residual and commonly transient variations from constancy, the weakness of our color memories and consequent poverty of reliable color vocabulary, it is little wonder that our everyday color concepts are rough-hewn indeed. It is only under carefully controlled, *standard* conditions rather than complex *normal* conditions that those theoretically vexing differences between material samples and, most particularly, between "normal" observers, are likely to be noticed or cared about. Over a wide variety of objects and circumstances, we have no difficulty at all in deciding what is green, or, to put it another way, in assigning the predicate 'green' to objects. But this has too frequently obscured the fact that we cannot with equal ease assign a particular "shade"[25] of green to objects.

Recall once more the puzzle about two normal observers who, under the same conditions and after careful observation, disagree about whether a particular material sample is unique green. We are perhaps initially inclined to say that at least one of them must be wrong as a matter of natural fact. But, since we have no independent physical criteria for the identity of hues, we are obliged to fall back on some form of stipulation. There are two well-worn strategies for handling situations of this sort. The first is to specify a standard observer, analogous to the 1931 C.I.E. *average observer,* an average of a largish sample of actual normal observers, and decree that the color judgments of the standard observer have normative force. But the consequence of any stipulation of this sort is that very large numbers, probably a majority, of "normal" observers would have unique hue loci at variance with those of the standard observer.[26] One would also have to make a similar stipulation of standard illumination, standard viewing conditions, etc., with comparable divergences among observers for these other illuminations and viewing conditions. By decree, there would then be a fact of the matter as to whether a particular stimulus under particular circumstances was unique green, though most people would fail to see it in its "true" colors. In a similar fashion, we could also establish a fact of the matter about the intrinsic worth of paintings and innumerable other puzzling concerns. The method has obvious advantages; they are, in Bertrand Russell's phrase, the advantages of theft over honest toil.

The second strategy is to relativize the ascriptions of colors to objects to the *particular* observer in a *particular* state of adaptation under *particular* viewing conditions and illuminants and. . . . This will do the job all right and not so high-handedly as the first strategy. But the result will be that any particular colored area will have *lots* of colors: it will be *F* for Smith under conditions *C*, *G* for Jones under the same conditions *C*, but *K* for Jones under different conditions *C'* etc., etc. Is this ontological payoff worth the bother?

The biological and adaptational basis of everyday color categories makes their employment useful and well-nigh inevitable. (You may have noticed that the author of the present essay has not eschewed the ascription of color predicates to material objects.) Although they are fine-grained enough for the tasks of ordinary life, everyday color categories are sufficiently crude for the inherent variabilities of their application to escape notice. When these become bothersome because the problem at hand requires more than usual precision, they are handled in a way that suits the character of the problem. Thus, the industrial supplier will want to effect a match that would be deemed acceptable by the intended users for the designated purposes under the appropriate conditions of use. One of the objectives of applied color science is to generalize across the conditions, contexts, and observers as much as possible, so as to make reliable and practical predictions and determinations of the values of the relevant variables. Color scientists will, of course, talk about "white" illuminants and "cyan" inks. But when they are concerned to predict what will happen when colorants are mixed, their language is that of transmittance, reflectance and the spectral components of light. They use the concepts and vocabulary best suited to the problem at hand.

The burden that some philosophers seem to want to put upon color concepts is different and far more difficult. They appear to want a purpose-free, context-free, individual-free method of deciding the colors of objects which will be consistent and continuous with common sense and common language. It has been argued here that there is no reason to suppose that such a method is possible or desirable. Common ascriptions of colors to objects are, for common purposes, correct enough, but there are, in the nature of the case, *no* such ascriptions that are both precise and correct. We are not, in the last analysis, entitled to say that, as a matter of fact, a determinably green physical object is determinately—for instance, uniquely—green. But if there are, in fact, bluish-green and yellowish-green physical objects, could it be that there is *no fact of the matter* about whether there is a green physical object that is neither bluish nor yellowish? Yet, if she is unwilling to avail herself of high-handed decrees and other such desperate expedients, this is the proposition to which the defender of extradermal colors seems to be committed.

It is not as if there were no plausible alternative to all these Ptolemaic epicycles. There is, and it is simply this: render unto matter what is matter's. Physical objects seem colored, but they need not be colored. They do have spectral reflectances and the like, and such properties are sufficient to give us a straightforward and detailed account of the stimuli of color perception. To account for the phenomena of color we need not ascribe any other properties to those stimuli, and we find, furthermore, that when we try to do so, the chief result is obscurity in our understanding and caprice in our tactics. So stop the sun and the stars, and start up the earth. The sun's motions, which we so plainly see, are illusory: the movement is on *our* end.

But if we are to make good on such a Copernican program, we must give an account of the analogue of those movements, the realizations of chromatic experiences within ourselves. This leads us directly to confront the following argument: We do sometimes see instances of determinate colors such as unique green, so something must be colored. If physical objects are not colored, there must be nonphysical colored objects. The argument's conclusion may seem hastily drawn, but in its favor we must observe that there do seem to be at least some plausible instances of seeing colors which we would, quite without regard to our previous considerations, be loath to characterize as cases of seeing the colors of physical objects.

Chromatic democracy

There is more than one way to see a color. Besides having cones catch the light from spectrally selective reflections, refractions, emissions, etc., color perceptions may be generated in a variety of ways, including

(a) pressure on the eyeball;

(b) relative movement between the eye and alternating dark and light regions (Benham disks and other phase effects);

(c) bombardment of the visual system by cosmic rays;

(d) electrical stimulation of the cortex;

(e) the onset of migraine headaches;

(f) the ingestion of certain drugs;

(g) the selective adaptation of visual receptors (successive contrast);

(h) the selective adaptation of higher-order visual cells (the McCullough aftereffect);

(i) "filling in" by higher-order visual cells;

(j) opponent interactions with surrounding visual tissue (simultaneous contrast).

Some of the products of these "nonstandard" color-generating processes are commonly called "subjective colors," and all of them have sometimes been referred to (mostly by philosophers) as "color illusions." But if our previous reflections are correct, such invidious distinctions among perceived colors are not deeply founded and may be downright misleading. Let us consider some cases.

(1) "Filling in" by higher-order visual cells occurs quite commonly when one sees colors. Otherwise there would, in monocular vision, be a hole in the visual field at the position of the blind spot. Like error correction in a digital audio or video system, this interpolation is normally so well done that it is never noticed. Indeed, one sort of filling in enables us to continue to see colors during eye blinks.

(2) Simultaneous contrast is a ubiquitous feature of visual experience, since it is integrally connected with the process of seeing. Even when one inspects color samples through an aperture, the color of the screen (usually a dark gray, approximating "brain gray") plays a role. The trick is to choose the aperture surround so as to minimize the interaction.[27] But, as we recall, black and brown are never available as aperture colors; they occur only in consequence of contrast. It would surely be perverse to single them out as illusory, but, if one does not, what principle can there be for calling other contrast colors illusory?

(3) The most commonly observed "illusory" colors result from successive contrast in the form of afterimages. Afterimage colors normally seem detached from object surfaces and are commonly labile. They obviously take their being from a change in the observer's adaptive state rather than from some external feature of the perceptual scene (excepting, of course, the stimulus for that adaptive change). But it is worth noticing that the colors of afterimages may be as precisely charted as the perceived colors of many other visual objects, and they generally mix subtractively with each other and the perceived colors of physical surfaces (Wilson and Brocklebank 1955;

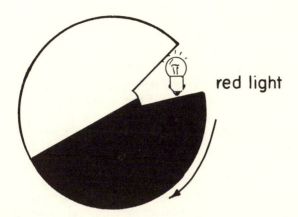

red light

Fig. II-8. *Bidwell's disk. A red lamp is briefly exposed with every revolution of a rapidly rotating half-black, half-white disk which is otherwise illuminated by a neutral light source. Under such circumstances, the wheel appears to be of a homogeneous blue-green color—the afterimage of the red light, which itself is never seen.*

Brown 1965). In fact, afterimages can also produce simultaneous contrast effects (recall plate 4). If these are illusory colors, they nonetheless do much of the work of real colors, so much so that one can set up situations in which afterimage colors will be taken to be the colors of particular physical objects or of the light that illuminates them. For example, one can walk into a room to see a rapidly rotating disk illuminated by a bright light. The surface of the disk is seen to be a homogeneous bluish green. But when the disk is stopped, it is seen to be half white and half black, with a radial segment cut out at the boundary (figure II-8). If the disk is stopped at a particular angle of rotation, a red light may be seen through the cutout. The color the rotating disk was seen to have was entirely afterimage color, produced by the brief flash of red light that occurred at every rotation; when the disk is rapidly turning the red light is never seen as red (Bidwell 1901).

(4) Since ordinary afterimages are produced by adaptation ("fatigue") of the receptors, they move with the eyes. This, along with the indeterminate distance which they appear to have from the front of the eyes and their tendency to fade rapidly, means that they are not commonly confused with perceived object surfaces. But there are other aftereffects with loci further up the neural-processing chain which have more striking properties. One of these is the *McCullough aftereffect*.[28] Although the effect is weak and takes quite a bit longer to establish than an afterimage, it is remarkable enough to be worth the

investment of the reader's time. See plate 5 and follow the instructions on the caption. In the adapting figure, the one grating is red, the other green. After examining the adapting figure for several minutes, look at the black-and-white test figure. You will see its gratings to be faintly but unmistakably tinged with color. Although the complementarity of the adapting and test colors might have been expected, the aftereffect's dependence on the orientation of the grating may come as a surprise. Furthermore, the effect depends on the grating spacing at the eye; vertical gratings with significantly wider or narrower bars (subtended at the eye) will not show the aftereffect color. A further difference from common afterimages is that the Mc-Cullough aftereffect can last for hours and, in some cases, even months. The duration of the effect may be prolonged by increased viewing of the adapting figure and decreased viewing of the test figure.

The McCullough aftereffect is usually explained by supposing that there are specialized cells ("feature detectors") in the visual cortex which preferentially respond to a stimulus with a particular color, spatial frequency, and orientation. Viewing the adapting stimulus excites the cells that are tuned to it more than it excites other cortical cells and causes them to lose sensitivity to continued exposure to any stimulus of the same type. To this extent, the principle is the same as that which operates with the retinal cells in chromatic adaptation. Similar adaptive effects occur for several other features of the stimulus, such as motion.[29] Aftereffects of these sorts lend credence to the picture of the visual cortex as consisting of networks of specialist cells performing selective analysis of the visual scene and leaving the imprint of their operations on the phenomenal character of experience.

(5) *Phosphenes* are colored regions in the visual field which are caused by means other than stimulation of the retina by light. These other means include cosmic ray bombardment (not recommended, but reported by astronauts) (Hurvich 1981, 14), electrical stimulation of the visual cortex (best avoided), and an occlusion of the blood supply brought about by pressing on the eyeballs with the palms of the hand through closed eyelids. The last procedure is safe if the pressure is not sustained too long. Try it. Fifteen or twenty seconds should be enough. Then relax the pressure, but keep your eyes covered for several seconds more and watch the show. What you get for your efforts are some colored geometric patterns, not so very different from those experienced by many migraine sufferers and some drug users, as well as a constellation of colored flashes.

It is very plain that phosphenes are internally generated, and yet they, like all colored regions of the visual field—even brain gray—are phenomenally located in front of the eyes. (It is also possible to see directly many objects and processes inside one's own eyes. They include the "floaters" in the vitreous humor, the macular pigment, the blood vessels in the retina, and "Purkinje arcs," which are probably the result of electrical discharges in the optic bundle coursing across the surface of the retina (Judd and Wyszecki 1963, 18–19). All of them appear as phenomena located outside the eyes.) But notice that, although they seem to be near the eyes, they do not appear to be any determinate distance from the eyes. This lack of determinateness frequently characterizes sensory phenomena. We shall have more to say about this shortly.

Most materialist accounts of color slight such phenomena as these, either by ignoring them entirely or by relegating them to the attic of illusion and then neglecting to give us an adequate account of how the illusion comes to be. It ill suits those who call themselves "scientific materialists" to throw away the data. One might look more kindly on this fault if those materialists at least had a proper story to tell about "real" and "objective" colors, but precisely that is what they (and we) now lack.

By contrast, one of the great virtues of sense-datum accounts is that they are very democratic when it comes to colors and perceptual objects. "Real" and "illusory" colors and objects alike find a common home as regions or qualities of regions of that very catholic object, the visual field. Furthermore, the ontological status assigned to them and the form of language used to describe them in sense-datum theories fit their phenomenological status as perceptual objects rather than as states of observers. This is unquestionably a point in favor of sense-datum theories, although it is by no means decisive. After all, we have repeatedly insisted that colors present themselves as properties of objects beyond the eyes, but this has proved to be an illusion, albeit a most durable one. We must also bear in mind the possibility of separating the act-object mode of describing visual phenomena from any commitment to a sense-datum ontology, preserving the former while rejecting the latter. We shall be entitled to do this if we can show how, at least in principle, we could eliminate sense-datum talk in favor of discourse that does not carry its ontological commitments and if we can show that those commitments are both unnecessary and undesirable. If we grant the program, manifest throughout our entire discussion, of explaining the phenomena of color vision in terms of physical and biological mechanisms, a commitment to sense data would certainly seem to be undesirable, because as they are usually construed, sense data are mental or at least nonphysical objects, and the difficulties of integrating such objects coherently into a world of material objects and processes are notorious.

Nevertheless, at this stage of our inquiry, there are reasons for thinking our argument has forced us into swallowing the bitter pill. Since colors cannot strictly be predicated of physical objects, it would seem that, if they are to be predicated of anything, they must be predicated of regions of the visual field. And what is the visual field if not an irreducibly mental—or at least nonphysical—entity? For, if it is physical, it should have a location in physical space, and it seems unreasonable to assign it one. Must we then conclude that, since there are colored objects, materialism must be false? Let us consider these questions by means of an examination of a recent and typical representative sense-datum theory, that of Frank Jackson (1977).

Sense data as color bearers

One attractive feature of Frank Jackson's theory of sense data is that he wishes to relieve sense data of many of their epistemic burdens, particularly incorrigibility. His aim is to show that the existence of sense data as immediate objects of perception and as the bearers of the properties objects look to have is essential for a correct analysis of such statements as 'I see a tomato'. In so doing, he proposes to "eschew such questions as: What is it not just to see a tomato, but to be conscious of seeing one, or, What is it to interpret one's personal experience as being of a tomato. . . . (These) are surely questions that presuppose what it is to see a tomato . . . and so, may reasonably be postponed" (p. 27). This implies that the character of a sense datum does not depend upon the way it is interpreted.

To what theses is any sense-datum theory committed? Jackson's answer is that

> . . . to accept (visual) sense-data is to accept that (i) whenever sensing occurs, there is a colored patch which is the immediate object of perception, and (ii) that this colored patch bears the apparent properties. . . . The immediate objects of perception have at least color, shape, and extension. (pp. 27, 88)

Furthermore, a sense datum's color, shape, and extension must be determinate. In this, Jackson accepts the classic empiricist stance, unequivocally expressed by Hume:

> No object can appear to the senses; or in otherwords, no impression can become present to the mind, without being determined in its degrees both

of quantity and quality. The confusion, in which impressions are sometimes involved, proceeds only from their faintness and unsteadiness, not from any capacity in the mind to receive any impression, which in its real existence has no particular degree nor proportion. That is a contradiction in terms; and even implies the flattest of all contradictions, viz. that 'tis possible for the same thing both to be and not to be. (Hume 1739; 1955, 19)

So according to Hume, cases of apparent indeterminacy are to be ascribed not to the inherent properties of impressions, but to their "faintness and unsteadiness". But if faintness and unsteadiness are properties of the impressions themselves, what could they be except indeterminacies in "degree of quantity or quality"? It must be, rather, that the mind has, under these circumstances, difficulty in making out the "particular degree or proportion" of the impression.

Compare this position with how Jackson treats the speckled hen, that stock example of the indeterminacy of perception:

A sensory item theorist needs merely to say that the item has a definite number of speckles, but that we are not perceptually aware of what this definite number is. . . . It is clear that every feature of which we are immediately perceptually aware must, on sensory item theories, be a feature of a sensory item. But it is not at all clear that every feature of a sensory item must be a feature of which we are perceptually aware. (p. 116)

Hume and Jackson thus share the view that indeterminateness is not a feature of the immediate object of perception, but arises from the manner in which the mind apprehends that object. Once again, it is not obvious that one can maintain this distinction and still hold that "sensory items are postulated to do justice to the phenomenological side of perception." But whereas Hume seems troubled with the difficulty of specifying the "degrees of quantity and quality" of an impression under difficult (often "threshold") conditions, Jackson largely regards the problem to be one of attention:

I am not, though, denying that if at the time of knowingly seeing an object I am asked to specify the relevant colored shape or apparent colored shape, I will, except in bizarre circumstances, be able to give a clear answer. There is a capacity of human beings, which we might call 'directing one's attention to one's perceptual experience' or 'putting oneself in the phenomenological frame of mind,' the exercise of which enables us to pick out a colored shape corresponding to any physical object we are seeing. (p. 26)

There is here the tacit but clear supposition that the act of attending to a sense datum makes it possible to discern its inherent properties without altering those properties.

In what follows we shall consider some examples that call into question the claim that whenever seeing occurs there exists a non-physical colored patch which is itself seen and has a determinate color and shape. These will be cases in which either something is knowingly seen without awareness of a colored patch, or a colored patch is knowingly seen but its properties are indefinite or even mutually contrary, or else the colored patch fails to bear the apparent properties of the object that is seen. Furthermore, consideration of these instances will oblige us to confront just those questions about the relations between interpreting and sensing which Jackson thinks can safely be postponed.

The first example concerns a common laboratory determination of visual threshold. A subject adapts her vision to a totally dark room. She is then exposed at random intervals to a 2-degree spot of monochromatic (say, 580 nm) light for 3 seconds. A stimulus of this sort, if seen by any non-color-deficient subject at moderate light levels, would invariably be described as yellow. But the subject in our experiment is given the stimulus at extremely low intensities. Care is taken to direct the stimulus at the fovea. At these levels, only a very few quanta of light are involved. Sometimes the stimulus will be detected and sometimes not; sensory thresholds are nowadays represented not by step functions but by probability curves. (This reflects a fundamental feature of thresholds. We shall return to this point later.) The subject is asked to report (1) whether she sees anything and (2) whether she sees the light as being of a particular color. She is permitted to use four color names: 'white', 'yellow', 'green', and 'red'. (If 'blue' were permitted, it would never be used when the stimulus is 580 nm.)

As the intensity level is gradually raised by very small increments, our subject begins to report seeing something which she is likely to describe as an "indefinite flicker". There will come an intensity point—call it 'A'—at which her reports that she sees a flicker will be correct 5 per cent of the time (figure II-9). But she will not report it as being any color—not even white. Just past A, those of her reports which correctly identify the stimulus as present will begin to ascribe color to the light, but the first of these will always be either "red" or "green," never "white" or "yellow."[30] By intensity point B, she will report seeing a light and be correct for 60 per cent of the stimulus presentations, Her color reports for those 60 per cent will be 15 per cent "green," 10 per cent "red," and 10 per cent "white." 25 per cent of the reports at B will be without a color attribution. Just after B the "yellow" reports begin. There comes an intensity point at

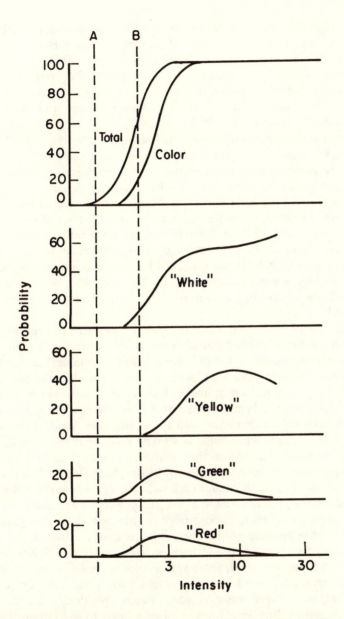

Fig. II-9. *The probability (in percent) of detecting a brief, faint light of 580 nm as a function of its intensity. The observer could simply report the presence of a light; these data are indicated by the total curve. The observer could also report the color of the light; the lower panels give the probability for the different color terms actually used by an observer.*

which the stimulus is seen 100 per cent of the time and ascribed a color 100 per cent of the time. (At an earlier point it is seen 100 per cent of the time, but seen as having a color just 80 per cent of the time.) At the 100 per cent color-response point, the "red" response has dropped to 5 per cent, the "green" response is 15 per cent, and the "yellow" and "white" responses are 30 per cent and 50 per cent respectively (Bouman and Walraven 1957).

Color scientists are interested in such experiments for the insight they give into the differences of performance of the visual system at very low as opposed to medium stimulus intensities. But our interests here are somewhat different. At what intensity did the subject first see the flash? If we opt for intensity A, we would seem to have to say that every time she saw the flash at A her seeing it did not involve her seeing a colored flash. Even if we choose the intensity for 100 per cent detection, on the rather stringent ground that anything less than 100 per cent visual detection should be regarded as guessing rather than seeing, we would still have to deal with the fact that at that point 20 per cent of the cases of seeing do not involve seeing anything colored.

One might reply that a colored patch was seen, but not noticed. Now if the term 'colored patch' is taken to refer to the stimulus, the reply is (at a certain level of discourse) unobjectionable, but this is not the sort of colored patch that Jackson—or anyone else who holds that sense data are nonphysical items—has in mind. If the sense datum is colored, why isn't its color noticed? It is surely not lack of attention: psychophysical subjects are paid to be attentive. And, if the sense datum is colored, what color is it? The color that the spot of light seems to have at moderate intensities? (At very high intensities it would seem to have yet a different color.) At intensity B, no spot is ever reported to be that color (yellow). The color that the other spot presentations appear to have at the 100 per cent detection level? But there are four colors to choose from in this case, with no reason beyond relative frequencies for choosing one over another. There seem to be only two remaining alternatives. We can say that, when no colored patch was reported, there was a colored sense datum nevertheless, even though we have no way of knowing its color. Or we can say that, since there was no colored patch, this does not count as a case of seeing. But would anyone be inclined to say either of these things, apart from a need to save a sense-datum theory from refutation?

There is a more familiar case of seeing something, and seeing one of its properties, without seeing a patch with either color or shape.

Our eyes are very good at detecting motion, and, for reasonably high speeds, we can often detect an object, distinguishing it from its background, without being able to distinguish its shape or its color. A similar set of tradeoffs prevails when one compares the center with the periphery of the visual field. The optical center of the retina is specialized for high spatial and chromatic resolution; the special strengths of the periphery lie in its detection of movement and dim light. One should therefore not be surprised to find that an object whose color and shape are clearly defined at the center of the visual field is amorphous in both shape and color when it appears near the visual field's edge. The visual field of a typical right eye extends as far as 110 degrees to the right of center, but an object of moderate size exhibits no chromatic color at all past 65 degrees, and red and green are unavailable beyond 40 degrees. As one goes much past 10 degrees to the right of center, both color and shape begin to lose distinctness. (It is largely a matter of size, though; all four hue families are detectable even in the far periphery provided that the target object is sufficiently large. However, at no target size is peripheral vision capable of the fovea's chromatic resolution (Moreland 1972).) The periphery is apt for the detection of motion, and we are indeed able to notice that something is moving in the far periphery without becoming cognizant of anything about its shape or color. We normally pay little attention to the characteristics of peripheral vision, because its natural function is to alert us to situations that demand motor avoidance or else inspection by the foveal region. Because of constant eye movements and the persistence of activation of visual receptors, we are able to build up a clear, wide-field visual representation of our surroundings. But even if we do fix our eyes and attend to the deliverances of peripheral vision, we cannot find there the determinateness of central vision. A peripherally presented color sample will match several distinct centrally presented samples equally well—or equally poorly; for if it were to match any one of them as well as any one of them could match another centrally presented sample, the peripheral sample would no longer appear indeterminate. This cannot be a question of the sense datum's having a determinate quality but our not being able to make it out, unless we are to give up the notion that sense data are to be the bearers of appearances. We must, rather, conclude either that, *contra* Hume and Jackson, sense data can be determinably qualified without being determinately qualified, or else that there are no sense data.

Let us now turn our attention to the paradigmatic domain of sense-datum theory, the phenomenal colors of foveally viewed, middle-sized, moderately illuminated objects that are not moving very fast. Even here the sense-datum account runs into severe difficulties. Consider the waterfall illusion: if one fixates on a waterfall for a few minutes and averts one's gaze to the nearby rocks, the rocks will seem to move in the opposite direction. There is no visible change of position of the rocks with respect to our bodies, and the relative rate of positional change between rocks and water remains the same, yet the rocks look as if they were moving. How is the sense-datum theorist to describe such a situation as this? Is the sense datum of the rocks both moving and not moving? Consistency precludes this. Is it neither moving nor not moving? Then bivalence is violated. Is it perhaps only moving? Or perhaps only still? Attention does not seem to enable us to choose one of these alternatives while rejecting the other, and either choice would violate the constraint that the sense datum should be the bearer of the appearances. Or is there perhaps no fact of the matter as to whether the datum moves or is still?

A comparable situation arises with the assimilation or *spreading effect* of von Bezold. The spreading effect is, in a way, the inverse of simultaneous contrast. Whereas the effect of contrast is to intensify large color differences and minimize small ones, the effect of assimilation is to minimize large color differences and intensify small ones. Contrast operates across relatively large areas, assimilation across small ones. Assimilation effects play a substantial role in the famous vibrant grays of Seurat's divisionist paintings. Adjacent red and green areas that subtend a relatively large angle at the eye vibrate against each other, but if they subtend a sufficiently small angle, they neutralize each other. This is optical fusion. As considerations of continuity might lead us to expect, there is a point before they fuse optically with each other at which the areas of color both neutralize and vibrate against each other. This is the point (in the case of Seurat's "Les Poseuses" it is about six feet from the canvas) at which the lustrous gray—and the spreading effect—appears.[31] Achromatic examples of the spreading effect may be found in any engraving, for example, the portrait of George Washington on a dollar bill. Shadows and variations in gray are rendered by fine black lines, so the darker areas have a higher line density, and lighter areas a lower density. If Washington's likeness is viewed with some slight magnification, the graying effect persists despite the fact that we see that the area consists solely of clearly distinguished black and white areas. We see an area as gray even as we see it as having no gray in it.

How is the appearance of gray to be accounted for according to the sense-datum theory? Does the sense datum of Washington's picture have areas that are grayer than other areas? But we can see that there are no differences in grayness. Is the sense datum free of grayness differences? Then how do the black lines on a white field convey the sense of grayness?

We might make some observations about this example. The appearance of grayness differences and of no grayness differences does not involve a gestalt switch, although the exact colors one sees may, under the proper conditions, depend in significant measure upon whether one attends carefully to the fine details of the scene or attends more casually to its more general features. With the proper stimulus objects, such as von Bezold's original illustrations (plate 6), it is possible to balance the factors tending toward assimilation against those tending toward contrast so that one is equally tempted to apply each member of a pair of contrary color predicates to the same area of the picture. Now it might be supposed that, since this equilibrium condition can often be readily upset by a change in the mode of a subject's attention,[32] the sense-datum theorist might be got off the hook by relativizing the perceived color to the particular way in which the scene is being attended to. But this maneuver will be completely successful only if the two modes of attending are strictly incompatible with each other, which some people, at least, do not find them to be. (You may differ; there tends to be some individual variation in these subjective effects, which is why it is wiser to rest one's arguments on a number of such examples.) Furthermore, there is a difficulty in principle for sense-datum theorists to relativize their ascriptions of colors to sense data in this way, since the proponent of sense data is committed to an act-object conception of sensory appearances in which the sense datum is to be the actual bearer of properties that the ostensible object of perception only appears to bear. This is presumably why the friends of sense data have usually insisted that attention reveals rather than enters into the constitution of the objects of direct perception. This is also why they have wanted to draw a sharp line between the sensed properties of an object and those which attach to it in virtue of interpretation.

Another possible way to rescue the sense-datum view would be to distinguish, for each pair of equally applicable contrary predicates, that member of the pair which seems phenomenally to apply from that which seems epistemically to apply, and to observe that the sense-datum theorist is obliged only to attribute the former to the sense datum. Thus, although the rocks in the waterfall illusion appear phenomenally to move, they appear epistemically to remain still: nobody believes, beyond a second or two, that the rocks really are moving. Now, although it is doubtless true that the rocks appear epistemically to remain still, it is also true that they appear phenomenally to remain still, insofar as we see them as not being displaced with respect to the rest of the scene; so the problem remains a problem. It is also certainly true that we want to say that in one way (the experience of absolute movement) the rocks look phenomenally as if they are moving, but in another way (the experience of relative displacement) they look phenomenally as if they are not moving. The problem for the proponent of sense data is to capture this difference in terms of two distinct but resembling properties of the direct object of perception. It is not obvious how this is to be done for the range of problem cases we have been considering.

There is a phenomenon that does depend on a gestalt switch, in which the perceived lightness of an area depends on the "reading" of an edge. The effect was first described by Ernst Mach, and bears his name (Mach 1897, 91). Mach's experiment may easily be carried out by the reader (figure II-10). Take a white file card, fold it lengthwise and set it down, tentlike, on a flat surface, oriented in such a way that the one surface faces the light and the other faces away from it. Now look down at the card from an angle of about 45 degrees and from a distance of about a foot (the exact angle and distance are not critical). Suppose that the light strikes the right-hand surface of the card. You will at first notice the card as a convex figure with the illuminated side a little lighter than the shadowed side. After a moment or two, the figure will "flip", gestalt-style, and you will see a concave figure opened toward you like a book. As your perception of the edge changes from that of a convex fold to that of a concave fold, you should see a change in the lightness of the two halves of the card. The right side will look translucent and significantly lighter than the left side. The strength of the effect seems to vary from one person to another, but it exists to some degree for almost everyone.

If the difference in appearance of the Mach card before and after the gestalt "flip" is due to there being two different sense data, it would appear that seeing X is inextricably bound up with seeing X as Y after all, and one cannot construct a theory of sense data and hope to separate sensory from interpretive factors in every case. If, on the other hand, the sense datum is the same in both cases, the lightness difference on the right side of the card must be due to attending to different features of the sense datum. But then to which feature of the sense datum must we attend to see its true lightness? And how are we to account for there being a merely apparent lightness? If both lightnesses of the right side are real features of the datum, bivalence is

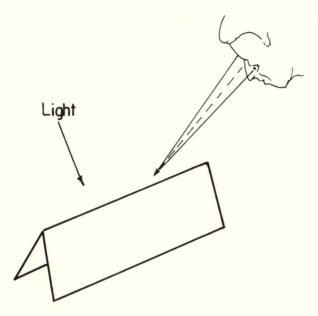

Fig. II-10. *The Mach card and how to view it.*

once more compromised. Finally, if there is no nonarbitrary way of deciding whether the lightness difference of the right side is sensory or interpretive, the sharp sensory-interpretive distinction is broken-backed.

We recall Jackson's remark that "what it is to interpret one's personal experience as being of a tomato . . . presupposes what it is to see a tomato." No doubt this is commonly so; but is it always so? Or could the color we see depend upon what we take ourselves to be seeing? The Mach card phenomenon suggests that it may.

Here is another phenomenon, often mentioned in the psychological literature: memory color, the tendency to see the colors one expects to see. Suppose a tree shape, a diamond shape and a star shape are cut out of pieces of the same green paper, and subjects are asked to match them to uniformly sized rectangles of the same green hue but of various saturations. If the reference rectangles and the test shapes are kept spatially separated, the tree shape will usually be matched to a rectangle of higher saturation than the star or diamond shapes will be. Stereotypically green shapes are thus seen as greener than shapes without a stereotypical color (Wasserman 1978, 110).

In another experiment, the indistinguishability of a figure from its background was used as a measure of perceived color. Using orange paper, the experimenter

> cut characteristically red figures (an apple, a heart, and a lobster), and figures which had no characteristic color (an oval, a triangle, and the letter V). The figures were placed in front of a red background, whose degree of redness was varied. The observer's task was to report, as the color of the background was varied from red to orange, when the figure was no longer visible. [The experimenter] found that figures having no characteristic color required less red in the background before they became indistinguishable from the background than figures having a characteristic red color required. (Beck 1972, 147–148)

The effects of memory color are fairly weak and require stimulus support (the heart shape could not have been cut from green paper and still have been taken to be red), but they seem nonetheless real. Perhaps they are to be understood as cases of interpretation altering sensation or perhaps as instances in which interpretation can no longer be separated from sensation (cf. Evans 1948, 178-180). In either event they make it clear that the epistemic order in which sensation precedes interpretation cannot in general be sustained.

The role of interpretation in the "look" of things becomes crucial

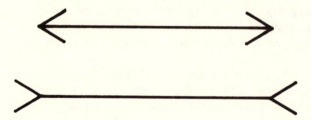

Fig. II-11A. *The Müller-Lyer illusion.*

when we attend to some of the classic illusions of space and shape. The Müller-Lyer illusion (figure II-11 A) is not a consequence of inference in the usual sense; you will probably find that the one line looks longer even when you have drawn the figure yourself. But a sense-datum account would not be helpful here: would the one sense-datum line be longer than the other sense-datum line? And if it were, then since the terminations of the lines remain as before, would it not look even longer?[33] Do you have a new sense datum each time the Necker cube (figure II-11 B) reverses itself? As with the dollar-bill engraving of Washington, the postulating of picturelike bearers of the appearances seems phenomenologically inappropriate. If the Müller-Lyer lines are placed so that one is immediately above the other, at the same time that you see one line as longer than the other, you also see them as being the same length; at the same time that you see the Necker cube as going into or out of the paper, you see it as a set of lines confined to the paper's plane. The nature of the dual awareness of contrary attributes in the spreading-effect cases, however, seems to involve two sensory channels, whereas in the classic illusions such as the Necker cube and Müller-Lyer lines, we are inclined to see a more-or-less sensory and more-or-less interpretive channel at work. The conflicting attributes seem to arise at different levels in the latter instances, and we feel that level difference. But the sense datum must bear the phenomenal properties on the same level, and thus fail to honor a difference that is latent in the experience itself.

Suppose we were to give an artist with appropriate philosophical indoctrination the task of drawing a representation of the sense da-

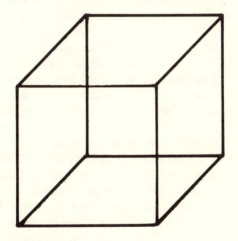

Fig. II-11B. *The Necker cube.*

tum one sees when one looks at a coin obliquely and with one eye shut. We would probably settle for an elliptically shaped drawing. In a similar fashion, such an artist could paint an afterimage which would, under appropriate circumstances, be seen to match or nearly match an actual afterimage. But how would an artist execute an instruction to draw a Necker-cube sense datum first with one face outermost and then with the other face outermost? She could do so only by altering the lines so that her drawing would fail to match what one sees when one views an actual Necker cube; the drawing would not look right. Thus is the level difference manifested within the experience itself.

We have examined cases in which seeing knowingly occurs, but either (i) there is no awareness of a colored patch, or (ii) the colored patch seems to have indefinite or, worse, contrary properties, or (iii) the colored patch does not bear the apparent properties of the object seen. Furthermore, the sensory appearance of a thing is sometimes dependent upon what it is taken to be. All the central tenets of Jackson's sense-datum theory are thus brought into question. Which of these theses is essential to any sense-datum theory? Surely the claim that, whenever seeing occurs, there must be a colored patch is not central and may safely be dropped. The matter of indeterminacy is another matter. The empirical evidence in favor of the indeterminacy of visual shape and color under various conditions of seeing seems quite overwhelming; we should take it to be a phenomenological fact. In this respect several sense-datum philosophers such as H. H. Price and C. D. Broad were prepared to break with Hume.[34] But accepting indeterminacy into phenomenology is one thing and incorporating it into ontology is another. Perhaps this is just a philosophical prejudice, and our holding to it shows that we have not yet learned our lesson from quantum mechanics. But the fact remains that many philosophers have viewed bivalence as the touchstone of realism, and have responded to indeterminacy in quantum mechanics either by interpreting that theory nonrealistically or by endorsing the position that quantum phenomena are to be understood as manifestations of a more fundamental level characterized by state variables that themselves take determinate values (these need not be classical state variables, however). It is not clear how the question of the ontological propriety of indeterminacy is to be settled decisively, but it certainly does seem that, in the absence of compelling evidence to the contrary, one should prefer a theory that regards the phenomenal realm as derivative from, or controlled by, a more fundamental domain in which determinacy prevails.

The sharp sensory-interpretive distinction seems to be consequent on a strict distinction between act and object of perception as well as on a single-level assignment of appearances. Drawing this distinction appears to be a core tactic of sense-datum theorists and leads in turn to the most damaging problem of all, the pressure to assign incompatible predicates to the same sense datum. The nervous system does go to considerable pains to resolve ambiguities and avoid inconsistency, so "catching it out" is very difficult, and the proper analysis of just how the resolution and avoidance occur is elusive, especially if one is restricted to the data of the phenomenal level. It may be possible to find and articulate appropriate pairs of phenomenal predicates which will capture relevant sensory differences and similarities between the way that the rocks in the waterfall illusion seem to move and the way that they do not seem to move, and likewise for the other paradoxical sensory presentations. But this seems not to have been done by any advocate of sense-datum theories, certainly not in any halfway systematic fashion, and the seriousness of the apparent counterexamples requires that this be done before the rest of us should be asked to take sense-datum ontology seriously.

Materialist reduction and the illusion of color

Two obvious and important questions remain for "the rest of us," however. The first is this: even if we renounce sense-datum ontology, how can we save phenomenal description from the very same problems which bedevil the friends of sense data? Secondly, since physical objects are not, in any fundamental way, colored and if we have no good reason to suppose that there are colored mental objects, what sense are we to make of the obvious fact that we have experiences as if of things colored? These two questions are closely related: by answering the first we may obtain a clue to what we should say in reply to the second.

In one way phenomenal description is not compromised by our paradoxical examples. As we have already said, areas of the engraved portrait of Washington look gray in one respect when they are partly covered by thin lines, but in another respect they do not, since one can see the continuity of the color of the paper between lined and unlined areas. A description such as this one asserts that there is a way in which areas of the paper appear gray and another way in which they do not, and it instructs us in the features to which we might attend in order to come into sensory contact with the apparent grayness and the apparent nongrayness, respectively. It does not, however, tell us how it is that the perceptions are sufficiently alike to be denominated as being from the same color category and yet sufficiently different that they can jointly occur. The complaint against such a description must then be that, until it is subsumed under more tractable rubrics, it is less penetrable by reason than one might wish. And our complaint against sense-datum theory is that it promises but does not deliver that more tractable set of rubrics; it does not further our understanding of the nature of sensing. The phenomenal description calls out for supplementation and further articulation.

This further understanding is potentially and at least in part actually forthcoming from perceptual psychology. Let us see to what extent explanations that psychologists have proposed for the spreading effect and for the waterfall illusion can clarify those phenomena. To take the spreading effect first: As we know, a retinal ganglion cell is responsive to stimulation of a retinal region—its receptive field—by virtue of its connection to an assemblage of receptors in that region. Different ganglion cells may have overlapping receptive fields and these fields may be of drastically different size. Let us think of each ganglion cell as responding to an appropriately weighted average of the net activity of the receptor cells to which it is connected. We would expect that a set of ganglion cells with small overlapping or adjacent receptive fields would be able to achieve a finer analysis of the configuration of stimulation of a given retinal region than a set of ganglion cells whose receptive field is the entire region. A typical retinal region in and around the fovea is usually represented by ganglion cells some of which provide coarse and some of which provide fine resolution. Now suppose that in a particular region the patterns of darkness and lightness corresponding to fine lines across a surface are analyzed by some cells and averaged by others. Although a considerable amount of integration of separate channels occurs as signals go up the neural processing chain (with consequent loss of information), a salient feature of the nervous system is the amount of parallel processing that takes place. Such processing carried out all the way to central cortical areas would result in fine detail being both discriminated *and* averaged, which corresponds pretty closely with what seems to happen in the spreading effect (Hurvich 1981).

The key idea is that the nervous system analyzes the same stimulus in a plurality of ways, and that plurality is sometimes sustained at the most central levels. We know, furthermore, that there are large numbers of cortical cells that respond preferentially to complex stimulus combinations. Although the outputs of "feature detectors" of related sorts may commonly tend in the same direction, circumstances may conspire to drive them in opposite directions. For instance, the visual cortex contains cells that are specialized for position detection but will also respond somewhat to changes in position, and other cells that respond strongly to movement alone. A circumstance may occur which adapts the one type of cell but not the other. Something of the sort probably happens in the waterfall illusion. Gazing at the waterfall adapts the detectors for movement in the direction of fall more than it adapts those position detectors which are more weakly sensitive to movement. The one sort of detector "affirms" movement, the other sort "denies" it, and we are able to sense not only the difference in the output but also the difference in the source.

Both the account of the spreading effect and the account of the waterfall illusion are obviously sketchy and much too simple, but they articulate, as the sense-datum account does not, what the experience shows but cannot say. They point the way to a further and deeper understanding of the sensory domain which remains beyond the reach of a theory that is confined to the appearances. Although we need not and cannot forego phenomenal description, we see that in order to get a clearer representation of the deliverances of experience, we must go beyond it, and the natural place to turn is to psychobiology.

The tactic that suggests itself is to show how phenomena of the visual field are represented in the visual cortex and then to show how descriptions of the visual field may be replaced by descriptions of neural processes. It will be argued in the chapters that follow that we have no good reasons for thinking that such a replacement of the one description by the other would leave anything out, with a consequent loss of information. On the contrary, we have reason to expect that a proper neural description would be richer, more complete, and, in principle, more penetrable by the intellect. Problems that are intractable either at the extradermal physical level or at the phenomenal level promise to yield to analysis in neurological terms. Of course, at the present rudimentary state of our knowledge of the visual system, most of this is promise, program, and principle. But enough has already been done to suggest that it is not mere hot air. Furthermore, there is plenty of evidence that all the alternative ways of proceeding are dead ends.

With this wave of the magic wand, we may resolve the problem of the ontological status of color in the following way: Since physical objects are not colored,[35] and we have no good reason to believe that there are nonphysical bearers of color phenomena, and colored objects would have to be physical or nonphysical, we have no good reason to believe that there are colored objects. Colored objects are illusions, but not unfounded illusions. We are normally in chromatic perceptual states, and these are neural states. Because perceptions of color differences and perceptions of boundaries are closely intertwined neural processes, we see colors and shapes together. Roughly speaking, as color goes, so goes visual shape. Consequently, there are no visual shapes in the ultimate sense, just as there are no colors.

But visual shapes have their structural analogues in the physical world, namely, shapes *simpliciter*, and colors do not.

A proper analysis of visual sensation might reasonably take as its analysandum the visual field as a whole, replete with colored and (visually) shaped regions, and as its analysans one of the hierarchy of mappings of retinal activity which are known to exist in the cortex (Cowey 1979; the mappings need not be spatial isomorphs of the retina). Which member of the hierarchy is to be selected will depend on the phenomenon; in general, the first point at which the neural embodiment of that phenomenon appears is the point to be chosen, for any phenomenon of which we are conscious will be represented at every higher level (how else would we be conscious of it?). Most interesting phenomena (e.g., the Necker cube) will involve several different levels (Uttal 1981), and the analysis should extend from the first appearance of the lowest-level feature to the first appearance of the highest-level feature, at which point it would terminate (for the sake of manageability) with a *caeteris paribus*, or in Davida Teller's felicitous phrase, a "provided that nothing mucks it up" clause (Teller 1980).

So much for a general sketch of where color phenomena ought to be located. We are to be eliminativists with respect to color as a property of objects, but reductivists with respect to color experiences. The value of a program to reduce chromatic experiences to neural processes can be determined only by its success—or at least reasonable promise of success—in dealing with otherwise intractable problems. To some of these we must now turn our attention.

III

Phenomenology and Physiology

THE RELATIONS OF COLORS TO EACH OTHER

The resemblances of colors

The relations which colors bear to each other—or which shapes bear to each other—have seemed to many philosophers to be particularly difficult to elucidate. In *A Theory of Universals*, David Armstrong lays out some desiderata for a satisfactory analysis:

> If we consider the class of shapes and the class of the colours, then both classes exhibit the following interesting but puzzling characteristics which it would be agreeable to understand:
> (a) the members of the two classes all have something in common (they are all shapes, they are all colours)
> (b) but while they have something in common, they differ in that very respect (they all differ as shapes, they all differ as colours)
> (c) they exhibit a resemblance-order based upon their intrinsic natures (*triangularity* is like *circularity, redness* is more like *orangeness* than *redness* is like *blueness*), where closeness of resemblance has a limit in identity
> (d) they form a set-of-incompatibles (the same particular cannot be simultaneously triangular and circular, or red and blue all over). (Armstrong 1978)

The perplexities about shapes can be effectively addressed by the devices of analytic geometry, which reduce questions about shapes to questions about equations. For example, we sense that circles are more like ellipses than like squares, and this set of similarities and differences is captured by the fact that circles and ellipses are represented by parametric differences in the same basic equation, whereas a square requires an equation of a quite different form. Furthermore, the difference between a circle and an ellipse is precisely represented by a difference in parameters such that, as the parameters approach each other in value, the corresponding figures approach each other in shape. A more puzzling determinable-determinate relationship, that which holds among that apparently heterogeneous collection of objects, the shapes, is thus reduced to a less puzzling one, that which holds among an apparently more homogeneous collection of objects, the numbers.

In a similar fashion we can map the relationships among the colors into a set of relationships among vectors, reducing questions about an apparently qualitatively heterogeneous collection of objects to questions about a qualitatively homogeneous set of objects. We shall see that the resulting account of the relationships among the colors will satisfy Armstrong's desiderata. Beyond that, by then transposing questions about phenomenal colors into questions about neural processes, we shall find that the way is open to explore some of the deepest features of the "internal relations" of colors, features that have proved almost totally resistant to other analyses.

We can approach our task by providing a simple perceptual model for *unrelated*—i.e., aperture—colors. These, we recall, are colors seen in isolation against a neutral background, for example, colored lights against a dark background or homogeneously colored papers seen through a gray reduction screen. We shall see how the treatment of unrelated colors may be paralleled for *related*, or surface, colors.

Unrelated colors may be characterized by hue, saturation, and brightness. For the sake of simplicity, let us consider a set of colors that have the same brightness. Our constant-brightness model (introduced and developed in Hurvich and Jameson 1956) will be a circle (figure III-1). The radii are to be lines of constant hue, with saturation increasing from zero at the center (the achromatic point) to 100 per cent at the circumference; saturation is here, as before, taken to be the ratio of chromatic to the sum of chromatic and achromatic responses. Hues are therefore to be represented by angles around the center. To make the opponent relationships salient, we shall let unique yellow be at 0 degrees, unique red at 90 degrees, unique blue at 180 degrees, and unique green at 270 degrees. So a diameter of the circle will connect cancellation complements[1] with one another, beginning with a hue at 100 per cent saturation, continuing with progressive desaturation of that hue to the achromatic point, passing beyond the achromatic point with increasing saturation of the opponent hue, ending with that opponent hue at 100 per cent saturation. Let us understand a *resemblance route* between color patches x and y to be

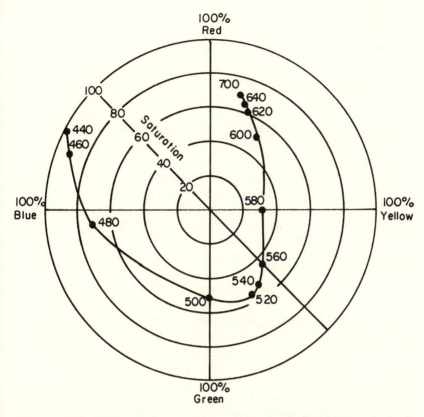

Fig. III-1. *H-S perceptual space: hue and saturation coefficients of spectral stimuli represented in a polar coordinate diagram. Hue is plotted circumferentially and saturation along the radius. The data are for a neutral state of adaptation.*

a sequence of distinct color patches with x and y as endpoints, which is such that each patch closely resembles its neighbors in hue, saturation, and brightness. There are thus just two kinds of resemblance routes between instances of opponent hues: routes that lead through the achromatic point, and routes that lead through a unique hue (which is distinct from both of the opponent hues in question if they are themselves unique). In our constant-brightness Hue-Saturation (H-S) space, every color sample of the given brightness is represented by a vector extending from the center. The length of the vector is the color's saturation, and its direction is the color's hue. We should notice that each such vector may be resolved into exactly two orthogonal components which lie along unique-hue vectors; in the case of the

115

unique-hue vectors themselves, one of the components is always zero. This is a direct consequence of the representation of the unique hues as vectors that lie along cartesian coordinate axes. H-S space is ideal, in that there are points in it which are unrealizable in normal perception. Colors of the spectrum, representing as they do mono-chromatic radiation, are maximally saturated; their loci are plotted in the figure. Any color locus with a saturation greater than that of the spectral color of the same hue (for example, a yellow of more than 40 per cent saturation) will not be filled by a normally realizable ex-ample.

Thus, the members of an equal-brightness color class

(a) are all representable by vectors in the same H-S space;

(b) differ in their vectoral components;

(c) exhibit a resemblance order modeled by the angular separa-tions and lengths of their vectors;

(d) form a set of incompatibles, in that no two distinct vectors can have both of their components in common.

So the relations that the colors bear to each other are neither more nor less puzzling than the relations borne to each other by a set of vectors extending from a common origin in a space with four pre-ferred directions.[2] Of course, what we have done here is simply to lay out in geometrical form some of the results at which we had ear-lier arrived. We have displayed the relations among the four unique hues, the binaries formed from them, and the achromatic colors in a degenerate, constant-brightness case. This degeneracy may now be removed by representing the achromatic series from dazzling to dim by a line orthogonal to our equal-brightness plane and passing through its center, and then constructing similar and parallel equal-brightness planes through each point on the achromatic sequence. The result is a three-dimensional Hue-Brightness-Saturation space.

The ideas of opponent-process theory which underlie the H-B-S space are also exemplified in a recently developed representation of some of the phenomenal relations that obtain among related colors. The Swedish Natural Color System (NCS) (Hård and Sivik 1981; Hård 1976) takes as basic six elementary colors, the achromatic colors Black and White, and the four chromatic colors: Yellow, Red, Blue, and Green. These paradigmatic *colors* (not, in this case, just hues, which may be construed to be classes of colors) are taken to be abso-lute mental-reference standards. The positions of all other colors in the system are to be determined by their degree of resemblance to the elementary colors. The grays, for example, are ordered in accord-ance with the respective percentages of black and white which they contain. A chromatic color will contain a certain percentage of black, a certain percentage of white, and a certain percentage of chromaticness, the three percentages adding up to 100. The chromatic component, in turn, will have a particular percentage of one member of each chromatic opponent pair—say, red and yellow or yellow and green. The structure of NCS space is in several respects similar to that of H-B-S space, with two perpendicular chromatic opponent axes orthogonal to a black-white (rather than a dim-brilliant) achromatic axis. The ideal chromatic colors of 100 per cent chromaticity (zero black and zero white content) are arranged in a circle. The span between two elementary colors is an elementary scale, and each such scale is divided into ten parts (figure III-2).

NCS scaling is achieved by asking the subject to rate the degree of resemblance in intervals of 10 per cent between a given material sample and a mental standard of an elementary, "pure" black, or red, etc. Such an instruction is apt to be greeted by philosophers with extreme skepticism, but this should be tempered by remembering the remarkable capacity of subjects in color-naming experiments to make reliable estimates of percentages of unique hues in randomly presented chromatic samples, estimates which correlate well with those same subjects' chromatic responses as determined in cancellation experiments. And, indeed, people prove to be remarkably apt at carrying out the NCS instructions in a ready and reliable fashion. Two of the developers of the system write:

> Within the R(esearch) & D(evelopment) work on these questions, we have also studied the reliability with which people are able to describe colors in this way. It is interesting that people without any previous knowledge of color assessment, other than with common color names, understand and rapidly acquire the NCS method of describing colors—less than 15 minutes is generally required. If, say, 20 naive observers assess a color, the confidence interval at the 0.05 level in most cases is less than 5% of the elementary scales.[3]

The ease with which the NCS system can be learned and accurately applied speaks to the naturalness of its assumptions, a point to which E. H. Rosch's work with color-name learning among the Dani also attests.

There is another important difference between the NCS and H-B-S constructions. Although the NCS elementary colors are ideal, the elementary chromatic colors are realized in the spectrum.[4] In the NCS atlas, a realization of the system by means of material stimuli, some of the loci are blank only because the corresponding color stim-

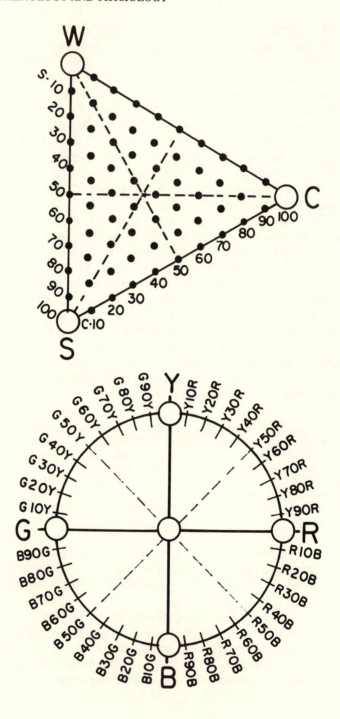

uli cannot be exemplified by reflective colorants at the present state of technology. They are not like the unfilled loci of H-B-S space. Why the difference? The answer lies in the somewhat different objectives of the systems. In H-B-S space, saturation steps are equal percentages of saturation as calculated from the opponent cancellation data. The diagram informs us that there are many more equal saturation steps from the achromatic point to the spectral unique blue than from that point to the spectral unique yellow. This is interpreted in opponent theory as being a consequence of the achromatic response of the visual system peaking close to the point in the 575 nm range at which the red-green response goes to zero, but being small at the other red-green null point. In the NCS system, on the other hand, 'saturation' is differently construed. The relevant basic variable is *chromaticness*, or degree of resemblance to the paradigmatic chromatic color. The term 'saturation' is used in the NCS system, but refers to increasing chromatic proportion. According to this use, elementary spectral yellow has 100 per cent saturation, and, although the number of chromaticness steps from the zero chromatic point to elementary yellow is the same as the number from the zero point to elementary blue, the size of the perceptual interval between any two steps along the constant-yellow line is much smaller than it is along the constant-blue line. It should also be noticed that, for both the H-B-S and NCS spaces, no attempt is made to secure constant perceptual size for equal hue intervals in the spaces, because to do so would obscure the psychological salience of the opponent relationships. The consequences of this decision are easily noticed when one compares the NCS atlas with the Munsell Book of Color, which is intended to be based on equal-sized perceptual hue steps; there are, for instance, many more perceptually equal intervals on the shortest path between unique red and unique blue than on the shortest path between unique red and unique yellow.[5] In the Munsell system, unique blue and yellow do not lie on the same diameter, nor do unique red and green.

By distorting certain phenomenal relationships, other relationships which are more suitable for the purposes at hand can be exhibited felicitously. Its compromises give NCS space a simple and intuitive character which would be sacrificed if accuracy in other respects were attempted. For instance, the Optical Society of America–Uniform Color Space has uniform perceptual intervals between each color

---

Fig. III-2. Facing page: *The Natural Color System coordinate scheme.* 'W' is *whiteness, 'S' is blackness, and 'C' is chromaticness.*

sample and its neighbors, but in it there exist no planes of constant hue (Kuehni 1983, 62–67). And if one demands not only that there be perceptual equality of intervals, but also that the sampling be done to the fineness of just-noticeable differences, it appears that the resulting space is not even Euclidean (Judd and Wyszecki, 1963, 309–310). If we want to go even further and represent phenomenal color relationships in a space that can accommodate the observations of deviant observers, we shall probably require several dimensions (Chang and Carroll 1980).

It should be understood that the issue is not that there cannot be a consistent scheme of representing phenomenal color, for there can. And, indeed, there is reason to suppose that the various representations can be mapped into each other (though the mapping relations will often be quite complex). The point is, rather, that one cannot expect any *single* representation to be serviceable for all purposes, not even if we restrict ourselves to the construction of psychological color spaces rather than, say, spaces whose primary use is in the mixing of colorants.

By representing the colors as we have, we succeed in explicating most of their relationships to each other. For instance, we are able to capture in perspicuous form the phenomenal features that make red more like orange than like blue: orange has red and yellow as components, and blue is not a component of red nor is red a component of blue. Likewise, we can show how it is that nothing is both blue and orange: any instance of orange has constituents of x per cent red and y per cent yellow, where the sum of x and y is 100 per cent, and neither red nor yellow has a blue component. Furthermore, since orange has a yellow component necessarily, and a yellow component is incompatible with a blue component, orange cannot have a blue component.

Answers such as these are perfectly adequate as far as they go, but, if pressed, they generate new questions. For example, unique green is more like unique blue than either is like unique red, but since all of these hues are unique and since the angular separation between blue and green is the same as the angular distance between blue and red, the component model is unable to represent the resemblance, and it seems that no other candidate is available within the phenomenal domain to give an account of this phenomenal fact. Even more fundamentally, it is perfectly clear that any two colors resemble each other much more closely than either resembles a sound or a smell, but we can find no phenomenal feature that all colors share beyond the resemblance itself. As for the exclusion of colors by other colors,

THE INCOMPATIBILITIES OF COLORS

our scheme exhibits the reduction of those exclusions to the separation of the unique hues from each other and the incompatibility that obtains between the members of an opponent pair. The incompatibility is a basic feature of the model, but the model does not, of course, explain it. What further account can be given of that incompatibility?

The incompatibilities of colors

We already have in hand the answer to this last question. A physiological process is responsible for the phenomenally basic opponency of colors, just as physiological processes are the foundation of that apparent motion without apparent displacement which is so perplexing as long as we confine our explanatory resources to the phenomenal domain (recall our discussion of this in Chapter II). Let us see in some detail how opponent physiological processes give us a deeper understanding of color incompatibility. This may in turn give us a clue as to where we should turn to improve our grasp of the more difficult problems of the resemblances of colors.

In his Carus Lectures, Brand Blanshard writes, concerning determinables and determinates,

> Thus determinates of the same determinable may be necessarily linked with each other. There is also a negative linkage: they exclude each other necessarily when asserted of the same subject. A surface that is pure red cannot, at the same time and to the same observer, be pure green. It has been alleged that this is an analytic statement, that it says only that the two colors are different, which is already involved in their being two. But the statement clearly goes beyond this. . . . What we have is a particular kind of incompatibility, based not on the form of the propositions but on the nature of the predicates. (Blanshard 1962, 439–440)

Blanshard is, alas, not forthcoming with a useful account of the "particular kind of incompatibility," and his discussion, like that of most philosophers on this issue, is couched in puzzling terms. What, for instance, is intended by 'pure' in the expressions 'pure red' and 'pure green'? If 'pure' means 'has no other color as a constituent', it is of course analytic that nothing is both pure green and *any* other color. If 'pure green' means 'homogeneously green', such statements need not be understood as analytic. But then, although nothing is "pure" green and "pure" red, there is something, namely turquoise, which *could* be regarded as "pure"—homogeneously—green and "pure" blue. Color exclusion would then not only fail to be necessary, but would, for many pairs of colors, not obtain at all. On the

121

other hand, perhaps we ought to adopt the principle that hue labels are to be hung on hues in such a way as to preclude any two distinct hues from receiving the same label, so we should then have to say, because of linguistic convention, that nothing could be both blue and turquoise.

It is plain that this last suggestion does capture some of our linguistic practice. We do not in fact normally describe turquoise as green *and* blue, but rather form a compound name, often with the help of an '-ish' suffix, so that turquoise is characterized as a bluish green, or a greenish blue, or else just a green-blue. There is, then, a soupçon of analyticity in the brew, arising from our conventions of language. But Blanshard is right when it comes to suggesting that there is more to the problem than linguistic fiat, and right in his choice of examples. The conventions of color naming may explain why we don't conjoin hue names, but they don't explain why we compound some hue names, as we do in 'reddish blue' or 'red-blue', but not others, as in 'bluish yellow' or 'blue-yellow'. This seems to reflect an incompatibility of a sort that lies outside language. The incompatibility seems to have a deep root; for not only do we fail to experience reddish greens, we seem not to be able to represent to ourselves what it would be like to experience reddish greens. Nothing, it seems, *could* be reddish green.

How to account for the modality? Perhaps not being red is part of the concept of being green. Yet it seems that all a normal human being has to do to have the concept of green is to experience green in an appropriately reflective fashion. To be sure, the green region must be distinguishable from its background, but that could occur in the total absence of a red region. There need be no occasion for a reflective green-seer to have had contact with red, and although such a person would doubtless be able to distinguish green from red were red ever to make itself known to her, there is no reason to suppose that the concept of not being red is thereby part of her concept of being green; after all, not being a mastodon isn't part of the concept of being a lampshade, even though reflective people would be readily able to distinguish mastodons from lampshades. If green is just a phenomenal property, its qualities are fully open to view and just what they seem to be. Excluding red does not seem to be one of those qualities nor any part of our reflective green-seer's concept of the hue. Is her concept of green *deficient* by comparison with ours because she hasn't experienced all the hues? Well, have most of us experienced all ten million or so colors[6] that can be experienced? If not, is our concept of that color which happens to be the color of stop signs thereby deficient?

If the mutual exclusion of red and green is not necessary *de dicto*, it is perhaps necessary *de re*. But it is hard to see how this could be the case if redness and greenness were merely phenomenal. Armstrong remarks about the relations of colors,

> What makes it difficult to accept the notion that properties such as the colours are epistemologically simple but ontologically complex is the idea that our grasp of colour is a *total* grasp. . . . We think that there can be no hidden depths in these qualities to which perception fails to reach. . . . In fact, however, perceived qualities and relations are as much epistemological icebergs as any other aspects of reality. (Armstrong 1978, 126)

Its author intended this to be a rallying cry for the objectivist view of colors. In the present case, it might be tempting to take such a path were we not already aware of the high degree of implausibility which attaches to objectivism and did we not have a much more satisfactory view of the matter already available to us. (As it is, it is easy to see how useless objectivism is for the red-green incompatibility problem. Take, for instance, the crude case in which being "pure" red is taken to be identical with sending 650 nm light and not other wavelengths, and being "pure" green is taken to be identical with sending 510 nm light and not other wavelengths. Then 'nothing is both pure red and pure green all over at the same time' becomes 'nothing sends 650 nm and 510 nm light to our eyes at the same time'. This is, of course, patently false, since the two lights can readily be superimposed. It is not hard to see that refining and complicating such an objectivist analysis won't help: it just gets off on the wrong foot.) It is far more satisfactory to say something like the following: What makes the things we call red typically look red to us is that they excite the red-green opponent channel, and what makes the things we call green typically look green to us is that they inhibit the red-green channel (you should festoon this statement with all the qualifications that have been previously detailed), and the red-green channel cannot be both excited and inhibited at the same time. So nothing can look reddish green, and since everything is ascribed a color only, as it were, by courtesy of color perceivers, nothing can be reddish green. A parallel analysis serves for yellowish blue, with a simple extension to all the opponent binaries. Colors are indeed epistemic icebergs, but the concealed part is within rather than without the perceiving animal.

Yet something of the original problem remains. How do we account for (1) the (purported) necessity of the nonexistence of reddish greens and (2) our knowledge of that necessity? What we can say about the first half of the question is that, if opponency not only prevails all the way from the retina to the visual cortex, but persists all the way through the central mechanisms of color vision, the necessity consists in the system's inability to be both excited and inhibited at the same time. But if opponency characterizes not those central mechanisms but only the usual inputs to them, the incompatibility of perceptual redness and greenness is *contingent* rather than necessary. If this analysis of the situation is correct, then there are two possibilities for our knowledge of the necessity of red-green incompatibility: (1) Opponency holds all the way up, and we know that red and green are necessarily incompatible. We therefore have a direct, intuitive grasp of a fact about our makeup which is denied to the discursive methods of present-day science. (2) Opponency may or may not hold all the way up, but in either case we *don't* know that red is necessarily incompatible with green. It is just that we never experience and can't imagine a reddish green, and thus take it to be impossible.[7]

That red is necessarily incompatible with green has been taken for granted by most philosophers who have discussed the issue. They have differed in their explication of the incompatibility and in their account of the ground of the necessity.[8] Yet, looked at from the present point of view, it seems more attractive to hold that we don't have such deep access to our internal workings and that, as long as we are obliged to rely on reflective introspection, unimaginability is as close to knowledge of impossibility as we can get in this matter. Some may of course maintain that, short of a demonstration of inconsistency, unimaginability is the best touchstone of impossibility that we can have. Perhaps, but we certainly have enough cases in the history of physics in which that which is unimaginable (collisions of rigid bodies, wave propagation in the electromagnetic field, quantum processes) proves nevertheless to be conceivable. More to the point, there has been an experiment recently published which, if taken at face value, suggests that a reddish green and a yellowish blue are not only possible, but have actually been experienced.

The experiment depends upon the phenomenon of the fading of stabilized images which is accompanied by "filling in" on the part of the visual system. We remember that edges and boundaries that fall on a retinal region without moving fade from view, and that the visual system fills in the affected area of the visual field with the type of information that is available in surrounding regions of the field. Because of filling in, the visual field corresponding to the blind spot on the retina is experienced not as a visual hole, but rather as a smooth continuation of the color or pattern of the adjacent area. In the experiment, Hewitt Crane and Thomas Piantanida (1983) used a complex device known as an *eye-tracker,* which can produce a fully stabilized image on a subject's retina without the use of a contact lens. Subjects were asked to observe an area in which the target object consisted of two adjacent bars, one red and one green. The boundary between the two bars, but not the rest of the image of the bars, was stabilized on the retina. Within a few seconds, the boundary faded from view. The visual system was thus required to fill in the washed-out area, but to do so on the basis of contrary cues, the display telling the brain's visual area, "Fill in red!" but also, "Fill in green!"

What did the subjects see? The responses fell into three groups. Reports of the first kind were that the border area was broken into a fine-textured pattern, with pebbles of red mixed in with pebbles of green. The second set of responses was that islands of red were floating in a sea of green, or vice versa. But the third set was the interesting one. Here, subjects reported seeing something they had never seen before, and had not expected to see, but had no trouble in identifying: a field of red and a field of green merging into a *reddish green* region in the middle. The experiments were repeated with yellow and blue bars, and the three classes of reports were once again produced. People who saw the red-green binary included naive subjects as well as a painter and the experimenters. The painter, who had a large color vocabulary, was nonplussed by what she saw.

Crane and Piantanida interpret the finding to mean that the opponent channels, which are the normal conduits of color information, do not extend all the way up the visual processing chain, and that the opponency may be superseded by the filling-in mechanism which is known to lie within the brain itself. The experiment, which has not received a published replication at the time of this writing, has, it is only fair to say, been greeted with widespread skepticism in the visual-science community, even though it comes from the laboratory of two respected visual scientists. We cannot judge whether or not the findings will be sustained. However, they are not contradicted by any secure scientific knowledge, and it would seem rash indeed for a layman to decide on a priori grounds that they must be rejected. (Would it not be equally rash to decide that there must be an experience of a red-green binary solely on the basis of reflective judgments by sincere observers about their immediate sense experience?[9]) But to agree that this is a matter to be settled by experiment is of course to agree that it is conceptually possible that something could look both red and green all over.

Furthermore, we should notice that if there do exist red-green or blue-yellow binaries, all existing three-dimensional color-order systems can be valid only for conditions of normal seeing. This is because, under the special conditions of the experiment, there are two quite different types of hue-resemblance paths that lead from a hue to its opponent hue. For instance, the normal sort of hue path from red to green leads through another unique hue, either yellow or blue. But under the new circumstance, there is another hue path, that which passes through red-green. Thus, if the experiment is valid, no resemblance ordering of *all* experienceable hues is possible in a three-dimensional color space.

Which properties of color qualities are essential to them and which ones are accidental? One could not be expected to have ready to hand a systematic answer to this question, but it is fair to say that most philosophers would readily locate some clear instances of each. At least some of the resemblances of colors would be taken to be essential to them. Crimson and pink, for example, resemble each other because they are both reds, and they could not be what they are, were they not reds. More careful reflection persuades us that there are other essential characteristics of colors, for instance, that orange could not retain its identity were it not reddish and yellowish. On the other side of the distinction, the property of being Sam's favorite color would generally be thought accidental to red. If pressed to spell out some principled way of making the distinction, one might think of putting it this way: those properties of colors that bear on the relations which colors have to each other are to be deemed essential; those which obtain only because of the existence and characteristics of other things (except, of course for the organisms who perceive them) are to be supposed accidental to them.

This plausible way of drawing the line is open to objections. We get the number of just-noticeable hue differences between two given colors just by attending to the relationships that these and other colors bear to each other, but it certainly does not seem that the *identity* of the colors depends upon there being, say, three rather than five just-noticeably-different hue steps between them.[10] There is significant variability between individuals in such discriminations, as well as diachronic variations with the same individual, and we do not generally suppose that this jeopardizes the identity of the colors unless it occurs in consequence of a dichromacy that alters the *constituents* of the colors or the dimensionality of the color space.

A more attractive view is that the constituents of colors are essential to them, along with the relations that obtain among them in virtue of those constituents. Yet this statement is also flawed; for the opponent relations between colors obtain by virtue of their constituents, yet we have seen that there is reason to think that, for example, opponency to green may not be essential to red. It is important to keep in mind the grounds of the caveat. That people claim to have seen a reddish green is one of the grounds, but not the only one. The other is that it is at the moment an open question whether opponent mechanisms are to be found throughout the post-receptoral processing chain for color vision. If we were to find strong independent evidence that they are, we should be obliged to reject or reinterpret the observation reports, especially if the experiment were not successfully replicated in other laboratories. On the other hand, successful replication and other appropriate evidence might well persuade us of the restricted character of opponent processing, however central a role it may play in normal color vision. For our present purposes, the important point is that the characteristics and relationships of colors depend upon their biological substrate, and we delude ourselves if we suppose it possible systematically to understand the relations colors bear to each other in isolation from that substrate.

Deeper problems

It is now time to look at the virtues and deficiencies of the account we have so far given of the resemblances of colors. We have found it possible, using the concepts of the NCS system, to give a completely adequate model of the resemblances that the colors bear to each other in terms of their resemblances to the six elementary colors white, black, red, green, yellow, and blue. (We can of course also give a similar perspicuous representation of the resemblances by means of the H-B-S space and its color vectors.) Since there are estimated to be between seven and ten million distinguishable colors, this amounts to a better than millionfold reduction of the problem. Two problems remain, however, and they are very fundamental and very difficult. The first is to account for the resemblances and differences among the elementary colors themselves. The second is to explicate that property which all colors share with each other and which none of them shares with other kinds of sensory qualities such as those of sounds and tastes. Our method of attacking the problems will be to suppose that phenomenal similarities and differences are rooted in and to be explicated by physiological similarities and differences. We must acknowledge at the outset that we cannot deliver solutions to either problem which are nearly as detailed or factually founded as our somewhat flawed and open-ended solution to the problem of the incompatibility of colors, nor nearly as persuasive as the reduction achieved by means of the H-B-S or NCS concepts. We can only hope by our speculations to open new ways to explore questions which have up until now seemed almost totally intractable.

We may take as our text a famous passage from Hume:

> It is evident, that even different simple ideas may have a similarity or resemblance to each other; nor is it necessary, that the point or circumstance of resemblance should be distinct or separable from that in which they differ. *Blue* and *green* are different simple ideas, but are more resembling than *blue* or *scarlet;* though their perfect simplicity excludes all possibility of separation or distinction. It is the same with particular sounds, and tastes, and smells. These admit of infinite resemblance upon the general appearance and comparison, without having any common circumstance the same. (*Treatise,* Bk. I, pt. I, Sect. vii.)

We need not say much about the "perfect simplicity" of colors, other than to remark that it is precisely the lack of such simplicity in colors which makes it possible to interpolate Hume's "missing shade of blue." On the other hand, the apparent "perfect simplicity" of the elementary colors or the unique hues does make Hume's problem about the relative resemblances of blue, green, and scarlet more daunting than Armstrong's red, orange, and blue. As we have already said, since red is a constituent of orange and not a constituent of blue, it is easy to see why it is that red resembles orange more than red resembles blue. Now if we take Hume's language very literally and insist on the particulars of the O.E.D. definition of 'scarlet' as "a brilliant vivid red color, inclining to orange," we can let the inclination to orange carry the weight, and handle Hume's case much as we handled Armstrong's. But if we more generously identify scarlet with elementary red and likewise take his green and blue to be elementary, we are in trouble, since each of these colors contains a zero amount of the others. The concepts of the opponent theory give us no basis for supposing there to be a stronger similarity between blue and green than between red and green. But the similarity is difficult to deny.

This similarity is part of a larger division of the hues which is salient and often commented upon, but very difficult to characterize intensionally except by analogy. Extensionally, this division of hues roughly corresponds to what one would get by segregating the long-wave spectral hues from the shortwave ones, the dividing region falling very roughly in the low-discrimination yellow-green region and, if we consider the whole phenomenal hue circuit, also in the purples, which don't appear in the spectrum. The division assigns red and yellow to one group, and green and blue to the other, with a reddish orange and a greenish blue or a blue seen by most people as psychologically furthest apart.

The most common analogical characterization of the difference labels red and yellow as the "warm" hues and green and blue as the "cool" hues. Some are inclined to use kinetic rather than thermal terms, so that red and yellow are "advancing" and blue and green are "receding." Still others assimilate the distinction to a variation in brightness, with red and yellow as "light" and green and blue as "dark." One can readily find particular and extrinsic reasons for each of these connections. *Warm-cool:* Red and yellow are the hues of fires, green and blue the colors of lakes. *Advancing-receding:* If the lens of the eye accommodates so that an image formed by middlewave light is focused on the retina, a shortwave image will focus in front of the retina, and a longwave image will focus behind it. Shortwave light thus focuses like light from a more distant object, and longwave light focuses like light from a closer object. To focus on a blue patch we must therefore accommodate our lenses as we would when we focus on a distant object, while focusing on a red patch requires that we accomodate as we do for nearby objects. It is sometimes claimed that afferent messages from the relevant eye muscles are among the clues we use to establish the respective distances of objects. *Light-dark:* The eye's sensitivity is much less at the spectral locus for blue and blue-violet than it is at the locus for yellow and yellow-orange. So, although a thing that looks blue may reflect as much light energy to the eye as a thing that looks yellow, the blue-looking thing will typically have most of its reflected energy in the neighborhood of 475 nm, where the eye is not só sensitive, and the yellow-looking thing will commonly reflect more of its energy at around 575 nm, where the eye is very sensitive. So the first thing will look darker than the second one.

These explanations are of varying degrees of persuasiveness, but they should at least caution us not to put too much weight on any single analogical formulation. However, they should not blind us to the striking fact that there is a remarkable clustering of oppositions which correlate with this hue division.[11] Here are some more: active-passive; exciting-inhibiting; up-down; positive-negative. The last pair is particularly interesting, because it is quite abstract, and yet most people have no difficulty in connecting it with the hue division, once it is made clear that 'positive' is not meant to express preference. If, however, 'positive' is taken to express preference, the correlation reverses. There is an outward physiological manifestation of the correlation, and this may give us a clue as to what is going on. People who briefly view the "warm" hues after adapting to gray surrounds tend to show elevated vital signs, such as increased pulse rate and blood pressure; those who briefly view "cool" hues display lowered vital signs.[12] The common theme that seems to run through all of this is a felt common *polarity*. We may continue to use the most frequent expression of it and refer to "warm" and "cool" hues, but have it understood that it is this polarity which is to be captured.

The pervasiveness of these associations suggests that their roots may be embedded deeply within our physical makeups. What kind of possible mechanisms might account for the polarities? The sketch about to be given must be regarded as only illustrative of the possibilities. Like most off-the-cuff speculations, it is probably wrong. In any event, although it is empirical in character, it is neither contravened nor supported by any hard evidence currently available.

We know that hue coding and transmission prior to the visual cortex are effected by increases or decreases in the base rate of neural firing. In speaking of, for example, the r-g channel, we assign ' + ' to the red response and ' − ' to the green response, but this is only by convention; we don't know what nature's assignment is. (Yet it is interesting to notice, as an expression of our inclination to assign polarity in one way rather than another, that the conventional assignment to all three opponent channels is just what we would have expected it to be on the basis of the foregoing considerations: ' + ' to red, yellow, and white.) The ultimate neural coding for hue response, however, takes place in the cortex; it is here that our speculative mechanisms are to be sited.

Let us suppose that it is the pattern of activity of many cortical cells rather than the firing of only a few which is crucial for sensory awareness. Among these cortical cells there will be many chromatically responsive ones. Let a substantial assembly of these latter be interconnected so that each is sensitive to the average activity level of the members of the assembly of which it is a part. Following a very general tendency of sensory neurons, the members of this assembly, we suppose, code information in terms of deviation from a base rate rather than by absolute intensity level. Let us, accordingly, postulate that when their owner views ripe lemons or McIntosh apples, the chromatic cell assembly in the visual cortex responds with an increase in activity level, and responds with a reduced level when ripe cucumbers or clear daylight sky are seen. Furthermore, let the central processing unit (the hypothetical neural correlate of "consciousness"—this is where our account becomes *really* sketchy) contain polarity-sensitive comparator cells which receive input from both the visual and the somatosensory systems. Finally, suppose that the cells of the central processing unit respond to the joint activity of the cortical chromatic cell assembly and the intermodal comparator cells, so that the chromatic experience comes labeled as "plus" or "minus."

That such intermodal comparator cells might exist is made plausible by at least three independent considerations. First, direct recordings have been made from cells that give their maximal response to a combination of auditory and visual inputs from the same region of space (Levine and Shefner 1981, 420). This shows that intermodal cells exist in vertebrates. Second, there is a considerable body of reliable cross-modal psychological connections documented in the experimental literature (Marks 1978). It is reasonable to suppose they have a neural substrate. Third, phylogenetic evidence suggests longwave and shortwave detecting mechanisms were originally separate, with each one connected to its own behavior-modifying or regulatory system. They later combined into proper visual systems, but the direct connections to other systems may have been retained (Menzel 1979). Such connections seem well documented in primates.[13]

This primitive sketch of a possible neural-process configuration contains elements that not only parallel the phenomenal similarities and differences, but also suggest how these relationships, which on the phenomenal level are at once strongly felt and cognitively opaque, may be explained. We are aware of a generic qualitative feature of the "cool" hues which not only differentiates them from a comparable but opposed feature of the "warm" hues, but which they share in a felt but even more cognitively opaque way with qualities in other sensory modalities. Occurrences within the phenomenal domain that are not explicable within the ambit of phenomenal concepts point to something beyond. But where could "beyond" be if not in the physiologies of human beings? It does not seem unreasonable to revive a point of view that dates back to the origins of psychophysics: regard perceived qualitative similarities and differences as an expression of the neural coding itself. Why not regard the phenomenal domain as being in some fashion *constituted* by a subset of neural codes?

Whatever sort of being colors might be supposed to have must, in the last analysis, have a sensuous, phenomenal character.[14] But phenomenal data are notoriously fragmented and limited. In seventeenth-century terminology they would be characterized as sometimes unclear, sometimes clear, but never distinct. They are sometimes unclear because it is not always evident, for example, whether a region of the visual field is colored, or what that color might be (think of the periphery of the visual field). A satisfactory materialist reduction of visual phenomenology must not only show how to replace visual-field talk by physiological talk, but also give an account of the circumstances and causes of our inability to regiment our phenomenal descriptions.

The data are also, in seventeenth-century terms, indistinct, because we always come to a point at which we sense more than we are able to say. We cannot, for example, specify, except trivially, the phenomenal feature that red and green share with each other but neither shares with a tone, a shape, or a taste. This is our other deep problem of resemblance: it is clear that the colors form a phenomenal family, but we are totally unable to give an account in phenomenal terms of what it is that connects them. The ground of the resemblance, if there is one, must come outside the phenomenal domain, and yet it must bear an *intrinsic* relationship to experienced color.

Does any solution to the problem exist if we are to be bound by such a double constraint? Heretofore, there seem to have been only two tactics for dealing with the problem. Some have despaired of finding any further basis for the resemblance, taking it to be irreducible. Others have followed Locke in proposing an extrinsic ground:

> For when White, Red, and Yellow, are all comprehended under the Genus or name Colour, it signifies no more, but such Ideas as are produced in the Mind only by the Sight, and have entrance only through the eyes. (Locke *Essay*, Bk. III, Ch. iv, sec. 16)

Locke's solution is manifestly an offspring of desperation. It seems more plausible and fruitful to propose that a commonality of neural coding is behind the the phenomenally irreducible and undeniable fact that the colors form a family. And we should want to make similar proposals about the auditory, tactile, and gustatory families, and about the analogies between sensory families.

The last point deserves some amplification. Subjects can readily and reliably match ratio changes in one mode with those in another: loudness with brightness with electric-shock intensity (Marks 1978, 53-75). In fact, the connection is so apparent that it is often seen as unproblematic: *of course* a louder sound is more like a brighter light than a dimmer one, *of course* a brighter light is more like a stronger shock than a weaker one. That such relationships seem immediately evident is doubtless because there is, in a wide range of cases, a rather direct relationship between stimulus intensity and sensory intensity, so we take ourselves to be directly reading off intensities in the physical world. In fact, things are seldom so simple in the realm of the senses, and sensory intensity is a function of stimulus size and duration as well as stimulus intensity. Furthermore, we can compare the brightness of two afterimages or the loudness of two "spurious" tones of internal origin. So what is it we are latching onto when we apprehend the similarity of the two ratios? Or, rather, what makes it possible that both can be expressed as ratios that covary so simply? The obvious supposition is that what covaries are the firing rates of populations of neurons (or, in some cases, the number of neurons that fire) and that our ability to make the comparison is just our ability to "read" these rates.

This may seem a rather minor point. Intensity is so ubiquitous that it tends to be put in a separate category: it pertains to sensory quantity but not to quality. Such a view is not without legitimacy, but it is difficult to sustain as a principled distinction. How far, for example, can the intensity of tickling be increased without an alteration in its quality? And at the inflection point, can we clearly distinguish qualitative from quantitative change and the quality of the tickling from its intensity?

If qualitative similarities and differences among sensory states amount, in the final analysis, to similarities and differences in sensory coding, we might expect not only that there be similarities across sensory modalities because of general similarities of neural processing, but that modalities whose physical substrates are more similar would show greater phenomenal similarities than those whose substrates are less similar. There is some indication that this is the case. Evolutionarily and embryologically, hearing and touch are much closer to each other than are hearing and sight. The most powerful hearing-sight analogical property is "brightness," which in sound is best represented as the product of pitch and loudness (Marks 1978, 53-75). The correlation between pitch and hue is much weaker, and not in the direction that stimulus dimensions, particularly wavelength, would have suggested. Furthermore, no one (not even synesthetes) would confuse a sight with a sound. With touch and hearing, the situation is quite different. The vibrational sensitivity of the skin is sufficiently analogous to the vibrational sensitivity of the ear for the related sensation to be referred to as vibratory "pitch." Perceived size and spatial location properties are closely similar. At very low frequencies, tactual feeling and hearing become so similar that in the 20 Hz region one is readily confused with the other. And when small puffs of air on the forehead are used to facilitate the subjective location of clicks that are fed to a subject through earphones, the puff is sometimes taken to be the click itself.[15]

These pieces of evidence suggest not only that a materialism is capable of dealing with the qualitative character of sensory experience, but that a materialist stance may lead us to a much deeper understanding of the resemblances and differences of phenomenal qualities than we would otherwise have. However, we should be under no illusion that these considerations in any way suffice to establish the correctness of a materialist perspective. For once materialists abandon attempts to dodge the qualia problem and face it squarely, the demands that must be placed on their position are severe. Sensory phenomenology must be taken very seriously, and the materialist, if he is to vindicate his ontological claim, must, in the last analysis, be able to account for the entire range of subjective sensory phenomena. Thus understood, reductive materialism is at once a research program and a risky hypothesis, albeit of a very general character.

OTHER MINDS

Spectral inversions and asymmetries

Despite the necessary character of the identity between heat and molecular motion, that identity is assertible on empirical grounds. But could one ever have comparable grounds for supposing that sensations of, say, red and green are identical to or reducible to brain processes? It has been often held that the issue could be settled by a thought experiment. Says Leibniz,

> It must be confessed, moreover, that *perception* and that which depends on it *are inexplicable by mechanical causes*, that is, by figures and motions. And, supposing that there were a machine so constructed as to think, feel and have perception, we could conceive of it as enlarged and yet preserving the same proportions, so that we might enter it as into a mill. And this granted, we should only find on visiting it, pieces which push one against another, but never anything by which to explain a perception. (*Monadology*, section 17)

What is this famous example supposed to show? We might gloss it this way: If the mill's perceiving were identical to some concatenation of its mechanical operations, reasonable knowledge of those operations should enable one at least to see that the mill is a thing fit for perceiving, and ideal knowledge of both mechanics and the psychology of perceiving would lead us to see it as inevitable that the mill should perceive. But, in fact, we need only visualize what it would be like to encounter an assemblage of levers and gears to realize that, no matter how complicated it is and no matter how mechanically clever we might be, nothing in its operations could ever lead us to guess that it is a perceiving thing. That it perceives must therefore be an *extrinsic* and thus *contingent* fact about the mill.

There is more than an echo of the mill argument in Joseph Levine's recent statement of the case against sensation/brain-process identity:

> Let's call the physical story for seeing red 'R' and the physical story for seeing green 'G'. . . . When we consider the qualitative character of our visual experiences when looking at ripe McIntosh apples, as opposed to looking at ripe cucumbers, the difference is not explained by appeal to **G** and **R**. For **R** doesn't really explain why I have the one kind of qualitative experience—the kind I have when looking at McIntosh apples—and not the other. As evidence for this, note that it seems just as easy to imagine **G** as to imagine **R** underlying the qualitative experience that is in fact associated with **R**. The reverse, of course, also seems quite imaginable. (Levine 1983, 357–358)

There is a striking feature which the arguments of Leibniz and Levine share with many others. It is the absence of detail. Leibniz did not think it important to tell us more about the construction of the mill, and Levine asks us to decide whether one could be in physical state **R** and yet have an experience of green, without letting us know anything about the particulars of **R**. At least one assumption that seems to underlie this casual confidence in the power of merely schematic imagination to decide such a difficult issue is that color experiences are fully open to view and structurally simple, so that no compounding of structural detail on the physical end will be of any avail.

We have by now sufficient reason to doubt that this is true. Just as thermodynamics provided a macrostructural map which could be both modeled and explained by the microstructure that statistical mechanics posited, so the psychophysically established map of color phenomena is both modeled and explained by a set of opponent neural processes. And, just as the theoretical entities postulated by statistical mechanics were confirmed by independent procedures in physics and chemistry, so direct cellular recordings established the basic opponent-process mechanisms.

In order to see how the neglect of detail may have compromised Levine's argument, let us look at an altered version of that argument. Take 'O' to denote the physical story for orange and 'R' the physical story for red. Is it just as easy to imagine **R** as to imagine **O** underlying the qualitative experience that is in fact associated with **O**? Rather than answer straightaway, let us reflect first on what we know about phenomenal orange and red and then see what the opponent theory would say about **O** and **R**.

All instances of perceived orange will contain red and yellow as phenomenal constituents. By comparison, a unique red will be neither yellowish nor bluish; it will have no phenomenal hue constituents beside red itself. The opponent theory tells us that there is an r-g channel and a y-b channel. The **O** story is that the r-g channel codes for r, while the y-b channel codes for y. The **R** story is that the r-g channel codes for r, whereas the y-b channel fires at its base rate, which is an achromatic coding. If we account for the experience of orange by appealing to the **O** story, we can explain the phenomenally binary character of the hue. No such explanation may be found in the **R** story. There is thus a reason for preferring the **O** story to the **R** story as an account of phenomenal orange; a human being of whose nervous system the **O** story may be told is a more fitting orange perceiver than one of whom the **R** story is true. It is, of course, in some fashion imaginable that the **R**-story person should nevertheless see orange, but it is likewise in some fashion imaginable that the heat of a gas should not be constituted by motion of its molecules. One should also notice, however, that it is far more difficult for the contemporary intellectually conscientious person to imagine the falsity of the kinetic-molecular theory of heat than it would have been for his early nineteenth-century counterpart; the alternative imagined account must be ever so much more complicated if it is not to be downright magical. The theory's *appearance of contingency* has been diminished by several orders of magnitude.

What we have done of course is to call into question not Levine's argument, but an altered version of that argument. The reason for altering the argument is to suggest, through its analysis, a line of attack on the argument in its original form. But make no mistake about it, what we have said about red and orange cannot give us a direct reason for preferring to ground experiences of green in the **G** story and experiences of red in the **R** story rather than the other way around. This is because green, unlike orange, is not a binary hue, and so the structural difference between the **O** and **R** stories will not appear in the **R** and **G** stories. If we are to employ a comparable tactic, we must find **R** and **G** stories that differ structurally from each other in some sense that is relevant to the experienced difference between red and green. Since our purpose is to show that there *could* be good reasons in the form of a preferred phenomenal-neural mapping for identifying color perceptions with a biological substrate, we require of a pair of candidate stories only that they be plausible.

Such a pair of stories is already available to us in our conjectural account of the basis for the distinction between "warm" and "cool" colors. Since green is cool and red warm, green is conformable to the "cool" account and red to the "warm" one. Our theory sketch went as follows: When their owner views ripe lemons or McIntosh apples, the chromatic cell assembly in the visual cortex increases its average level of activity, but decreases it when ripe cucumbers or clear daylight are seen. The central processing unit contains polarity-sensitive comparator cells which receive input from both the visual and the somatosensory systems, and so the chromatic experience comes labeled as "plus" or "minus."

In order to see whether this gives us the sort of distinction we want, we shall try it out on a hypothetical case of hue exchange between Dick and Jane. We suppose Jane to be wired according to the specifications of our sketch. She sees ripe McIntosh apples as red and ripe cucumbers as green. By virtue of the operation of her comparator, she sees red as positive and green as negative. Her beliefs about the qualities of the colors she is seeing are brought about by her color experiences, and her color behavior reflects her beliefs. We can account for Jane's color behavior by appealing either to her wiring or to her color perception, depending upon the particular demands of the explanatory context.

Dick's hues are inverted with respect to Jane's; so whenever Jane sees a particular hue, Dick sees its complement. Dick sees ripe McIntosh apples as green (though he describes them as "red") and sees ripe cucumbers as red (though he describes them as "green"). We don't know how Dick is wired up. Since Dick's yellow-red pair will correspond to Jane's blue-green pair, paradigmatic objects that look similar to Dick will also look similar to Jane, and vice versa. Can we spin a coherent yarn in which Dick's hue exchange vis-à-vis Jane is undetectable?

Well, suppose that Jane describes the hue of ripe McIntosh apples as "warm" and "positive." What will Dick say?

Case 1. Dick says that the apple hue is "cool" and "negative." He says this in consequence of his wiring. We may conclude (in the absence of contravening information) that Dick is hooked up differently from Jane.

Case 2A. Dick's wiring is the same as Jane's; so in consequence of his wiring he says, as Jane does, that the apple is "red" and "warm" and "positive." But normal causality has failed in this portion of

Dick's innards; the physiological processes that cause experiences of redness and warmth and positiveness in Jane inexplicably cause experiences of greenness and coolness and negativeness in Dick. Dick's hue sensations are epiphenomenal prisoners of his nervous system, having nothing to do with his actions. But either he has beliefs about the colors he sees which he can neither express nor even attempt to express (because his beliefs are epiphenomenal and hooked to his perceptions but not to his actions), or else his beliefs can issue in behavior but are causally detached from his perceptions, so he believes that the phenomenal green he is now experiencing is positive and warm even though he doesn't experience it as positive and warm.

Case 2B. Normal causality prevails, but Dick's wiring differs from Jane's. The apple that rouses experiences of redness in Jane evokes experiences of greenness in Dick. But Dick's comparator is wired in reverse; so Dick sees greens and blues as positive and warm, and reds and yellows as negative and cool. So his behavior, and in particular his linguistic behavior, will accord with Jane's; but his experiences will be very different. Can we coherently represent to ourselves just what those experiences will be? Dick will, we say, see green as positive and warm. But exactly how could phenomenal green be experienced as positive and warm and yet be green? If there is a "residue" of green which is separable from its polarity, that residue would seem to correspond to nothing in experience or imagination, yet it is only the ostensible imaginability of the hue inversion which makes its possibility intuitively plausible.[16]

Our theory sketch thus enables us, in a standard example of spectral inversion, either to decide, as in case 1, that Dick's wiring is inverted with respect to Jane's—a respectable empirical conclusion—or to see, as in cases 2A and B, that the supposition that there could be an undetectable spectral inversion has absurd consequences. Although case 2B is perilously close to conceptual incoherence, 2A seems merely outlandish. One interesting result of all of this is that dualism, rather than reductive materialism, comes to seem counterintuitive; for, if our story of chromatic mechanisms is correct, a dualism that permits the possibility of the spectral inversion we have envisaged does not comfortably satisfy the intuitive demand that perceptual experience be the chief determinant of perceptual belief and that perceptual belief find expression in behavior.

Of course, it is true that cases 2A and B may in some sense be possible; there may be a case 2 Dick around. If so, the identity claim is simply false. But likewise, as far as we know, some gases may behave as they do because of thin shells of caloric around their submicroscopic parts, and our confidence in the explanatory efficacy of the kinetic theory is misplaced. There is an inevitable explanatory gap between theories and their data, but it is the gap of underdetermination, that bane of epistemic realism, rather than some separate explanatory gap peculiar to the mind-body problem. Though sensory experience/brain process identity, if it holds, must hold necessarily, our grounds for asserting it or any comparable reductive claim will, in the last analysis, be empirical, and the principles that guide such claims should be quite similar to those which guided the analogous claims in the kinetic-molecular theory of heat.

The argument we have just given does not constitute a systematic refutation of the possibility of a hue inversion of some sort. There are several reasons for this. First of all, one can just live with some of the anomalies, such as those which follow in the train of epiphenomenalism. Why one should be willing to do this is another question. Second, the physiological story we have given is only a story. Our insistence throughout has been that the issue is empirical, and such questions are not settled by thought experiments, the only purposes of which are heuristic and rhetorical. Third, we have not canvassed all the possibilities. Let us dwell on this point for a while.

Think of the hues as arrayed in the H-S space of figure III-1. Every possible hue inversion can be represented as a rotation around the achromatic point or as a reflection around an axis passing through a pair of opponent hues. The requirement that any rotation or reflection carry unique hues into unique hues or binary hues into binary hues is a very powerful constraint, since it rules out all but a very few possibilities. The restriction is a consequence of the demand that hue shifts be undetectable by noninvasive means. The unique hues provide benchmarks for the coordination of physical samples with phenomenal color experiences, and in practice they are used as a measure of the variation among normal observers; recall our discussion of interobserver variations in the spectral locus of unique green. Up to this point, the possibilities have been constrained by straightforward phenomenal features intrinsic to the hues themselves: that hue which is unique red could not have been binary, nor could any hue that is in fact orange have been unique. The further restriction that "warm" hues be mapped into "warm" hues and "cool" hues into "cool" ones rests on rather more subtle phenomenal features, but features that reflection makes persuasive, especially once one abstracts from the nuances of 'warm' and 'cool' to the underlying polarities. It is hard to see how unique blue could have been "warm." What we also did was to see how these phenomenal saliences might be appropriately modeled in the domain of neural processes, with the suggestion that this could give us good grounds for taking the color experiences to be constituted by those processes.

But a problem arises when we consider the following mapping: let red go into yellow, and yellow into red; let green go into blue and blue into green. This satisfies all the preceding constraints. Psychophysiologically, it has the y-b channel evoking the phenomenal red-green responses, and the r-g channel evoking the yellow-blue responses. Now such an exchange will not amount to a swap of the *elementary color* yellow for the *elementary color* red (to use the NCS concepts); for elementary red has a much greater absolute chromatic content than elementary yellow. To put this in H-B-S terms, spectral yellow has a far lower saturation than spectral red, and an exchange of one for the other would be easily detectable, for it would entail a substantial and easily measurable shift in achromatic sensitivity. What must be involved, rather, is a replacement of one *hue* by the other, with the result that viewing a moderate-level spectrum at the normal locus for unique yellow, the hue-shifted person would see a very desaturated red, while at the longwave end she would see a dark, rich supersaturated yellow. The former could readily be imagined, indeed duplicated by us, but the latter could be imagined only by an *extrapolation* of a process involving a series of yellows of increasing saturation. (This can be contrasted with Hume's missing shade of blue, which involves a far easier *interpolation* of the desired color between two given colors.) One can have an experience of a phenomenal yellow more saturated than a spectral yellow by first fixating on a spectral blue and then looking quickly at the spectral yellow. The afterimage color adds to that resulting from direct stimulation without any additional achromatic excitation. However, the result will fall well short of the required supersaturation.

One can multiply examples of phenomenal asymmetries that will not map well into the proposed hue exchange. The most striking of these results from the fact we have just discussed, that elementary yellow *color* has high lightness and low chromatic content. Those surface colors which are of yellow *hue* but of substantially lower lightness will take on a characteristic appearance of their own. If the yellow tends toward red, i.e., if it is orangeish, it looks *brown*, and if it has a greenish cast it looks *olive*. Brown corresponds to one of eleven basic color categories in the comparative linguistic investigations of Berlin and Kay (Berlin and Kay 1969). Olive does not correspond to a basic category in the Berlin-Kay scheme, but 'olive' does appear as one of thirteen basic color names in the Inter-Society Color Council—National Bureau of Standards scheme (Kelly and Judd 1976). We shall examine both classifications when we later turn our attention to color language. The perceptual difference between "standard" yellow or orange and their blackened counterparts is striking. For example, surround a spot of light that matches an orange (the fruit) in color by an annulus of white light that comes from a source of adjustable brightness. Keeping the orange spot constant in intensity, increase the intensity of the white spot. Simultaneous contrast mechanisms will blacken the orange, and, with a sufficiently bright surround, the orange spot will now match a chocolate bar. This suggests that we might simply take brown to *be* a blackened orange and take olive to *be* a blackened greenish yellow. If this were so, we should expect that subjects in color-naming experiments would be able to estimate percentage components of red, yellow, green, and black in browns and olives so that the total would add up to 100 per cent. Similar experiments have shown that orange and purple and pink could be completely described using the names for the four unique hues along with black and white, and there was no difficulty in doing the same thing for blackened reds, greens, and blues under the same conditions in which brown was produced. But some experimental work suggests that, although browns can be generated by achromatic contrast with yellows and reddish yellows, they cannot be fully described with the restricted set of color names.[17] The experiments were not conducted for olive as well, though one might expect similar results. The physiological basis for this special phenomenal character of browns is simply not understood.

For a somewhat more subtle instance of asymmetry, consider purple, a binary which, like orange, has a very salient character. It is, along with the unique hues, one of the five basic hue categories in the Munsell system of color appearance, and it shows up frequently as a basic color category in many languages. By contrast, yellow-green, the hue-shift counterpart of purple, does not appear as basic in the color vocabulary of any known language. One tends to see yellow-greens either as modified yellows or as modified greens rather than as having a pronounced quality of their own. A similar remark might be made about pinks, a perceptually salient family of colors, and their hue-shift counterparts, the array of light, desaturated greenish yellows, which have no such distinctive quality.

One is not inclined to put too much weight on these and other caveats, such as the substantially different number of perceptually equal hue steps in the interval between yellow and green (18) as compared with the hue-shift counterpart interval, red to blue (31) (Kuehni 1983, 60). The reason is that they do not seem, in a convincing way, to capture differences between *intrinsic* features of the respective hues, and this is what we were after. The other problem, given our present objectives, is that there seem to be no readily available neural mechanisms, either actual or hypothetical, that can account for these phenomenal asymmetries in even simple causal terms, let alone mechanisms with the nice isomorphisms required by our strong identity conditions. There are, for instance, many known psychophysical differences between the r-g and y-b channels, and they exhibit themselves in many ways, such as in the Bezold—Brücke effect, but there is no obvious way of connecting them or their physiological underpinnings sufficiently tightly to the differences in hue quality which we have here been concerned to capture. Until visual scientists know much more about central chromatic processes, this deficiency is not likely to be made up. All of this only shows that the stronger program—establishing the truth of a reductive materialism for color experience—remains, and probably will for some time remain, a program. On the other hand, our business here has been to pursue a weaker program, to show both that such a materialism is possible and that it has significant advantages over its metaphysical rivals.

Internalism and externalism

The first philosopher to attack the possibility of an inverted spectrum on the empirical ground that no inversion could be both undetectable and preserve the asymmetries of phenomenal color space was Bernard Harrison (Harrison 1973). Harrison's approach was simply to point out the heterogeneous manner in which the basic color categories in a variety of languages divide up phenomenal color space as specified by the Munsell system. If Harrison had proceeded to connect this division of color space with the underlying mechanisms that account for it and had shown how these mechanisms capture at least some of the essential qualities of phenomenal color, his way of attacking the problem would not have invited the charge that he was simply trading on some accidental features of human color perception. As it is, Sydney Shoemaker's reaction to Harrison's attempt to rule out the possibility of spectral inversion seems justified:

> The question of whether our color experience does have a structure that allows for such a mapping—whether it is "invertible"—is an empirical question about our psychological makeup. And it is one I intend to by-

pass. Even if our color experience is not invertible, it seems obviously possible that there should be creatures, otherwise very much like ourselves, whose color experience does have a structure that allows for such a mapping—creatures whose color experience *is* invertible. And the mere possibility of such creatures is sufficient to raise the philosophical problems the possibility of spectrum inversion has been seen as posing. (Shoemaker 1984, 336)

Shoemaker goes on to say that even if, as a matter of fact, human spectral inversion were impossible, the possibility of spectral inversion for some creatures poses a problem for the adequacy of functionalist analyses of qualitative experience. Furthermore, says Shoemaker, the impossibility of spectral inversion for human beings does not rule out the possibility that some people might have systems of color qualia whose elements are radically different from any of those of other people, even though the relations that each person's qualia bear to one another might be closely similar—even isomorphic—to the relations that any other person's qualia bear to one another. Let us now discuss these two issues, not only for their intrinsic importance, but to see whether our approach has anything to contribute to them.

Although Shoemaker does not mention it, Harrison does raise the question of whether two people could have radically different color qualia even though their color spaces are closely similar:

Why should not Jones, instead of seeing exactly those colours which Dick sees, only transposed in some way, see a range of qualities quite different from any perceived by Dick, but related amongst themselves in exactly the ways in which the qualities which Dick calls 'colours' are related? (Harrison 1973, 119-120)

He then argues that this is conceptually impossible:

First, what can be meant by 'quite different'? It can only mean, I think, that the qualities in question would not be given, by Dick, any place in the colour array as he sees it, for any qualities given a place in that array would be, by that very fact, numbered among the colour presentations capable in principle of being seen by Dick. It follows that we cannot have intermediate sceptical hypotheses, in which Jones sees some of the colours seen by Dick, but with others of Dick's colours replaced by radically different qualities having the same relationship to Jones' residual Dick colours as the Dick-colours which Jones has lost; the reason being that such hypotheses are incoherent. For a presentation to be placed next to a given shade of light blue in the colour array is just for it to *be* the next adjacent shade of light blue: for that is all that 'having the same relationship' to the first shade can consist in. What Jones calls 'colours' then, are presentations which Dick would not call 'colours' at all, and neither perceives anything which the other calls a colour, but because the presentations which each calls 'colours' are related amongst themselves in exactly the same way as those which the other calls colours, discourse neutrality is preserved. (*ibid.*)

What, asks Harrison, could this relational way be? It is not sufficient that Jones's "color" space be isomorphic in a purely formal sense to Dick's color space. Rather, the relations among the Jones elements must be *color* similarities and differences. But then how are we to understand 'color', except by reference to red and green and white and such? There is no more general sortal in terms of which color can be understood. If there are to be qualities different from these, qualities that could count as colors, they must *resemble* red, etc.—the "standard" colors. And if they were to resemble the standard colors, it could only be with respect to hue, brightness (or lightness), and saturation. But color space is closed under these relations; if there were, for example, a novel hue, it would have to fit on the hue loop, and it could not do so without introducing a discontinuity on that loop. There can therefore be no novel hue, and, without a novel hue, there can be no novel colors. (A hueless color is achromatic, and the existence of black, white, and gray is presumably not at issue.) The skeptic "is claiming both that his array is qualitatively radically disparate from the colour array, and that it is at the same time qualitatively continuous with it" (*ibid.*, 127).

Let us contrast this "internalist" position of Harrison's with the more widely held "externalist" position exemplified by what Paul Churchland says about the type-identity conditions for sensations of red:

. . . the qualitative character of your sensation-of-red might be different from the qualitative character of my sensation-of-red, slightly ·or substantially, and a third person's sensation-of-red might be different again. But so long as all three states are standardly caused by red objects and standardly cause all three of us to believe that something is red, then all three states are sensations-of-red, whatever their intrinsic qualitative character. (Churchland 1984, 39–40)

It is not difficult for us, at this point, to see the problems with Churchland's defense of this functionalist position. For such functionalists, mental states are characterized by sensory inputs, behavioral outputs, and their relations to other mental states. Here, the behavioral outputs are presumably various bits of discriminating behavior. The inputs are stimulations of the visual receptors "standardly caused by red things." As we know, what is to be accounted a "red thing" must depend upon our sensations-of-red. As for other mental states, the most relevant are various beliefs "that something is red." Such beliefs are presumably to be individuated in part by reference to their content. But how is their content to be specified unless it be in terms of sensations-of-red? (And couldn't one sensation-of-red be of the same type as another even though either or both of them produced no beliefs at all?) Identifying sensations-of-red thus depends upon identifying red things and beliefs about red things, but both of these must in turn be identified by appeal to sensations-of-red.

Other colors, other minds

It very much looks as though we must answer Harrison's argument if we are to be able to speak meaningfully of alien colors, that is, sensory qualities that may be said to have a hue, but a hue that is not identical with red, yellow, blue, green, or any of their binaries. Our problem is to ensure that the alien hue, H, has the appropriate resemblance relation with the standard hues. That in turn would seem to require that both H and at least one of the standard hues occur within the consciousness of a single individual, and thus that Harrison's "intermediate skeptical hypothesis" be possible. But where would H fit, as it must, into the hue array? We recall Harrison's assertion: "For a presentation to be placed next to a given shade of light blue in the colour array is just for it to *be* the next adjacent shade of light blue: for that is all that 'having the same relationship' can consist in."

Consider a true red-green dichromat, who has only blue, yellow, and the achromatic colors available to him. His world is one whose colors consist of two unique hues variously desaturated, and his hue space is a line. Such a dichromat's r-g system is inoperative. Relative to his experience, red and green are alien hues. He can form no notion of them beyond an appreciation of their functional role in the lives of others, although he is likely to suppose that when other people speak of green, they refer to that point on the spectrum which is flanked by a barely discernible tint of blue and an equally washed-out bit of yellow, and looks very like red, which is situated out there where yellow tails off and the darkness begins. The contrast between red and green that most people claim to find so striking puzzles him. A flatlander, he wonders what the talk of a color sphere[18] is all about.

But perhaps the dichromat's hue experience is only formally similar to ours; perhaps what he sees is incommensurable with what we see. How could we know? We *do* know, and in two ways. First, people do sometimes acquire dichromacy through accident or disease after they have learned the use of color language. Second, there are a few people who are dichromatic in one eye and almost color normal in the other. They compare what they see through each eye, and their descriptions of what dichromats see tally fairly well with what scientists had come to expect (Boynton 1979, 380–382). No doubt about it, dichromatic vision is a degenerate case of normal color vision.

Here is a hypothetical case. A person has a mutation that causes her cones to cross-connect in such a way as to give her a normal r-g channel, no y-b channel at all, and a new chromatic channel, the w-z channel. The opponent-response w-z curves are distinctly different in shape and crossing points from those of a y-b channel, but she has a normal-looking set of r-g curves. Her wavelength discriminations and hue categorizations differ markedly from ours, but we can map her color responses on an H'-B-S space with a w-z axis drawn perpendicular to an r-g axis. Would it not be reasonable to say that she has two unique hues like ours, and two unique hues unlike ours? Notice that all her binary hues would then be at least somewhat different from ours; she could not have our binaries *and* fit two new unique hues into a three-dimensional color space. It is this latter sort of situation that Harrison seems to have thought to be necessary to the "intermediate skeptical hypothesis."

Perhaps, though, one could claim that we need not suppose the last example in order to show the possibility of novel hues, but would need only a distortion of our usual hue structure, achieved by deviant means in the early stages of visual processing. Very well then, consider a hypothetical visual superwoman with an extra cone type and *three* chromatic opponent systems, two just like ours and a third, call it the "c-d" opponent system, involving cross-connections between the regular three cone types and the new cone type. She understands our color vocabulary very readily and can use it as well as we, but she pities our visual degeneracy, for she is a *tetrachromat*. Her visual hyperspace requires four dimensions for its adequate depiction, with her c-d opponent axis and her achromatic, r-g and y-b opponent axes all mutually perpendicular. She claims to see not only the binary hues that we see, but ternary ones as well. Here, it becomes downright unreasonable to deny that hers is a color space, unless we would be prepared to go along meekly when, some time in the future, dichromats come to be the majority and rule that trichromatic color space is only "color" space, but not really *color* space.

By appealing to the biological substrate of color vision, we can begin with the human case, in which we know there to be genuine color perception, and extend the concept of a color perceiver outward to other species. We can also appeal to behavior wherever we can reasonably suppose that similar behavior is linked to similar biological mechanisms. Now this last remark is apt to sound perverse, since we commonly ascribe color vision to other animals before knowing very much at all about their underlying biology, and we are inclined to say that people knew (philosophical fun and games aside) that their fellow human beings had color experience like theirs long before they had any accurate knowledge of the mechanisms of vision. But what did they know, and when did they know it? It is a notorious fact about humankind that it readily ascribes its thoughts, feelings, and capacities to everything in sight as well as to some things invisible. Our species supplicates large rocks or the clouds or images of its own making, admires the moral virtues of animals, talks to houseplants. If foreigners do not understand our native language, whose meaning is so transparent, it must be because they are either deaf or dim. We accordingly make them understand us by speaking slowly and loudly. Even when we think ourselves sophisticated, we may be shocked to discover that our color-anomalous friends cannot make out the numerals on color-deficiency test plates, for those numerals are so plainly there, right in front of the eyes: "Perhaps," we feel inclined to say, "you weren't paying attention. If you'll just look again. . . ."

Since most people make the same color classifications as we, there may be nothing to produce cognitive dissonance with our tacit assumption that they see what we see. And when reflection on such matters begins, human similarities in behavior and outward form lead us readily to take it that human beings are all of a kind. When we come to this point in our intellectual development, we can begin to entertain questions about whether other kinds of animals see as we see, think as we think, feel as we feel. Assumptions about physical nature do in fact govern our more reflective views about what goes on in other people. Hazy though we may be about mechanisms, we make the minimal supposition that these mechanisms are of the same sort for individuals of the same kind. As far as we know, this assumption is at least roughly correct in the case of color vision. So, in this instance, people either take for granted or reflectively assume that which is in fact the case. That this constitutes *knowledge* is certainly open to question.

Once reflection on these matters begins, and a common human

nature is explicitly supposed, the question of what, if any, part of this nature is shared by other things becomes a live issue. The answers proffered to this question can both guide and be guided by specific empirical investigations.

At our present state of knowledge, we see that three broad types of considerations are relevant to inferences about the color vision of other species: (1) wavelength-dependent discrimination and classification behavior; (2) similarity of physiological systems and their functional arrangements; (3) evolutionary closeness. In empirical studies of these matters, scientists usually take (1) to be decisive for determining whether or not a species has "color vision"; the issue of whether other animals have hue or huelike *experiences* at all is generally avoided; it is sufficient that their behavior should group visual stimuli in an appropriately huelike classification, or even have similar detection and discrimination behavior. It is interesting to see how often some scientists will talk uncritically about a particular animal's ability to see red or blue and how other scientists will occasionally issue warnings about the confusions engendered by applying human hue labels to the wavelength-dependent perceptual groupings of other animals.

As one might expect, even those visual scientists who rely almost exclusively on behavioral criteria for color vision become uneasy in speaking about the color vision of animals as the evolutionary distance between those animals and ourselves increases. Very primitive animals such as the single-celled Euglena show differential responses to light of long and short wavelengths, but nobody is prepared to speak seriously about the animal's color vision, even though its behavior is discussed in systematic surveys of invertebrate color vision (eg., Menzel 1979). Perhaps this is because we can see in such organisms the precursors of color vision and because we do not know how to make a principled division between color seers and mere wavelength responders.

If Euglena is at one end of this continuum, human beings, apes, and old-world monkeys are at the other. The details of wavelength discriminations and metameric matching by macaque are so closely similar to ours, and they share so much of our evolutionary history and general physiology, that scientists feel relatively comfortable in drawing extensive inferences from the physiological mechanisms of macaque color vision to those of homo sapiens. And rhesus monkeys, also extensively used in color-vision studies, prove to have strong, consistent color preferences. It is very difficult indeed for an unbiased observer to avoid the conclusion that these animals have color experi-

OTHER COLORS, OTHER MINDS

ences very much like ours. How much like ours? One expects that, as we get clearer about the ties between our phenomenology and neurophysiology, the use of imaginative analogy, carefully controlled by behavioral and physiological studies of the other animals, is capable of yielding an intuitive understanding of a quality not much inferior to the intuitive understanding that men and women have for the inner lives of one another. (This may not strike some of the more cynical readers as being much of an achievement.)

One must, however, draw conclusions with due caution. In one experiment, Gregory Keating tested five rhesus monkeys on a variety of visual tasks involving shape and velocity discrimination as well as a two-choice wavelength discrimination.

> At the start of a trial a door in front of the monkey was raised and the animal faced a plexiglas projection screen. The screen stood at arm's length from the monkey and had two foodwells cut out of it, each covered by a door. A blue field appeared on the screen over one of the foodwells, a yellow field over the other. The monkey reached through the door under the blue stimulus for a food reward. (Keating 1979, 379)

After discussing the precautions he took to ensure that the monkeys were not responding to brightness rather than wavelength cues (an essential but not always properly carried out part of color-vision experiments), Keating describes the rest of the protocol:

> The monkeys received 50 trials a day selected from the 20 blue/yellow slides. The left-right position of the blue stimulus and its relative brightness varied from trial to trial in an unpredictable manner. After a monkey reached a criterion of 45/50 correct responses in a session, it was switched to a similar set of blue/green slides. In normal animals stable performance of a wavelength discrimination will generally be indicated by good transfer to a second pair of stimuli containing a novel unrewarded hue. (*ibid.*, 380–381)

After many training trials the animals reached the criterion performance level of 90 per cent correct, and after certain further perturbations, three of the five relearned the task at or near the criterion level. These three "were switched to a blue/green discrimination and showed fairly good transfer to this novel pair of stimuli" (*ibid.*, 381).

There seems nothing at all extraordinary about this experiment unless one knows that the animals were performing the first task after having their primary visual (striate) cortexes surgically removed. The three who successfully performed the relearning of the task did so following the removal of their preoccipital cortexes as well. The postoperative relearning was, as one might have expected, much slower than the preoperative learning—300 preoperative versus 1500 postoperative trials, in the median case—and the quality of the discriminations was considerably poorer. Normal rhesus monkeys are trichromatic, whereas the postoperative monkeys were rather poor dichromats.

When human beings are deprived of the corresponding parts of their visual cortexes, they have, without exception, no visual experiences whatever. They are *cortically blind*. However, in cases in which human patients have lost the visual cortex on one side of their brains and hence suffer blindness in one half of their visual fields (hemianopia), it sometimes happens that there is a form of "seeing" in the blind visual field. One patient of Weiskrantz,

> having lost his right visual cortex, had a normal hemifield on the right and was blind in the left hemifield. Into this blind region Weiskrantz projected light in patterns of X's and O's in random order. As expected, the subject, when asked, stated that he saw nothing. When urged to make a choice, however, he guessed correctly in twenty-seven out of thirty trials. In another run the choice was between horizontal and vertical stripes. This time he was correct thirty times in thirty trials. The patient continued to maintain that he was unaware of seeing *anything* and showed surprise when informed of his success rate. (Harth 1982, 128)

The supposition is that, in both the human and rhesus-monkey cases, visual information is reaching the brain through pathways in the thalamus whose principal function seems to be to regulate eye movement. But visual information is not visual experience, and there is a very fundamental sense in which neither Weiskrantz' patient nor (one supposes) Keating's rhesus monkeys could be said to be able to see. There are, so far, no good published experiments in which human hemianopic patients were systematically tested for "blind sight" color vision. However, the monkey experiments would lead us to think that there is a good chance that some might be found. It is in any case clear that until we gain a much better understanding of matters such as the essential difference between how the brain handles visual information that comes to it from the visual cortex and how it handles information that arrives by way of the thalamus, we shall not be able to determine what the physiological difference between color vision—phenomenal awareness—and "color vision"—as specified by behavioral criteria—really comes to. In the balance of our discussion of other animals, we shall sometimes omit the double quotes and simply say 'color vision'. But the difference between the two should always be kept in mind.

Well-developed "color vision" is widespread in the animal world. It is interesting to notice that there are many species of mammals which, although relatively close to human beings, seem to be dichromatic, whereas the evolutionarily more distant insects often have excellent trichromatic vision. Honey bees are a well-known case. They have three receptor types, with higher-order neurons which display spectral opponency. They are sensitive to simultaneous contrast effects. Their color mixing obeys Grassman's laws pretty nearly, and their spectral hue circle, like ours, is closed by an extraspectral hue analogous to our purple and thus dubbed "bee purple" (Menzel 1979, 560–565).

Yet, for all of these similarities to our own case, there is very much about bees that makes one tempted to put those double quotes back around words like 'hue', 'color', and perhaps 'vision'. For if consciousness is evolutionarily valuable for us, enabling us to perform complex higher-order tasks involving a great deal of behavioral plasticity, it looks very much as if insects can do very well with a highly modular nervous system, devoted to carrying out a limited number of behavioral routines in a less flexible but highly reliable manner. What one finds in the visual systems of many infra-ape species is that specialized neurons of a sort to be found in the cortexes of human beings and monkeys, occur in the retinas of these other species, and thus at a much earlier stage of neural processing. These other animals have fewer and simpler analyzers with fewer connections to other specialist cells and, indeed, several orders of magnitude fewer total numbers of neurons and neural connections. If one were able to account for the entire behavioral repertoire of, say, a fly, by appealing entirely to a relatively small set of interconnected modules, one would have little reason for supposing the animal to have anything remotely like experience. Here is a comment about the modularity of fly color behavior. Whether or not the fly acts as if it "sees color" seems to depend on what sort of thing it is doing:

> Only recently were flies successfully trained to react to spectral lights and were found able to discriminate between blue and yellow. Since color discrimination is not present in all aspects of visual orientation, the failure or success of demonstrating optomotor responses to wavelength contrast, or selective color mixture effects in phototaxis, does not simultaneously exclude or prove wavelength discrimination in goal-oriented behavior such as prey catching, food collection, courtship behavior, and host selection. (*ibid.*, 560)

For its part, "The bee discriminates colors in the behavioral context of collecting nectar and pollen from flowers and during orientation at the hive entrance, but is color-blind during other behaviors" (ibid., 565). While engaging in those "other behaviors", does the bee see colors but ignore them? Or does it see them in some contexts and fail to see them in others? Or should we eschew 'seeing' and 'colors' in such contexts?

If bees do see colors, what do they see? The use of the names of human hues is rampant in the literature. Thus:

> . . . for these insects the color complementary to yellow is not blue, but a mixture of violet and ultraviolet. . . . Daumer also found that bees can distinguish very different spectral radiations as well as very similar ones, like shades of blue, green and other colors. Mazokhin-Porshnyakov, using better methods of training bees to distinguish colors than Daumer did, also ascertained that bees can recognize green, yellow, and orange from one another, which had been denied by other investigators. (Mazokhin-Porshnyakov 1969, 184)

We should regard such talk as a convenient façcon de parler for the more accurate but cumbersome specification of the stimulus in nanometers. But it may lead the unwary to suppose that at the wavelength where the bee's sensitivity overlaps ours, what the bee sees (if it can be regarded as having visual sensations) is similar to what we see. And if we do not suppose that, we might be tempted to think that human hue classifications are at least useful in specifying the type-identity of color perceptions. But to think so obscures the fact that human hue categories may carve up bee color space well away from the joints. For example, for us the mixture complements of wavelengths are other wavelengths (or mixtures of wavelengths) in our visible range. But the mixture complements for bees of the wavelengths to which we are also sensitive are all in the ultraviolet. Human hues cannot, then, have the same opponents as the bee "hues" to which they are matched by these type-identity conditions.

The reverse problem may also occur. Wright and Cummings (1971) devised an interesting way of extracting information about spectral appearance in pigeons. The experiment, summarized by Jacobs, is sufficiently interesting on its own account to merit description here. It should be compared with the "color naming" experiments with both adult and infant human subjects which we have already discussed.

The paradigm employed a three-key, matching-to-sample task in which the pigeon was presented with three spectral stimuli and was trained to peck at the wavelength appearing on one of the side keys that matched the wavelength presented on the center key. For example, if a 570-nm light appeared on the center key with 510- and 570-nm lights on the two side keys, then the bird was reinforced for pecking on the side key that was illuminated with the 570-nm light. Once the birds were thoroughly trained in this task for several different wavelengths, on some trials a test (probe) stimulus appeared on the center key. Thus, if the bird had been trained with both 572- and 512-nm lights appearing on both center and side keys, on test trials the 572- and 512-nm lights were presented on side keys and a probe wavelength (say, 540 nm) was presented on the center key. The experimental question was, given the 540-nm stimulus, does the bird match it to the 572-nm or the 512-nm light? Because these wavelength differences are much greater than those required for mere discrimination, it was argued that the bird's response must be based on placing two of the stimuli in the same category. Repetition of this procedure for a large range of test wavelengths resulted in the categorization functions shown in figure III-3.

The implication of the data shown in figure III-3 is that the pigeon is able to consistently group adjacent wavelengths into categories (possibly hues). Furthermore, the transitional boundaries between these categories are clear-cut. As shown in figure III-3, Wright and Cumming replicated the basic experiment with a second set of training wavelengths. The results from these two experiments are similar enough to imply that the hue categories formed by the pigeons are not simply artifacts of the particular wavelengths used. . . . These categories are quite different from those obtained in color-naming experiments with humans. Thus, as Wright and Cumming point out, wavelengths on either side of 540-nm fall into differ-

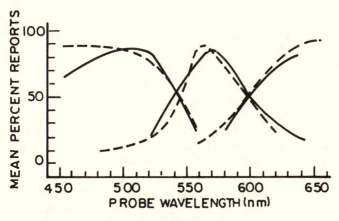

Fig. III-3. *The pigeon's categorization (into hues?) of spectral wavelengths. Dashed and solid curves show the results from two different experiments.*

ent categories for the pigeon, whereas they clearly do not for the normal human observer tested on a similar task. (Jacobs 1981, 117–118)

Normal human observers at moderate light levels see the region from 530 nm to 560 nm as consisting of yellowish greens. As Jacobs remarks, ''this result strongly emphasizes how misleading it may be to use human hue designations to describe color vision in nonhuman species'' (*ibid.*, 118). On the other hand, it might in the last analysis be *appropriate* to use human hue categories. For instance, suppose it turned out that we had good grounds for taking pigeons to be bearers of conscious sensations. Certainly even now we have much better reasons for supposing this for birds than for insects. And suppose that the post-receptoral visual stages of pigeons turned out to be like ours in the relevant respects. (Based on what is known about the comparative anatomy of the visual systems of pigeons and people, this does not seem likely.) Should we then maintain that pigeon hues are qualitatively unlike human hues because pigeon hue categories divide at different points in the spectrum? Such an inference would be hasty. The pigeon retina contains oil droplets that play an important but still badly understood role in the bird's color vision. One thing they seem to do is to shift the peak cone absorbance to a greater or lesser extent toward the longer wavelengths (*ibid.*, 109–119). The pigeon chromatic responses might, therefore, differ from that of human beings only with respect to their spectral loci but not with respect to their basic characteristics, just as some people have their unique hue loci shifted (though to a much lesser extent) with respect to those of other people. Of course if pigeon color vision differs in some major respect from ours—some researchers have suspected, for example, that pigeons are tetrachromatic—we would not be entitled to such a conclusion.

In asking whether there are color perceptions in minds other than human, we have encountered many more problems than solutions, and to many of our questions there may be no answers that are humanly obtainable. The complexities of brains may simply prove too much for us. But in taking color perceptions to be the outcome of biological processes, and by controlling our speculations by what we can find out about the biological similarities and differences between our own and other species, we may hope to advance such questions if not solve them. It may be more fun to engage in functionalist fantasies about Martians whose physiology is based on cream cheese, but there is something to be said in favor of attending to collections of humble neurons: we *know* that at least some of them *do* generate color perceptions. This should be our Archimedean fulcrum.

COLOR LANGUAGE

Foci

> I cannot learn the colour unless I can see it; but I cannot learn it without language either. I know it because I know the language. . . . I can remember the sensation I had, just as I can remember the color I saw. I feel the same sensation, and that is the same color. But identity—the sameness—comes from the language.
>
> *Rush Rhees, philosopher (1954, 81)*

> There is a continuous gradation of color from one end of the spectrum to the other. Yet an American describing it will list the hues as red, orange, yellow, green, blue, purple, or something of the kind. There is nothing inherent either in the spectrum or the human perception of it which would compel its division in this way.
>
> *H. A. Gleason, social anthropologist (1961)[19]*

So went the prevailing wisdom of the 1950s, when anthropological relativism and nonopponent color theory were in full flower.[20] No physical feature of the spectrum divides it into sections. The perceptual counterpart of this fact is that one portion of the rainbow blends continuously into the next. If color vision is founded upon the additive mixing of the outputs of the three cone types, such spectral blending is just what one should expect. So any division of the spectrum must be the product of a classification imposed on this sensory continuum from the outside. We classify with words, and words are the expression of a way of life, a culture. For its part, culture is shaped by a variety of geographical, economic, and historical accidents. As needs and circumstances vary, so do cultures, and, as cultures vary, so do linguistic practices. Empirical studies of language reveal that the color predicates of one people carve up the chromatic world in ways quite at variance with those of another people:

> The Shona speaker forms a color category from what we call *orange, red,* and *purple,* giving them all the same unpronounceable (sic) name. But he also makes a distinction within the band we term *green.* Here we have a clear case of speakers of different languages slicing up the perceptual world differently. And, of course, it is also the case that the kinds of slices one makes are related to the names for the slices available in his language. (Krauss 1968, 268–269)[21]

In 1537, there appeared a treatise, *Geometrical Gunnery,* by one Walter Ryff. The text was a pedestrian discussion of projectile motion along well-worn neo-Aristotelian lines: the cannonball's path consists of a straight portion of "forced" motion, followed by a circular part in which natural and forced motion conflict with each other. This is in turn succeeded by a vertical drop in which the ball, freed of its initial impetus, hastens toward its natural place, the earth's center. The frontispiece of *Geometrical Gunnery* shows a town under artillery fire. The artist represented the trajectories of the cannon shots: they are indistinguishable from parabolas (Dijksterhuis 1961). One may entertain a parallel fantasy about a philosophical essay on color, circa 1950. The text solemnly assures us that the spectrum is the very paradigm of continuity and its division the product of cultural accident embedded in language. The frontispiece is a pleasing photograph of a rainbow, whose most prominent feature is that it consists of a small set of clearly differentiated colored regions.[22]

The perceptual salience of certain spectral hues suggests the existence of a natural, biologically induced set of hue categories which may in turn leave its traces in a variety of natural languages. That there is a striking correspondence of color categories across a variety of unrelated languages was persuasively argued by Brent Berlin and Paul Kay in their now famous *Basic Color Terms*. The authors were well aware that their study lent itself to interpretation in terms of underlying physiological mechanisms:

> Our essentially linguistic investigations have led, seemingly inescapably, to the conclusion that the eleven basic color categories are pan-human perceptual universals. But we can offer no physical or physiological explanation for the apparently greater perceptual salience of the particular eleven color stimuli, nor can we explain in any satisfying way the relative ordering among them. Existing theories of color perception, both classical and recent, offer several plausible suggestions for parts of the observed pattern, but none will serve as the basis of an adequate explanation. (Berlin and Kay 1969, 109)

Since the publication of *Basic Color Terms*, which has by and large successfully passed the critical scrutiny of linguists and anthropologists, (e.g., Conklin 1973) there have been attempts, notably by Marc Bornstein (1973) and Floyd Ratliff (1976), to produce more comprehensive psychophysiological explanations of the Berlin-Kay data. It is instructive to see what can be solidly concluded in this matter, since it yields an intriguing scheme in which biology determines phenomenology and, in consequence, a piece of semantic structure. We shall proceed by sketching Berlin and Kay's procedure and chief results and then apply what we have learned about color perception to the interpretation of these results.

What are the criteria for a color term's counting as *basic?* Berlin and Kay give four principal criteria:

(i) It is *monolexic;* that is, its meaning is not predictable from the meanings of its parts.
(ii) Its signification is not included in that of any other color term.
(iii) Its application must not be restricted to a narrow class of objects.
(iv) It must be psychologically salient for all informants. Indices of psychological salience include, among others, (1) a tendency to occur at the beginning of elicited lists of color terms, (2) stability of reference across informants and across occasions of use, and (3) occurrence in the ideolects of all informants. (Berlin and Kay 1969, 6)

Having determined the color terms in twenty languages which were to count as basic, the authors assembled a set of 329 color chips from the Munsell Color Company, representing "forty equally spaced hues and eight degrees of brightness, all at maximum saturation, and nine chips of neutral hue (white, black and grays)" (*ibid.,* 5). The set was formed in the array shown in figure III-4. Each native informant "was given a black grease pencil and asked to indicate for each basic color term *x:*

(1) all those chips which he would under any conditions call *x:*
(2) the best, most typical examples of *x.*" (*ibid.,* 7)

Figure III-4 shows the placement of focal examples for the twenty languages. Several points should be kept in mind when viewing the chart.

(1) Although eleven basic color categories are given, several languages had fewer than eleven basic terms.

(2) "The location of color foci varies no more between speakers of different languages than between speakers of the same language." (*ibid.,* 10)

(3) "Repeated mapping trials with the same informant and also across informants showed that category foci placements are highly reliable. . . . Category boundaries, however, are not reliable, even for repeated trials with the same informant" (ibid., 13). The boundaries shown in the figure represent the spread among foci. They are *not* category boundaries. We shall discuss the problems of fixing category boundaries later.

(4) The data point at Hue 2.5 Blue and Value 3 and the point at Hue 7.5 Blue-Green and Value 4 mark the foci of terms, in Vietnamese and Korean, respectively, which make no clear distinction between what we would call "blue" and what we would call "green".[23] If these two points were disregarded, the foci for the blue and green categories

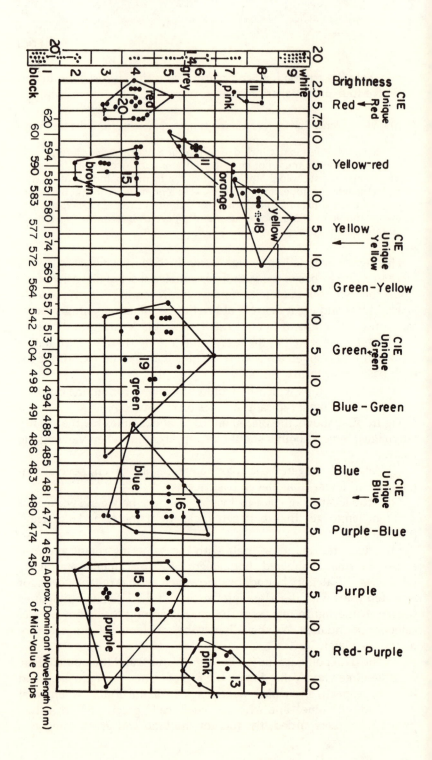

would appear to be much more closely bunched. (This is *not* one of the comments of Berlin and Kay, who do not feel as free to throw away data.)

The next several paragraphs of the present essay first give a brief account of the Munsell color system and then give arguments for supposing that the Berlin-Kay foci for RED, YELLOW, GREEN, and BLUE cluster around the unique hue loci for normal observers. Those who are willing to take this result on faith may skip the next six paragraphs, which are marked by an asterisk. Those with a taste for more technical detail are, of course, encouraged to read them.

*We begin with a brief account of some of the features of the Munsell color system. In 1905, Albert H. Munsell published the first edition of "A Color Notation,"[24] in which he propounded a system based upon equally spaced perceptual steps of Hue, Value (lightness), and Chroma (roughly, saturation).[25] Chroma extends from 0 (achromatic) to the highest materially attainable purity level for a given combination of Hue and Value. The Hues, with which we shall be chiefly concerned, were divided by Munsell into five primary and five secondary categories of ten steps each. At this point architectonic considerations begin to control empirical determinations to some extent. There are, for instance, too many Munsell steps between certain pairs of Hues, such as Munsell Blue and Green, compared with other pairs of equal perceptual difference. In 1943 a subcommittee of the Optical Society of America proposed an extensive revision of the Munsell system intended to make the intervals between the standard color chips approximate more closely the ideal of perceptual equispacing. This is known as the "Munsell renotation," and subsequent editions of the *Book of Color* have conformed to its specifications. The Hues 5 Red, 5 Yellow, 5 Green, and 5 Blue correspond fairly well with the unique hue loci for the 1932 C.I.E. Average Observer; the actual loci are 5 Red, 8 Yellow, 6 Green, and 4 Purple Blue (which is obviously the greatest deviation from the nominal Munsell value). One must also always bear in mind individual differences in unique hue loci. Whatever its drawbacks, the Munsell system has proved to be of great utility as an appearance standard, and is widely employed in America among artists (for whom it was originally intended), manu-

---

Fig. III-4. Facing page: *Normalized foci of basic color terms in twenty languages. Numerals along the upper border of the chart refer to the Munsell system of color notation. Numerals on the body of the chart refer to the number of languages in the sample of twenty which encode the corresponding color category. The smallest possible number of lines are used to enclose each color area. Numerals along the lower border are explained in the text.*

facturers, and psychologists. The Munsell samples are meant to be viewed separately, under rather strict conditions of illumination (6500–7500 degrees Kelvin color temperature—North Daylight) and neutrality of background. Berlin and Kay's subjects did not view the chips under these standard conditions (they used a high-intensity lamp rather than North Daylight), but the authors argue that this did not materially bias the results (Berlin and Kay 1969, 162–163 n. 13). (Given the essentially approximative nature of the whole enterprise, their judgment is probably right.)

*Since the Munsell system employs three variables, the Munsell color samples form a three-dimensional array. As a practical matter, Berlin and Kay chose a two-dimensional array, employing, for each Value and Hue, the chip with the highest available Chroma (effectively maximum saturation). Their procedure is sensible, but it may lead to some distortion in the case of brown, which is a family of *colors* rather than *hues*. Notice also that the chromatic chips selected by Berlin and Kay are 2.5 Munsell Hue steps apart.

*For our purposes, but not for Berlin and Kay's, it is useful to associate the color chips with dominant wavelengths.[26] This is possible with the Munsell samples because they have very smooth spectral reflectance curves (and hence a low degree of appearance variability with illumination changes) and are manufactured to close tolerances. Using the published Munsell-C.I.E. conversion charts (Wyszecki and Stiles 1967), one can arrive at a reasonable estimate of the dominant wavelength of each Hue designation (standardized on Value 5—an approximation for the sake of convenience which will introduce some nonfatal error into the results). These dominant wavelength estimates are shown along the bottom line of figure III-4. Such wavelength specifications enable us to compare the Berlin-Kay chart of color foci with psychophysical data such as the chromatic and achromatic response curves of figure I-14. This figure represents the responses in absolute terms. It is also helpful to express the same chromatic information in relative terms. Figure III-5 plots wavelength against percentage of chromatic response. Let us now see how these two figures might assist us in understanding the data contained in the Berlin-Kay chart. In the discussion that follows, Berlin-Kay hue categories will be designated with upper-case letters to distinguish them from the color terms of English.

*We would expect the foci for RED, YELLOW, GREEN and BLUE to cluster around the average values for the unique hues. This is indeed the case. The foci for YELLOW range from 586 nm to 572 nm, with most of the foci on the 580 nm chip. Unique yellow is at about 580

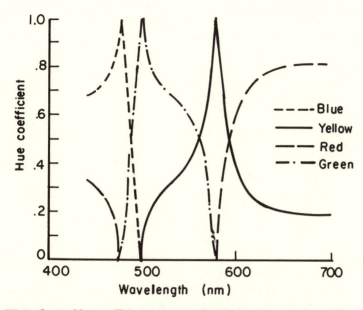

Fig. III-5. *Spectral hue coefficients represent the relative amounts of paired hues seen at each wavelength. These are values for an average observer at a moderate light level.*

nm for most observers. Excluding the two data points we have mentioned before, which represent terms that extend across both GREEN and BLUE, we see that BLUE foci are on chips extending from 481 nm to 474 nm. Unique blue is around 475 nm for most observers. The spread of foci for GREEN is considerably larger: chips from 557 nm to 494 nm were picked out by the respondents. The average for unique green is about 503nm. But the disparity here between the placement of the foci and the psychophysical data is not nearly as large as the size of the wavelength interval might suggest, for two reasons. The first is that Munsell chips 7.5 Green-Yellow, 10 Green-Yellow and 2.5 Green span an area of poor hue discrimination, as the flatness of the curve for the 557-513 nm range in figure III-5 indicates. Remember that the spacings between the Munsell chips represent approximately equal *perceptual* steps, which do not typically correspond to equal wavelength intervals. Attending only to Hue intervals, the foci in GREEN range over seven chips (ignoring the pair of data points we previously mentioned), while BLUE extends over four, YELLOW over five, and RED over three. This is the proper basis for comparison. The second point is that there is substantially more variation from one observer to another in the placement of unique green than for any of the other unique hues. We recall that Hurvich and Jameson, in a study of fifty normal subjects, found that unique green was located by five subjects at about 490 nm, by eleven at about 500nm, by fifteen at around 503 nm, by twelve at about 507 nm by five around 513 nm, and by two at 517 nm. This is a Hue span of six Berlin-Kay Munsell chips! It must be emphasized that the typical variation in unique hue settings from one trial to another for the same subject is much smaller than this, on the order of ± 2 nm.[27]

*As we recall, there is no spectral equivalent for unique red, because for all wavelengths from 590 nm to 700 nm—the region in which the red response predominates—there is always some yellow response. This yellow response must be canceled by blue if a unique red is to be seen. The foci for RED are on a three-chip-wide Hue expanse. Of these three hue steps, only 7.5 Red can be characterized by a single wavelength, 620 nm. The other two chips contain some small admixture of short, "blue" wavelengths. 5 Red is unique red for the C.I.E. average observer.

*These lines of analysis are confirmed by direct experimental investigation. Reporting the findings of an unpublished dissertation, Floyd Ratliff tells us, "Indeed, an experiment by McDaniel in which persons matched their choice of focal chips for these four categories with a patch of light of variable wavelength showed that the perceptually equivalent monochromatic hues were, under those conditions, the unique hues" (Ratliff 1976, 321). We may conclude that these four hue categories reflect the perceptual salience of the unique hues.

One might also have supposed that there would be basic hue categories corresponding to the four balanced binary hues, red-yellow, yellow-green, green-blue and blue-red. In fact, only two of these are to be found: red-yellow (orange) and blue-red (purple). Balanced purple is extraspectral and thus not represented by anything in figure III-5, but its corresponding hue category PURPLE is placed neatly between BLUE and RED, where we would have expected it. (A stretch of purples, usually called "violet," is in the perceived spectrum, below unique blue. This class of binaries is seen because of an increase in red response at very short wavelengths. The reason for this increase is still unclear.) Orange ought to be centered near the spectral locus at which the red and yellow response curves intersect. Figure III-5 tells us that the curves cross at 590 nm, which corresponds to chip 5 Yellow-Red, the mid-point of the ORANGE category.

Why are there no categories for yellow-green and green-blue? It is interesting to notice that the two vary considerably in perceptual salience. This is marked in English by the fact that there are several common words for green-blue: 'aqua', 'turquoise', and 'cyan' come readily to mind, but finding generally recognized (as opposed to decorators' fantasy) words for yellow-green will tax even those with large color vocabularies. We have commented previously on this lack of special identity for yellow-green, but then, as now, we could not find a persuasive explanation for it. One possible reason for the absence of common names for yellow-green is simply that people tend not to like it! In a pair of studies, college students and four-month-old infants judged the pleasantness of various hues, the students with a rating scale, the infants with time spent looking at them. The preference curves for the two age groups agreed pretty well, and both curves took a nosedive in the 550 nm region (Bornstein and Marks 1982, 66; Teller and Bornstein 1982). An explanation for this phenomenon is, alas, not forthcoming.

There is a somewhat better reason for green-blue's absence from the basic hue category list, as well as for the tendency in some languages to lump blues and greens into a common category. R. W. Pickford compared groups of subjects on their performance on a set of color-matching tests. His purpose was to explore anomalies of color vision, but in so doing he turned up some interesting variations among normal subjects. The results of his red-yellow, yellow-green, green-blue and blue-red matching tests showed decidedly larger variations from one individual to another in the blue-green test than in any of the other three:

> Since the differences of the standard deviations of the red-yellow, yellow-green and blue-red tests are about the same as their own standard errors, the subjects are on the whole equally sensitive in these colour comparisons. Since the difference between the standard deviations for the blue-green test and the next larger, that of the blue-red test is more than six times its own standard error, the subjects are on the whole much less sensitive to the green-blue distinction than to any.of the other three. This strongly confirms the general impression from everyday life, that the distinctions between near shades of green and blue are more often disputed than any other colour distinctions. It supports the view that these differences are not due to mere differences of naming, but are the result of real differences of colour sensitivity among the persons concerned. The evidence collected from this series and other tests indicates that these differences are most often due to varying sensitivities to blue. Varying sensitivities to green result in differences of opinion about pale greens and yellows, or about pale greens and pinks, while varying sensitivities to blue result in differences of opinion about blues and greens which are desaturated and about the same brightness. Thus the frequent assertions that Cambridge blue is really a kind of green are due to blue weaknesses. Cambridge blue is a desaturated blue-green, to most people predominantly

blueish, but those who have a weakness in blue are less sensitive to the blue in it than the normal, and see it predominantly as greenish. "Eau de Nil" is a similar colour, but predominantly green to the normal, and is therefore less subject to this variation for the blue-weak. "Electric blue", peacock and even turquoise are often called "green". (Pickford 1951, 245–246)

So far, we have concentrated our attention on the *hues* of the Berlin-Kay focal colors, thus confining ourselves to differences in the horizontal direction of their Munsell chart. This has involved some distortion in our manner of speaking of the chips, which are, after all, *color* chips. But some of the most striking features of the chart are color features, in particular, the locations of focal ORANGE, YELLOW, BROWN, and PINK. Why does YELLOW have such a high Munsell Value, and why are there no basic lightness variants of basic hues other than these last three? These two questions are probably related. Compare the placement of YELLOW at Value 8, with the placement of RED, GREEN, or BLUE, all of which center between Values 4 and 5. The special feature of the yellows to which this is related is their low relative chromatic content, to which we have previously referred. At the region of the spectrum where the y-b system gives its strongest positive response, the achromatic system's response is almost at its peak, so the ratio of the yellow response to the whiteness response—a measure of saturation—is less for unique yellow than it is for any of the other unique hues. The difference is most apparent when we compare yellow with blue. As a result, if we wish to select a yellow sample whose absolute chromatic content—its yellowness—is to come nearest to the chromatic content of a blue chip, the yellow chip must be lighter than the blue one. (Blues will always be relatively dark because of the lower sensitivity of the eye to short wavelengths.) So a "good" yellow will be of higher Munsell Value than a "good" blue. As a further consequence, focal orange should be intermediate in Value between "best"—i.e., most chromatic—yellow and "best" red. The relative positioning of ORANGE, YELLOW, and RED on the Berlin-Kay chart bears out this expectation.

A consequence of the high Value assigned to YELLOW and, to a lesser extent, ORANGE is that beneath their representative chips there is a substantial gamut of chips of the same Hue but lesser Value. These low-Value orange-yellows are the objects of the category BROWN. That browns are related to but markedly distinct from high-lightness oranges and yellows is something on which we have already commented and for which we have no ready explanation. One can *blacken* reds or greens or blues by simultaneous contrast and get effects which are somewhat different from the *dim* reds or greens that are available as aperture colors (a dim orange or yellow does not look brown), but the perceptual difference between a "clear" red and a blackened red is not striking. One possibility that might be relevant is this. The blackening is operating on the achromatic content of the red, and, if this is low, as it is in a "clear" red, so will be the perceptual shift. With yellow, however, the achromatic content is always high, and the perceptual shift is accordingly more dramatic. So the desaturation of yellow *may* be responsible both for the high-Value placement of YELLOW and for the distinctive appearance of brown; hence the emergence of BROWN as a basic color category.

That PINK should appear as a basic category is not easily explained. Like balanced purple, pink is not a spectral color. It is a desaturated red with a relatively small blue component. It could be described as a desaturated, very reddish purple. Since the mean focal placements of RED and PURPLE are slightly lower in value than those of GREEN and BLUE, there is more Value "space" above PURPLE and RED than above those other hues. This suggests an analogy with the ORANGE-YELLOW and BROWN case. In both instances a shift in the Value "center-of-gravity" away from the average focal Value for the basic colors as a whole is compensated for by an approximately equal and opposite shift. Low-Value BROWN "counterbalances" high-Value OR-ANGE and YELLOW, whereas the smaller downward deviation of RED and PURPLE is offset by a corresponding upward deviation in PINK. But whereas brown is a contrast color, pink is not; the distinguishing features of brown have no exact parallel in the case of pink. We still lack an adequate explanation of PINK as a basic linguistic color category.

The evolution of color categories

We have not yet discussed a second major finding of Berlin and Kay: an invariant or near-invariant sequence of stages in the evolution of basic color terms. Not all languages have the full complement of basic color terms: some have only two basic color terms, some only three, and so on. What emerged from the Berlin-Kay study is the following remarkable set of rules:

(1) All languages contain terms for white and black.

(2) If a language contains three terms, then it contains a term for red.

(3) If a language contains four terms, then it contains a term for either green or yellow (but not both).

(4) If a language contains five terms, then it contains terms for both green and yellow.

(5) If a language contains six terms, then it contains a term for blue.

(6) If a language contains seven terms, then it contains a term for brown.

(7) If a language contains eight or more terms, then it contains a term for purple, pink, orange, grey, or some combination of these. (Berlin and Kay 1969, 2–3)

It should be mentioned that, for languages with fewer color terms, the semantic boundaries of the terms tend to be broader than they are in those languages with more color terms, although the foci tend to stay fixed. In a "Stage I" (two-term) language, for example, the category BLACK tends to encompass the "dark" and "cool" chromatic colors, whereas the category WHITE tends to encompass the "light" and "warm" chromatic colors. The two categories thus do not correspond in extension to the English 'black' and 'white'.

The regularities captured by these rules cry out for explanation. Once again, we can deliver enough of an account to satisfy ourselves that at least most of what is involved is rooted in the mode of functioning of the visual system, but we must equally acknowledge that some things remain to be explained. It should not, for instance, surprise us that the first chromatic terms to appear always pick out the categories centering upon the four unique hues. But why do they appear in that particular order, with RED first and BLUE last?

It is plain that more factors are at work than can be exhibited in the chromatic response data taken alone, and it is not clear whether these factors are built into human biology or are constraints arising from near-universal environmental imperatives. That RED is the first of the chromatic categories may, for example, depend in part upon the fact that fire and blood are stereotypically red. But there may be sorts of biological tendencies other than those we have so far considered. For instance, not all the nerves proceeding from the Lateral Geniculate Nucleus go to the cortex; some lead to the "lower" brain centers which are often implicated in emotional response. Do they have something to do with pronounced human emotional reactions to colors? It is known that, when a subject is brought from a neutral to a red environment, his blood pressure, temperature, and respiration rate increase immediately, then fall below their base rate in five or ten minutes' time. Just the reverse happens when a subject moves from neutral to blue surroundings (Gerard 1958; cited in Kaiser 1984). It may also be relevant that infants (but not older children) have a distinct preference for red.

Claims of biological effects of various colors and color combinations on both man and beast abound. To take just one example, it has recently been maintained that disturbed people are markedly calmed when placed in a bubblegum-pink room. One football coach attributed his team's success on its home field in part to the deliberate use of that same bubblegum-pink as the overall color of the visiting team's locker room! The testimony of athletic coaches on color schemes is hardly probative; some have placed their trust in the efficacy of plexiglass pyramids; others assiduously calculate players' biorhythms. There is an enormous amount of folklore on color and the emotions, a fair amount of semiscientific work on the subject, and the occasional competent experiment. It seems plain that there are genuine phenomena to be studied here, and equally plain that there is at present no well validated set of principles on the basis of which they can be understood.

For whatever reason, red is perceptually salient as well as emotionally arousing, and we should not be overly surprised that it should be the focus of the first chromatic category.[28] (Have you ever noticed that when philosophers want to refer to a color for the sake of an example, they overwhelmingly prefer red? Is this purely accidental?) The next two categories are also those we might expect. Green is the color of vegetation as well as red's opponent hue, and its complement (or near-complement) on any color system. Yellow's claim is based on its high luminosity; it is, as we know, the color associated with the wavelengths to which the eye is most sensitive. Blue is the last of the psychologically primary hues to be distinguished by a basic linguistic color category. Why does it finish fourth? In an elaborate and interesting paper, Marc Bornstein has argued that the native speakers of languages that lack a BLUE category tend to be concentrated near the equator (Bornstein 1973). The people in these regions have more yellow macular pigmentation than those closer to the poles, with the consequence that less shortwave light reaches their retinas, rendering them comparatively less sensitive to blue and less able to distinguish it from green. Although the filtering effect is demonstrable and in fact accounts for a considerable amount of the variation among color normals, it does not seem to be of sufficient magnitude to produce a profound shared difficulty in differentiating green from blue. (*Variations* in macular pigmentation, as we have seen, are quite capable of producing disagreements among people about whether an object in the blue-green region is "really" blue or "really" green.) Most middle-aged Caucasians have little difficulty with the discrimination of blue from green (except in the borderline cases), despite a comparable filtering attributable to the yellowing of the lens with age. Finally, the Dani people of New Guinea have just a three-term basic color vocabulary, but E. H. Rosch, who showed that focal color terms could be learned by the Dani more easily than nonfocal ones, reported that her subjects had no particular difficulty with distinguishing blue from green.[29] The invariable fourth-place finish of BLUE in the Berlin and Kay sweepstakes remains to be explained.

It should now be apparent that, far from language carving out categories from a structureless color space, the basic linguistic categories themselves have been induced by perceptual saliences common to the human race. The similarity between these semantic universals and the widely discussed universals of syntax and phonology was not lost on Berlin and Kay:

> Chomsky and Lenneberg have argued that the complexities of language structure, together with some known limitations of human neurophysiology, imply that human language cannot be considered simply a manifestation of human intelligence. Rather it must be recognized as a species-specific ability, ultimately based on species-specific bio-morphological structures. What the particular biological structures underlying particular linguistic functions may be, it is not possible to say at this time in any detail {More has subsequently been said—CLH}. The study of the biological foundations of the most peculiarly and exclusively human set of behavioral abilities—language—is just beginning, but sufficient evidence has accumulated to show that such connections must exist for the linguistic realms of syntax and phonology. The findings reported here concerning the universality and evolution of basic color lexicon suggest that such connections are also to be found in the realm of semantics. (Berlin and Kay 1969, 109–110)

Are there some other examples of biology influencing semantics? One was first pointed out by the famous acoustician Georg von Békésy and discussed by Ratliff, to whose examination of the Berlin-Kay work the present discussion is deeply indebted (Ratliff 1976, 326–328; von Békésy 1970). In English, elevation words are used to refer to pitches: short-wavelength sounds are called "high," and long wavelengths are called "low." The surprising fact is that the very same connection between pitch and elevation words occurs in eleven languages as diverse as Hungarian and Mandarin. There seems to be no basis in inanimate nature to account for this association, but there are two sorts of phenomena associated with human beings that seem pertinent to it. The first is that high-pitched sounds are produced in the upper vocal cavities and low-pitched sounds are produced in the lower cavities. You may test this for yourself by singing a scale or noticing the bodily sources of the initial 'e' in 'ether' or the 'u' in 'rug'. The second appears most noticeably with headphones (though the origins of the linguistic practice can hardly be traced to this particular way of observing the phenomenon). If one listens to a sequence of pure tones, the lowest (say, 150 Hz) are localized low in the head, and the highest (say, 5,000 Hz) are localized high in the head, or even *above* it. Similar but less striking pitch-height effects may be noticed with other acoustic sources; the sound of a triangle sometimes seems to "fly" *over* the orchestra.

An attempt to bring color science to bear on Berlin and Kay's results is worth while because it goes beyond an argument like Chomsky's, which tries to show *that* biology shapes language, and provides a case study of *how* biology shapes language. The case is, inevitably, primitively and incompletely presented, but the interesting thing is that it can be presented at all. The reason it can is that the eye is a brain extension which can fruitfully be subjected to a few simple (by neurophysiological standards) micro pokes and prods without investigators getting involved in the incredible tangle of connections that constitute the neural basis of most linguistic performances. The Berlin-Kay basic color categories are simply the product of a set of filters at an early stage of neural processing. We gain advantage from the twin facts that the filters can be separately studied and that the shaping the filters impose on the incoming signal is largely preserved through the entire processing chain.

Boundaries and indeterminacy

There has been a very important omission up to this point in our discussion of color language: the semantic boundaries of color terms. Berlin and Kay found the fixing of boundaries to be very different from the fixing of foci.

Repeated mapping trials with the same informant and also across informants showed that category foci placements are highly reliable. It is rare that a category focus is displaced by more than two adjacent chips. Category boundaries, however, are not reliable, even for repeated trials with the same informant. This is reflected in the ease with which informants designated foci, in contrast with their difficulty in placing boundaries. Subjects hesitated for long periods before performing the latter task, demanded clarification of the instructions, and otherwise indicated that this task is more difficult than assigning foci. In fact, in marked contrast to the foci, category boundaries proved to be so unreliable, even for an individual informant, that they have been accorded a relatively minor place in the analysis. Consequently, whenever we speak of color categories, *we refer to the foci of categories, rather than to their boundaries or total area,* except when specifically stating otherwise. (Berlin and Kay 1969, 13; emphasis in text.)

Yet boundaries of color terms do somehow get established. It is apparent, however, that they are not fixed rigidly, and some philosophers have argued that this means that there can be no coherent account of the semantics of color terms. Such a thesis has been propounded by Crispin Wright:

Colour predicates, it is plausible to suppose, are in the following sense purely *observational:* if one can tell at all what colour something is, one can tell just by looking at it. The look of an object decides its colour, as the feel of an object decides its texture or the sound of a note its pitch. . . . Since colour predicates are observational, any pair of objects indistinguishable in point of colour must satisfy the condition that any basic colour predicate applicable to either is applicable to both. It is, however, familiar that we may construct a series of suitable, homogeneously coloured patches, in such a way as to give the impression of a smooth transition from red to orange, where each patch is *indiscriminable* in colour from those immediately next to it; it is the non-transitivity of indiscriminability which generates this possibility. So, since precise matching is to be sufficient for sameness of colour, we can force the application of 'red' to all the patches in the series, some of which are not red but orange. That is: since 'red' is observational, its sense must be such that from the premises, that x is red and that x looks just like y, it follows that y is red, no matter what objects x and y may be. This rule enables us to conclude that each successive patch in our series is red, given only the true premise that the first patch is red.
    If we hold that predicates of colour are tolerant with respect to marginal changes of shade, we shall be forced to regard identity of shade as a non-observational notion. We shall be admitting that changes in shade take place between adjacent patches where none *seem* to have taken place, where the most minute mutual comparison reveals no difference.[30]

The difficulty, says Wright, cannot be avoided by invoking a "notion standing to the concept of shade as that of real position stands to phenomenal position" or by simply stipulating the boundaries of color terms, for to do either would be to abandon our "conception, viz. the *look* of a thing, of what justifies the application of these predicates" (*ibid.*). And to abandon that, he holds, is to abandon hope of accounting in any systematic way for the use of color terms in everyday life.

Let us investigate this question of boundaries by inquiring into the sources and resolution of indeterminacy in (1) individual color perceptions, (2) perceptual matching and discrimination of closely resembling color presentations in the laboratory, and (3) the drawing of color-term boundaries in common practice. It will turn out that the indeterminacy of individual color perceptions may well be connected with the difficulties of fine-grained perceptual matching, but that neither will have a great deal to do with the way color boundaries are established in daily life. We shall see that, although biology and culture both have a part in the establishment of these boundaries, context and purpose play the leading roles.

We have already had several encounters with the indeterminacy of color perceptions. The phenomenal fact that colors and shapes that are seen in the periphery of the visual field are indeterminate[31] is a matter of substantial embarrassment to the sense-datum theorist, for if sense data are ontologically irreducible, there must be entities that have determinable but not determinate properties. We suggested that a materialist reduction of visual objects and qualities would be ontologically advantageous if it would replace indeterminately qualified objects and processes with determinately qualified objects and processes. We now need to consider how the statistical features of determinate neural coding could represent the chromatic indeterminacy of a visual sense experience.

As we well know, many sensory neurons display incessant spontaneous activity, discharging randomly in the absence of stimulation. The effect of a stimulus on lower-level visual neurons may be either to facilitate or to inhibit their firing with respect to that spontaneous base rate. The success of higher-level neurons in detecting and decoding a sensory message will depend upon their being able to uncover changes in the frequency of the outputs of those lower-level neurons. Since lower-level neurons fire at an irregular base rate, higher-level neurons will have to sample the input from these neurons over a stretch of time if they are to establish that a particular criterion value has been met. The fundamental principles involved here are illustrated in figure III-6. Although this figure depicts the behavior of a peripheral neuron that originates on a skin receptor and terminates on a second-order neuron in the spinal chord, its mode of function is closely similar to that of a typical post-receptoral visual cell.

In figure III-6, (a) shows a train of action potentials—voltage spikes—resulting from the application of a stimulus. In either the stimulated state or the spontaneous firing state the interspike interval is irregular. The two are therefore to be distinguished only by a difference in the average number of impulses in a given time period. In the same figure, (b) plots the average number of impulses over sev-

171

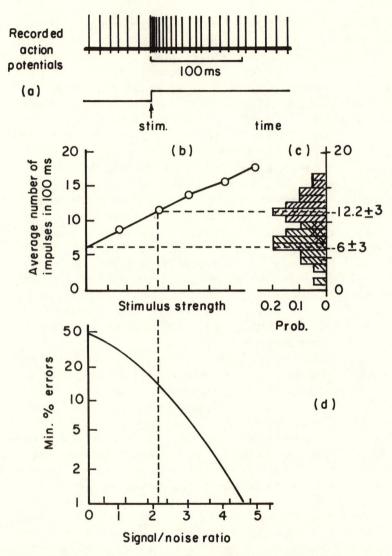

Fig. III-6. *Signal detection as a probabilistic process at the neural level.*

eral 100-millisecond periods following stimuli of various strengths. Notice that the average number increases smoothly with increases in stimulus strength. If we turn our attention to the distribution of pulses during each 100-ms period, we see substantial variation. In (c) two histograms are displayed, showing the proportions of impulses during several 100-ms periods, ranging from 2 to 17 impulses per 100

ms. The lower histogram is a no-stimulus (spontaneous firing) record, with an average of 6 impulses; the upper histogram, with an
average of 12.2 impulses, represents the effects of a moderate stimulus. Both of these distributions have a standard deviation of ± 3 impulses. The reliability of detecting a stimulus depends on the signal/
noise ratio, which is (12.2–6)/3 = 2.1 for a stimulus of the strength
shown here. Because these distributions overlap, errors are unavoidable when judging whether or not a stimulus was present from the
number of impulses in a pulse train, and (d) shows that for a signal/
noise ratio of 2.1 the error rate would be at least 15 per cent on average. A stronger stimulus would separate the distributions shown in
(c), and the error rate would fall as shown in (d).[32]

Think of the higher-level neurons as making a statistical summary
of the firing rates of the lower-level neurons that synapse onto them.
For strong stimuli, the summary could be approximated by a normal
distribution curve, with the value of the maximum amplitude of the
curve taken as the message-rate frequency and the width of the curve
as representing the uncertainty of the message. As the signal strength
increases, the width of the curve decreases. Perfect transmission of
the message would be represented by a curve of zero width. As the
signal strength decreases, the curve spreads and flattens, several different neighboring message rates are represented as having maximal
amplitude, and the central tendency of the distribution may fluctuate
over time. If higher-order portions of the visual system represent
both the central tendency of a set of signals and their dispersion, that
is, represent both the probable value of the signal and its transmission
quality, we can readily understand that whether we experience a particular visual field region as having a more or a less determinate chromatic character will depend upon the net signal strength that the system receives.

The indeterminacy of perceived color for a given region in the visual periphery is entirely a function of encoding adequacy. The entire
retina is populated with cones, but their density decreases with distance from the fovea, so they can deliver a chromatic message equivalent to one from a foveal region only if an equivalent number of them
are stimulated (or, up to a point, a smaller number for a longer period
of time). This means that, for a peripheral region, as the stimulus size
increases, there should be an increase in the strength of the signal
and thus an increase in the determinateness of the color that appears
in that region. This is exactly what happens (van Esch et al. 1984).
There is, of course, a maximum achievable ratio of signal to noise for
the system or subsystem. Once that is attained, further increases in

stimulus strength do nothing to improve the quality of message transmission.

If this analysis is essentially correct, it means that (1) visual system noise should manifest itself perceptually in the absence of stimulation, and (2) even foveal color perception under optimal circumstances should show some indeterminacy because of the upper limit to the achievable signal to noise ratio. As we already know, visual noise shows up as "brain gray," and subjects in visual threshold experiments do report seeing occasional small flashes when no stimuli are presented. Indeterminacy in foveal color perception is difficult to lay hands on, but it is worth pondering whether it might be a factor in phenomena that happen in the course of precise observational work in psychophysical laboratories, like this occurrence in one of Werner and Wooten's hue-naming experiments:

> Variability in hue naming responses did not appear to vary systematically with wavelength. In some cases, particularly around the unique hue loci, the hue was described as a large percentage of one hue and a very small percentage of a second hue. When there was a very small percentage, the observers reported difficulty in detecting the minor hue component. For example, around unique blue, the hue may sometimes have been described as 96% blue and 4% red and at other times as 96% blue and 4% green. In these cases, we plotted the mean percentage for the terms that were used most often. (Werner and Wooten 1979, 427)

Let us take this occasion to examine our next concern, situations in which laboratory subjects are engaged in making small discriminations between stimuli, for example, in judging whether two samples match or differ in color. We shall subsequently see how these discrimination tasks may be related to the indeterminacy of individual perceptions as we have described them.

When philosophers write about whether or not one homogeneously colored patch is discriminable in color from another, it is easy to get the impression that one could decide whether or not one had a match rather easily, just by giving a good straight look. If a difference between the patches falls above the threshold of discriminability and the conditions of seeing are optimal, the straight look will reveal that difference, but if the difference falls below the threshold, neither that look nor any succedding look will uncover the discrepancy, and the samples will match perfectly.

Actual attempts to match and discriminate closely similar material color samples are, by contrast, typical cases of decision making under conditions of uncertainty. If one compares the matches a subject makes or rejects with the spectral characteristics of the material samples to be matched, one discovers that some of the rejected matches are of samples that are physically extremely close, whereas some of the accepted matches are between samples that are physically further apart.[33] In fact, when the same samples are presented on another occasion, several of the previously accepted matches will now be rejected, and several of the heretofore rejected matches will now be accepted. How, then, is one to decide what the limits of discrimination are? The appropriate procedure seems fairly clear, and analogous to that generally applied in observational sciences such as astronomy, which must extract meaningful observational information from a babel of perturbing influences: assume that the sources of error are random, use that assumption to factor out biases, and then select and apply a criterion of statistical significance. But if we follow this procedure, we get a *statistical* distribution of discriminations. What is to become of the "classical" conception of the fixed, sharp threshold? Answer: it must be abandoned, and has in fact been abandoned in psychophysics for many years.

A common experimental method for establishing a metric of color differences is to have the observer adjust the wavelength composition of a comparison spot of light so as to generate a visual match for a test spot. When the procedure is repeated a number of times, it provides a statistical measure of the observer's visual tolerance of physical variation and thus estimates the same human capability that threshold measurements are intended to capture. Here is Erwin Schrödinger commenting (in 1926) on these two procedures:

> Instead of the threshold, sometimes the mean adjustment error for repeated production of the color match is determined. This method has many advantages: it is more objective, freer from prejudice because the observer does not have to decide the question of whether the fields are distinguishable, but has only to match them as well as possible. The mean errors are proportional to the thresholds; they therefore, for reasons given above, serve the same purpose. The proportionality factor can probably not be stated generally. If the threshold itself were a sharply defined quantity, then each adjustment outside the threshold ought to be impossible, each adjustment within it ought to be equally probable; therefore, a "square curve" would be expected as the error distribution. Instead, of course, an ordinary Gaussian [34] error distribution is obtained. Therefore, the threshold is not a precisely defined quantity, but, for each stimulation difference, the probability for correct evaluation of the difference increases towards unity with increasing stimulus difference. (Schrödinger 1970)

There are various methods that have come into use in recent years for dealing with threshold-determination problems. They generally

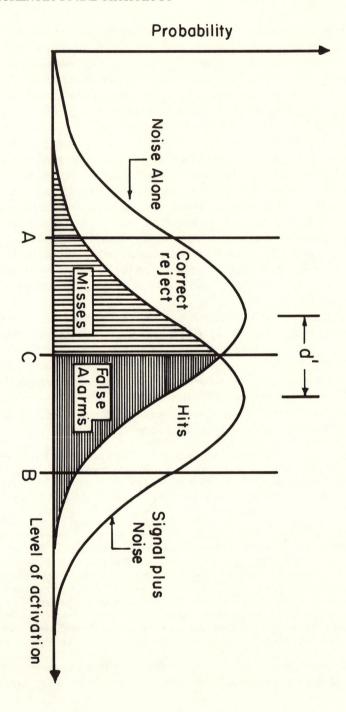

involve regarding the threshold as a statistical concept, tagged to a conventionally established criterion of significance. It is a feature of statistical ensembles that small differences between them can be progressively brought to light by increasing the size of the samples drawn from them. What this comes to in psychophysical experiments is that a subject's sensitivity to a small stimulus difference that cannot be detected in a single observational trial may be detected over a larger number of trials. For instance, suppose that the subject's task is to make out whether, in a given interval of time, a sound of a particular audible frequency has been transmitted over a noisy channel.[35] The signal/noise ratio is low, so she will generally be uncertain about whether she hears it or not. She is to answer 'yes' if she thinks she hears it, 'no' if she thinks she hears only noise. She is obliged to make one of these two responses for each presented interval. If she says 'yes' and there is a signal, the experimenter is to score a *hit*, but if she says 'yes' and there is no signal, it is to be scored as a *false alarm*. If she says 'no' and there is a signal, it is a *miss*, and if she says 'no' and there is no signal, it is a *correct rejection*. (See figure III-7.)

It can be shown that it does not matter whether the subject is bold and guesses 'yes' a lot, or is timid and tends to say 'no' for most trials. In the first case, she will have more hits but she will also have more false alarms. In the second case, she will have fewer false alarms but also fewer hits. What matters is her *sensitivity*, her ability to detect the difference between the noise alone and the noise with signal added, and her sensitivity is determined by the ratio of hits to false alarms in her responses. If the noise alone and the signal plus noise both have normal distributions, the sensitivity will be the difference between the means of the two curves, measured in standard deviations. Ideally, if the subject's boldness or timidity remains constant over time (technically: her *criterion* remains the same) and if her sensi-

---

Fig. III-7. Facing page: *Threshold perception according to signal-detection theory. The left-hand curve represents the probability distribution of sensory activation produced by noise alone, and the right-hand curve is the probability distribution due to the combination of signal and noise. The difference* d' *(in standard deviations) between the means of the two curves is the observer's sensitivity.* 'A', 'B', *and* 'C' *represent three different criteria that a subject might employ in deciding whether or not she is detecting a signal. An activation to the right of the criterion point will elicit a* "yes, there is a signal" *response, whereas an activation to the left of the criterion point will elicit a* "no, there is no signal" *response.* 'A' *thus represents the criterion of a* "bold" *subject, and* 'B' *the criterion of a* "timid" *subject. The subject's sensitivity,* d', *is independent of the positioning of the subject's criterion.*

tivity does not change, any signal plus noise distribution could be distinguished from the distribution of noise alone by the proportion of hits to false alarms. All that is required is that the number of trials be large enough to distinguish the two proportions. By extension, under the same assumptions, any two distinct, repeatedly presented signals above the noise level may be distinguished from each other by the differences in their proportions of hits to false alarms. The task of matching or distinguishing two closely resembling color samples falls under this latter rubric.

To claim that there is in theory no lower perceptual discrimination limit save that imposed by quantum mechanics sounds quite unreasonable, but it takes only a moment to see that it is not much different from saying that someone could die of asphyxiation because all the molecules of the air happened to be someplace else for five minutes or that the water in a teapot might freeze rather than boil when put over a flame. These two events are allowed by statistical mechanics, but the probability that they will happen in a reasonable number of trials is virtually nil.

In psychophysics as in physics, one imposes cutoff points in order to get on with the business at hand. The cutoff point will vary with the needs one has. The "just-noticeable differences" in color that are used in the exploration of the metric of perceptual color spaces are, from a certain point of view, rather large. Wyszecki and Stiles, discussing some aspect's of D. F. MacAdam's important work on this subject, tell us that "MacAdam's extensive auxiliary experiments on just-noticeable color differences indicated that for the same observer these are proportional to the corresponding standard deviations of color matching, the just-noticeable difference being about three times as large as the corresponding standard deviation" (Wyszecki and Stiles 1967, 529). The emphasis in work of the sort MacAdam was doing is to find a satisfactory tradeoff between smallness of observational difference and reliability of its detection. Reliability is here given a relatively heavy weight: three standard deviations corresponds to 75 hits for every false alarm. The detection of very small color differences is demanding, tedious work, and one doesn't want to have to add endless retracing of one's footsteps to the burden, especially when it would serve no useful purpose for the task at hand.

In his argument against the possibility of a coherent semantics for color terms, Wright takes it as obvious that there exist color patches x, y, and z such that x is indiscriminable in color from y, and y from z, but x is discriminable in color from z. This assumption seems to be widely shared among philosophers and is rarely, if ever, examined. Here, for instance, is an extract from an argument by David Armstrong:

> Now suppose that we have three samples of cloth, *A*, *B* and *C*, which are exactly alike except that they differ very slightly in colour. Suppose further, however, that *A* and *B* are perceptually completely *indistinguishable* in respect of colour, and *B* and *C* are perceptually completely indistinguishable in respect of colour. Suppose, however, that *A* and *C* can be perceptually distinguished from each other in this respect. . . . (Armstrong 1968, 218)

It is plain that Armstrong takes indistinguishability to be an all-or-nothing affair. In passages such as this, the notion of a *criterion* or *test* of perceptual indistinguishability never makes an appearance, yet we know that this makes a real difference. And if we take 'completely' at full strength, then if *A* and *B* are completely indistinguishable, any *C* that is distinguishable from the one will be distinguishable from the other as well.

We now have sufficient reason for rejecting this view of perceptual indistinguishability and for suspecting all arguments that take it for granted. But we are obliged to answer three questions about our analysis of matching situations. (1) When philosophers have used the term 'perceptual indistinguishability,' they have meant it to refer to a single observational act, or, if you will, to the observer's sense impressions at a particular moment. Isn't the statistical view of observation that is the backbone of the present analysis really addressed to a different question, so that one can attack the standard view only by changing the subject? (2) Observations have on the present account been treated as statistical in two different ways. In the first, which is concerned with the indeterminate quality of individual color perceptions, the perception itself is, from the neural point of view, *constituted* by a statistical summary of the relevant internal substates of the observer; in the second, which is the one relevant to the discrimination between two color samples, the statistics relate to an ensemble of distinct sensory states. How are the two notions related, if at all? (3) What purchase does this analysis give us on the matter of the semantic boundaries of color predicates?

(1) It is useful to ask ourselves what actually happens when we have to make a considered color-matching judgment when extremely fine discriminations are at stake. Our estimates vacillate, and we become uncertain about whether we do or do not see a difference. If we have any sophistication and commitment to objectivity about our

own perceptual states, we shall have recourse to a statistical analysis of our own performances. The very fact that a sequence of observational judgments uncovers a sensitivity to differences that are not revealed by single observational judgments shows that there is information about our sensory states which is not fully accessible to introspection. It is, however, interesting to notice that, if subjects are asked to rate the accuracy of their judgments, about all of which they are uncertain, their relative level of confidence in their reports generally correlates well with their discrimination rates, although they tend to underestimate how accurately they perform (Vickers 1979, 185).

We should also observe that "individual" sense experiences take time to develop and, therefore, for reasons we have already given, involve statistical estimates on the part of the nervous system, estimates which are a function of time. That this is so is evidenced by many psychophysical experiments which show that very brief sensory events of moderate intensity have rather different characteristics from longer ones (Hood and Finkelstein 1983). We discussed an example of very small, brief stimuli in connection with our critique of sense data. There are many more such examples. Visual sensory phenomena are only one of many types of natural phenomena whose character is bound up with the time they take and are thus incapable of existing at an instant. Any phenomenon that can be interpreted as constituted by a wave packet will illustrate the point.[36]

(2) In connection with our speculative modeling of qualitatively indeterminate sense impressions by a sensory estimate of the dispersion and central tendency of neural firings, it was postulated that two sorts of things happen under conditions of weak stimulation. The first is that the dispersion increases. The representation of that in the visual system is the indeterminate quality of the perception. But the other thing that might be supposed to happen when the stimulus gets weaker still and the discrete nature of the neural response makes itself felt, is that the approximation to a normal distribution begins to break down, and the central tendency of the distribution begins to fluctuate from one moment to the next.

We can see how this relates to the sensory-discrimination case by considering that in this instance, the signal that is to be discriminated from the noise is the *difference* in receptoral response to stimulation from the two color samples. Even though the two stimuli may be quite strong, so that there is no question about the reliable discrimination of either one, when the two provoke closely similar response in the receptors, the difference signal will be very weak, and show the fluctuations characteristic (according to the hypothesis) of very low signal/noise ratios. The variability in subjects' responses may not lie, then, in fluctuations in their response criteria, but rather in the perceptions themselves. Perceptions do, on this view, fluctuate with time; so their statistics are to be represented by an ensemble analysis. But there is no reason to suppose that there is a natural length of time which is required for a single perception to occur and which could therefore serve to individuate that perception from another. There is in such cases no hard and fast distinction between the statistically constituted individual perception and the statistically characterized ensemble of individual perceptions. Rather, how the perceptual continuum is to be divided into blocks will be dictated largely by the requirements of the particular analysis.

Supposing that there is a color-difference signal that receives separate treatment by the visual system is not quite as gratuitous as it may seem to be. We have already seen in the discussion of sense data that various constituents of a perception which commonly go together are capable of being experienced apart from one another; the waterfall illusion is an illustration of this. Such phenomena suggest that these features receive separate analysis, and, as we know, the cortex contains numerous cells with "preferences" for certain features of the visual scene. And, in particular, there are cells that respond primarily to chromatic *difference* without caring much about the particular chromaticities involved (Jacobs 1981, 85).

(It must once again be emphasized that the theoretical sketch given here is quite speculative, like the earlier attempt to suggest a neural ground for the felt quality difference between red and green. It is subject to more precise formulation and empirical refutation. The purpose of such sketches is to provide fresh approaches to stagnant problems.)

(3) If the previous discussion is on the right track, it tells us that color predicates that are defined at very fussy levels of discrimination are to be regarded as statistical in character, and so they must be specified by a central tendency as well as by a measure of dispersion. The extensions of such color predicates therefore overlap, and our ability to decide, given two predicates, which one applies to a given color instance will be a direct function of their degree of overlap. This is how observational measures are generally treated in science; a report of a quantitative measurement without an expression of probable error is automatically suspect. What has troubled philosophers about this rather obvious way of dealing with color predicates is presumably that they believe that phenomenal colors are perfectly determi-

nate and exclude each other. To the extent that colors are determinate, they do exclude each other in the sense of 'exclusion' which is explicated by the opponent theory. But, at these very fine levels, the indeterminacy of phenomenal colors makes itself strongly felt, and the relationships of exclusion are correspondingly weakened.

Establishing boundaries

When fine-grained predicates of color appearance are actually employed in color science or technology—they usually take the form of interpolations between Munsell color chips—their limits of accuracy are tacitly understood; hue interpolations by practiced observers are accurate to about half of a Munsell step. This is not the limit of hue discriminability, however, but it is something like the limit of useful naming of phenomenal colors, since the perceptual differences between individuals at a given time and between observations by the same individual at different times have at this point come to swamp the fine discriminations of which any one observer is capable. Ralph Evans remarks,

> It is not realized ordinarily how great is the variation of observers in this respect. A rough estimate indicates that a perfect match by a perfect "average" observer would probably be unsatisfactory for something like 90 percent of all observers because variation between observers is very much greater than the smallest color differences which they can distinguish. Any observer whose variation from the standard was much greater than his ability to distinguish differences would be dissatisfied with the match. (Evans 1948, 196–197)

Even if the assumption that there is a nontransitive "observational" indistinguishability of colors were correct and a sorites argument of Wright's sort could be launched, it would have little bearing on a rational reconstruction of the rules governing color predicates in a public language, since such predicates are necessarily *much* coarser than the fine grain of just noticeably different colors that are perceivable by particular individuals.

We recall the estimate that a trained normal observer can, under optimal conditions, discriminate something on the order of ten million surface colors. About half a million colors are considered to be commercially different (Judd and Wyszecki 1963, 359). But the number of color names in use in English is much smaller; the Inter-Society Color Council—National Bureau of Standards *Method of Designating*

Colors lists some 7,500 color names, and reduces these to 267 equivalence classes (Kelly and Judd 1976). The names assigned to these classes are, in turn, compounded of just ten hue names, three achromatic names and a few modifiers such as 'dark', 'light', 'very' and '-ish'. Berlin and Kay found that eleven English color terms satisfied their criteria of basicness; all the terms on their basic list are included in the Bureau of Standards basic list. A survey of seventeen best sellers showed that, of a total of 4,416 color term tokens, 4,081 are occurrences of just twelve terms, and half of the total number are tokens of 'white', 'black,' and 'gray' (Evans 1948, 230).

We previously mentioned several reasons for the enormous disparity between the number of possible color discriminations and the number of color terms in normal use. One of them is variability between observers. A second is the great difficulty people have in comparing colors under *normal* as opposed to *standard* conditions of observation. Changing light, shadows, contrast, inhomogeneity of color across surfaces, and surface differences among materials, such as texture and glossiness, all make color-appearance comparisons highly problematic. A third reason is that it is far more difficult to compare a perceived color with a mental standard than with another color seen at the same time, except for such "natural" mental standards as the NCS elementary colors.

Because quite different purposes and standards are at work in identifying and discriminating colors in everyday life than are involved in laboratory color matching, we should not expect that the range of considerations required in an account of the latter should have a great deal to tell us about the former. So we need to inquire as to what phenomenal features do seem to underlie the ascriptions of colors to objects in ordinary language, and, in particular, to ask how and why boundaries between colors get drawn as they do. It would also be helpful to know how the everyday uses of color language tie in with more specialized and precise employments of color predicates. To these tasks we shall now turn.

Let us address the problem of fixing color boundaries by considering a simplified case: the hue boundary between orange and red. We shall examine in imagination the phenomenal hue stretch between unique red and unique yellow. (One must always bear in mind that imagination is but an *ersatz* for experience and that promissory notes issued here must—and can—be backed by experiment.) The stretch will be represented by estimated percentages of phenomenal red and yellow in each of five hues in the range, along with the hue names associated with them.

100% red	(unique) red
75% red, 25% yellow	yellowish red
50% red, 50% yellow	yellow-red (orange)
25% red, 75% yellow	reddish yellow
100% yellow	(unique) yellow

The three intermediate hues exhibit a perceptual tension between red and yellow. Yellowish red seems more red than yellow; reddish yellow seems more yellow than red. The boundary of red in the broadest sense extends to the immediate neighborhood of unique yellow, and the breadth of that spread we acknowledge by our use of the modifier 'reddish'. But, in a somewhat narrower sense, the boundary between red and yellow falls at the point at which the perceptual "pull" of yellow is equal to that of red. This point is, of course, orange. But once we introduce orange as a distinct hue category, its boundary with red is at issue, and the extension of 'red' must be contracted to make room for the oranges. The natural red-orange boundary would seem to fall at the 75 per cent red, 25 per cent yellow region which was well within the scope we took 'red' to have when we were concerned to compare red with yellow.[37]

The principle that appears to be operating is that the unique hues are at the core of (humanly) natural color categories, the extent of which will be governed by the phenomenal tensions between them and by the number of intermediate categories that come to be defined by a person's culture and subculture as well as by the pragmatic requirements of the task at hand. And, as is usual in such cases, experts draw the boundaries more precisely and reliably than laymen. In the instance of colors, the common system of classification is simplified and made more precise and regular for expert use up to the point of precision of discrimination at which it begins to lose its value (because, for instance, individual differences have come to play too large a role).

These ideas are exemplified in the hierarchy of color terms developed in the *Universal Color Language* of the Bureau of Standards and the Inter-Society Color Council. The language is divided into six levels. Level 1, the least precise, consists of 13 terms, the 11 of Berlin and Kay and 'violet' and 'olive.' Level 2 consists of the terms of Level 1 plus sixteen combination terms such as 'purplish pink.' Level 3 comprises the 267 color terms of the ISCC-NBS *Method of Designating Colors* to which we have previously referred (Kelly and Judd 1976). Level 4 is based on color-order systems such as the Munsell system and uses their designations. It comprises about 5,000 terms. Level 5 has about 100,000 designations, which represent visually based extrapolations and interpolations from the standard samples of the Munsell or other systems and are expressed in their notation. Level 6 abandons visual criteria for defining the stimulus and instead relies upon instrumental specification.[38]

The question: What are the boundaries of red? has, in and of itself, no well-defined answer. It is first necessary to specify, explicitly or tacitly, a *context* and a *level of precision* and to realize the margin of error or indeterminacy which that context and level carry with them. This is a lesson we can carry over from our discussion of the laboratory matching cases. Another lesson we must carry over is that we must not be hypnotized by the dogma that color predicates at the same level of specificity and, indeed, colors themselves, exclude each other. For neighboring unique hues and the predicates that go with them, this simply is not so, as that yellow-red which we call 'orange' adequately testifies. Hue exclusions may be handled properly by observing two principles governing binaries: (1) no binary may have complementary hues as its constituents; (2) the sum of the percentages of the constituents of a binary must be 100 per cent. For its part, orange can and does have red as a phenomenal constituent, so worrying about borderline cases between orange and red because orange *excludes* red is disturbing one's peace quite gratuitously.

For each *real-life* color-boundary question, there is a level at which it may be asked and answered in a reasonably objective way, even if the answer is that one is free to legislate as one likes. To settle the question of whether a casually viewed piece of material is orange or red, one could look at it again and consult one's more color-aware mate, treating the question as one to be answered on Level 2, perhaps. If one were stymied and sought further assistance, the sample could be compared under ISSCC-NBS standard conditions to a set of Munsell papers, making as close a match as possible and then referring to the *Method of Designating Colors* for a determination. This would be to ask a Level 3 question. But suppose one were in a fussy frame of mind, noticed that the match was inexact, went to the Really Big Book of Munsell papers, and found that the closest match was to 7R 5/8, which is directly on the boundary between "15—moderate red" and "37—moderate redish orange". What to do? The answer is plain: call it red or reddish orange—as you like. At this stage, one could try visual interpolation, to see whether the sample is really a Munsell 6.5R or perhaps a 7.5R, and decide the issue that way. But this would be to misuse the nomenclature of Level 3 by invoking Level 4 standards of accuracy with respect to which Level 3 concepts are undefined. There is, to be sure, still a fact of the matter as to what color the object appears to have for an individual observer at a particular time, and of how that color is to be specified. But there is *no* fact of the matter as to whether it is correct to label it as red rather than reddish orange.

To recognize that there is, in such a situation, no fact of the matter is to abandon neither realism nor hope of formulating semantic rules, but simply to realize that the nature of our purposes and the capabilities of our natures impose limits on the precision of our utterances.

A P P E N D I X

Land's Retinex Theory of Color Vision

In the 1950s, physicist and inventor Edwin Land, founder of the Polaroid Corporation, was busy with research into the problems involved in devising a self-developing color film for his new instant camera. He had three projectors casting superimposed images of the same still-life on a screen. One projector contained a black-and-white negative of the scene which had been taken with a blue filter and which was projected through a blue filter of the same composition. Another contained a negative taken with and projected through a green filter, while the third held a negative taken with and projected through a red filter. The resultant image contained a full range of natural-looking colors. This was not surprising, since the procedure employed the conventional principles of color photography.

During the course of the work, the blue filter was accidentally removed from its projector, but its omission went unnoticed for a while, because the blues did not vanish from the projected picture. Land found this deeply puzzling, for it flew in the face of what he took to be the standard conception of color vision, first adumbrated by Newton, whom Land is fond of quoting in this context: "Every body reflects the Rays of its own Colour more copiously than the rest, and from their excess and predominance in the reflected Light has its Colour."[1] Land then conducted a series of experiments to investigate the precise conditions under which two-filter color images are generated and how the resultant image colors change with changes in the filters. He concluded that established color theory could not account for these effects, because it was committed to two false propositions: (1) the composition of the light from an area normally specifies the perceived color of that area, and (2) receptoral adaptation suffices to compensate for deviations from normal illumination conditions. Thus, he held, a new approach to the subject was called for, and he set to work to lay the foundations for a novel theory of color vision, the Retinex (*retina-cortex*) Theory.

This burgeoning revolution in color science was extravagantly hailed in many sectors of the popular press and warmly, though more moderately, embraced by the *Scientific American*, which ran Land's "Experiments in Color Vision" as a cover article in 1959. In the succeeding years, that estimable journal has contained no mention whatever of the opponent-process theory which *did* revolutionize color science, although it featured a second cover article by Land in 1977. This, more than anything else, accounts for the widely prevailing assumption among scientifically literate nonspecialists that retinex theory is *the* advanced scientific account of color perception.[2]

Among most visual scientists a very different opinion has prevailed. Land's views were given sharp and detailed criticism by a number of writers (Walls 1960, Judd 1960, and Wilson and Brocklebank 1961). As Land soon acknowledged, the two-filter effects were, at root, colored-shadow phenomena, described in some detail by J. W. Goethe (Goethe 1840; 1970, Part I, section VI) and, even earlier, by Count Rumford. What Land had done (in ignorance of these previous observations) was to devise particularly sophisticated and effective demonstrations of colored shadows, rather similar to those shown in the 1940s by Ralph Evans of Kodak. Indeed, as Leo Hurvich remarked (Hurvich 1969, 162),

> Not widely noticed in the same *Scientific American* issue of 1959 in which Land presented an account of his findings, was the "50 and 100 years ago" column in the front of the magazine which contained a summary of an article published in May 1909 that began: "George Albert Smith and Charles Urban have exhibited very satisfactory moving pictures in approximately natural hues, using only two colors, with the aid of colored lighting projection."

This question of priority is in itself of no great importance, but the fact that colored shadow phenomena were well known to visual scientists, who could not have been blind to their obvious implications (as, indeed, Goethe was not), suggests that Land's description of the tenets of prevailing color-vision theories might represent the understanding of a physicist rather than the understanding of a visual scientist.

How were colored shadows understood by visual scientists? There were, in fact, two chief interpretations, corresponding to the general theories of vision held by the followers of Young and Helmholtz on the one hand, and Hering on the other. Both camps agreed that part of the effect was due to an adaptive von Kries-type shift in the sensitivity of the receptors, and another part due to the effects of simultaneous contrast. They differed, however, in their interpretations of the latter phenomenon. The Helmholtzians, who were in the majority, took simultaneous contrast to involve a quasi-conceptual "discounting of the illuminant", which takes place when one is in possession of various clues about objects and light sources to be had when one typically views a natural scene with recognizable three-dimensional objects, especially objects whose usual color appearance is known to us from previous experiences.[3] Land did successfully undercut this last point by producing an effective two-projector demonstration of an American flag in reversed colors. But such a demonstration could have no force against the position defended by the then-minority of Hering supporters, who held simultaneous contrast to be a biologically based phenomenon of purely automatic character, admitting of no modification by judgmental or judgement-like processes (Hurvich 1969; Walls 1960). The precise anatomical site or sites of such contrast processes was (and to some extent still is) an open question, although opponent-process supporters and Land have tended to agree that post-receptoral neural mechanisms must be involved. But Land's theory gave no new guidance on these points of detail. It was obviously incumbent upon Land to demonstrate the inadequacy of *all* reputable existing analyses of simultaneous contrast or of simultaneous contrast accounts of the "Land effects" if he was to be entitled to the claim that a drastically new theory of color vision was called for. This he did not do, and it is interesting to observe that even the most recent versions of retinex theory, which do allow for opponent processing, do not have any explicit role for simultaneous contrast phenomena (see Shapley 1986).

It is thus apparent that Hering supporters did not in fact acknowledge either of the tenets that Land took to be fundamental to existing color theories, and, indeed, even the advocates of the Young-Helmholtz view would not have embraced them in unqualified form. Despite the criticism from the visual-science community, which was in fact far more detailed than what we have adumbrated here, Land pursued the development of retinex theory for the next twenty-five years, with the assistance of a number of able visual-science collaborators. The larger community of visual scientists found the theory either wrong-headed or gratuitous and, after the initial round of criticism, simply ignored it. Other factors contributed to their neglect: the rehabilitation of the opponent theory at the same time as the first formulation of retinex theory led to a great burst of new work in psychophysics as well as neurophysiology, and the problems of lightness and color constancy fell into the background.

But others who worked outside of traditional psychophysics, particularly those who were interested in machine vision, found Land's work very interesting indeed. For what Land tried to do was to develop retinex theory so as to be simple in principle, general in character, quantitative, and, above all, capable of representation as an algorithm. The last was particularly attractive, for it led to the possibility of constructing computational models of human color vision, and as interest in such models grew, interest in Land's theory grew as well, for it and its variants[4] were the only contenders in the field until the advent of G. Buchsbaum's spatial-processor model (Buchsbaum 1980). Since that time, there has been a surge of interest among visual scientists in algorithmic models of lightness and color constancy.[5] Because retinex theory has been preeminent in this domain, those who wish to displace it must first criticize it. The welcome result has been a set of detailed discussions of its virtues and vices.

The objectives and methods of recent versions of retinex theory are clearly and succinctly laid out by A. Blake (1985):

> The Retinex theory of lightness perception is described in Land and McCann 1971 and in Land 1983. It explains how it is possible, in the restricted world of "Mondrian" images, to compute lightness—the psychophysical correlate of surface reflection—even under highly non-uniform illumination. The theory was motivated by the notable ability of human vision to perceive surface reflectance in apparently adverse illumination conditions: a uniform, white piece of paper continues to look white when moved into shadow, and still appears to be of uniform colour even under a steep illumination gradient (for example, from a nearby point source). Moreover, the theory explains some but not all simultaneous contrast illusions (Marr 1982).
>
> A Mondrian image is defined to consist entirely of patches of uniform reflectance, separated by step edges. In such a restricted world, reflectance variations are not confounded with illumination variations: the reflectance function is piecewise constant—all its variations are assumed to be step changes—whereas the illumination function is assumed everywhere to have a finite gradient. Image intensity is the product of reflectance and illumination so that step changes in intensity indicate step changes in reflectance and any gradual change in intensity corresponds to a variation in illumination. Thus, in principle, the reflectance and illumination functions can be recovered from the image intensity.

Land and McCann propose to perform the recovery in the following way. First colour is treated by identical but independent retinex processes in three colour channels, so that each retinex is effectively a monochrome process. Now, given one of the three intensity functions, step changes in intensity are detected. By measuring the *ratio* of intensities on either side of a step, all information about reflectance is extracted. Within boundaries delineated by step changes, reflectance is constant and the ratio of reflectances in adjacent patches is given by the intensity ratio across their common boundary. The reflectance function can be reconstructed explicitly by first choosing one patch arbitrarily to have reflectance value 1, then the reflectance of any other patch is determined by following a path back to the 1st patch and calculating the product of intensity ratios across all boundaries crossed. The result is independent of the path chosen, for Mondrian images. In this way the reflectance is determined up to a multiplicative constant; Land and McCann suggest that, in a monochrome image, the reflectance function be normalised by finding the patch of highest reflectance in the image, and calling it white. More recently however, Land (1983) has demonstrated an alternative method that involves, for each patch, computing reflectance relative to a number of other patches. For a given waveband, the average of those relative reflectances then forms an absolute designator for that patch and waveband.

There are two fundamental questions to be asked about a scheme such as this. First, do the values that it assigns to the chromatic and achromatic patches in the scene correspond to those seen by human eyes? Second, is it reasonable to believe, given what we now know about the workings of primate visual systems, that a retinex type of scheme is biologically realized in ourselves and our kin? At present, the answers to both questions seem to be qualifiedly negative. Let us consider them in turn.

First, it needs to be said that, given an illuminant consisting of three narrow-band light sources whose relative intensities may be varied and a "Mondrian" of a large number and variety of Munsell colored papers, the Land-McCann retinex scheme's predictions agree with the color estimates made by human observers as well as the observers' estimates agree with one another.[6] But if other, for example, monochromatic, light sources are employed or if papers are used which display a higher degree of metamerism than do the Munsell papers, the Land-McCann algorithm predicts a higher degree of color constancy than the eye will see (Worthey 1985). If, on the other hand, one selects a set of simple Mondrians, each with the same three Munsell test papers as the others but with a different set of six "background" Munsell papers, and a C.I.E. "daylight" illuminant, the 1983 Land algorithm will predict large variations in the appearance of the test papers as the background papers are varied, whereas the human eye will see virtually complete constancy.[7] Finally, it is a distinguishing characteristic of the retinex theory that it sees color processing as based on a more fundamental process, the computation of lightnesses within a particular waveband. This should give one pause, since we now have reason to believe that chromatic and achromatic information is handled in rather different ways by the visual system and that this difference shows up psychophysically in high spatial and temporal achromatic resolution as opposed to low spatial and temporal chromatic resolution (Lennie 1984). In particular, achromatic contrast is facilitated by sharp boundaries between visual areas, whereas chromatic contrast is aided by blurring boundaries. Be this as it may, it should nevertheless be the case that retinex theory should get the perceived lightnesses right in a Mondrian consisting only of achromatic papers. But, because it lacks general resources for handling simultaneous contrast, retinex predictions can be readily falsified by a variety of achromatic Mondrian-type displays (Shapley 1986; cf. Marr 1982, 250–267). And a Mondrian seen in highly chromatic illumination will display chromatic contrast effects which are much better predicted by the old Helson-Judd empirical formulae (Helson 1938, Judd 1940, Judd 1960) than by retinex theory (Jameson 1985).

Predictive failures of a theory are quite as often invitations to improve it as they are grounds for rejecting it, and one's degree of sanguinity about the theory's prospects will be a function of the extent to which one sees the failures as due to oversimplifications, omissions, and the like, rather than to flaws in the basic conceptual structure of the theory. Expert opinion on the prospects of the retinex theory is divided, but it seems clear that it is not the smashing predictive success that some of its advocates take it to be.[8]

How likely is it that mechanisms of the sort posited by retinex theory are embodied in primate visual systems? Some of the most interesting recent words on this subject were written by one of Land's warmest advocates among neurophysiologists, Semir Zeki (1985, 38–39):

> In general, then, one can see that retinex theory, more than the classical theories of colour vision, can provide a framework for cortical experiments in colour vision. But this does not mean that the mode of operation of the nervous system in generating colours is identical, or even similar, to that postulated by retinex theory. Indeed the opposite is the case, for retinex theory supposes that there are three channels, identical to the cone channels, which are maintained separate from the retina to the comparison site somewhere in the central nervous system. The physiological evidence, by contrast, is unequivocal in showing that the signals are mixed at the post-

receptoral level, with the input from one set of cones being opposed by an input of opposite polarity from another. In retinex theory, there is no place for opponency and all colours can be generated by comparing lightnesses generated by each channel.[9] The physiological evidence, by contrast, shows that opponency is an ubiquitous phenomenon of the colour pathways, even if the recent evidence that is reviewed above raises the question of the precise function of such an opponence system. Finally, retinex theory supposes that there are three channels that input to the comparison stage. If one were to judge by the physiological evidence on the peak sensitivities of the double opponent cells (which, to repeat, probably represent an initial stage in the lightness generating system) one could make an argument for the presence of multiple channels that input to the comparison system in the cortex because the peak sensitivities of such cells, unlike the absorption spectra of the cones, are widely distributed throughout the visible spectrum. Hence there are differences between the mechanisms postulated by retinex theory and those used by the nervous system to generate colours, but the end result of both is the same. In other words, whereas the details of the implementation may differ, both types of operation lead to the generation of colour and, moreover, to colours which change little, if at all, with profound changes in the wavelength composition reflected from a single surface.

Whatever one's ultimate assessment of the retinex theory may be, the attention now being given to it gives us good reason to hope that we shall soon have a more detailed, precise and unified account of the mechanisms whereby animals like ourselves are able to distinguish illuminance from reflectance, and a more adequate understanding of the limitations of those mechanisms.

N O T E S

Notes to Chapter I

1. It is about 1/80th of the range of the electromagnetic spectrum (Nassau 1983, p. 24).

2. Nassau 1980, 154. Virtually all of the information about the physics and chemistry of color which is to be found in this section is derived from this source as well as from Nassau 1983. The latter book is the most complete and accessible work on its topic to be found in the literature. What little bit Nassau says about color vision is, however, considerably less authoritative.

3. This is of course in the form of biological signals—"come here," "stay away"—rather than theoretically revealing information. The evolution of wavelength-sensitive receptors in turn prompted the coevolution of color displays in plants and animals.

4. Were it not for the peculiarities of the hydrogen bond that forms when water is in its liquid state, the molecular vibrational energies would be too low for any visible light to be absorbed, and liquid water would have the colorless appearance of live steam.

5. People are often able to see the images of their retinal blood vessels projected on the ceiling when they first open their eyes in the morning, and sudden illumination changes sometimes make the Maxwell spot briefly visible.

6. Actual ganglion cells are more diverse and complex than the following discussion will suggest, but the simplification will suffice for our purposes.

7. Wyszecki and Stiles 1967, 239. The C.I.E. (Commission Internationale de l'Éclairage) average observer is also called the "standard observer." As we shall soon see, there are likely to be small but significant differences between the color perceptions of a given particular observer and one whose performance corresponds to that of the C.I.E. average observer.

8. Grassman's laws are four in number (Grassman 1853):
(1) Every impression of light may be analyzed into three mathematically determinable elements, the hue, the brightness of color, and the brightness of the intermixed white.
(2) If one of two mingling lights is continuously altered (while the other re-

mains unchanged), the impression of the mixed light is also continuously changed.
(3) Two colors, both of which have the same hue and the same proportion of intermixed white, also give identical mixed colors, no matter of what homogeneous colors they may be composed.
(4) The total intensity of any mixture is the sum of the intensities of the lights mixed.

9. The continued use of this terminology is, however, warmly defended in Boynton 1975, 191 fn. The notation that seems to be predominant at present is to label the longwave, middlewave and shortwave cones 'R', 'G', and 'B' respectively. As might be expected, this occasionally produces confusion.

10. This is often called the "Young-Helmholtz theory" and sometimes the "component theory." The terms are nowadays used only historically, since all contemporary theories call for a Young-Helmholtz type of first stage and a Hering type of second stage. A historical discussion of color vision theories may be found in Wasserman 1978.

11. The need for a good wavelength-differentiation system to employ ratios of receptor excitations makes it clear that, given differencing processes between receptor outputs, substantial overlap of those responses is highly *advantageous*.

12. It would not be useful to attempt to survey them here, and a survey would inevitably be both incomplete and out of date. The interested reader is referred to such standard journals as the *Journal of the Optical Society of America, Vision Research,* and *Color Research and Application*. But we shall cite one recent example: Hunt 1982.

13. A very thorough and accessible discussion of chromatic response is to be found in Hurvich 1981, to which much of the present chapter is deeply indebted.

14. Bornstein, Kessen, and Weiskopf 1976. See also the review article, Teller and Bornstein (in press). The Bornstein *et al.* 1976 study has, however, been criticized on the ground that infants have, as Bornstein himself has shown, initial color preferences, so that the infant may stare at *B* more than at *A* even without habituation.

15. When two colorants such as pigments are mixed, the wavelengths that are reflected from the mixture will be the proportional amounts of the wavelengths of the incident light *minus* the proportional amounts of those wavelengths which are absorbed by the two colorants. So the spectral reflectance of the mixed medium which results will depend on the absorbtion spectra of its constituents. Since two materials with the same dominant wavelength may nevertheless have quite different spectral absorption profiles, one cannot tell by the appearance of a colorant exactly what its effect will be as a constituent of a mixture. Experienced painters well know that pigments from

different manufacturers which are nominally the same and look the same often mix differently. Because hue names for colorants underspecify their mixtures properties, the usual "laws" of subtractive color mixture and the "primary colors" which play a role in them are only rough approximations. So colorant mixing is often a complex empirical matter for painters and a difficult calculational problem for industrial users.

16.   The jagged spectral emission profile of fluorescent light tubes is responsible for their notorious color rendering properties, especially with artificial colorants that may themselves have peaky reflectances. Metamerism is usually not a serious problem with natural illuminants and materials, which typically have smoother spectral profiles.

17.   Land, Hubel and Livingstone 1983. A similar situation seems to obtain for simultaneous contrast as well. Retinal models do nicely for Mach-type (short range) lateral inhibition, but not for Hering-type (long range) inhibition, such as that exemplified in figure I-9. The argument for the involvement of higher-level processes in these phenomena of lightness and chromatic contrast is made in Uttal 1981, 849–861.

18.   The issues are vigorously discussed in the various contributions to Ottoson and Zeki (eds.) 1985. See particularly the articles by Jameson and MacLeod. The importance of retinal mechanisms is also stressed in Worthey 1985 and Shapley 1986, although the latter is chiefly concerned with achromatic adaptation.

19.   Derrington, Krauskopf and Lennie, 1984. Hurvich 1985 questions their interpretation of the data.

20.   This has become standard textbook fare. It is well discussed in, e.g., Levine and Shefner 1981, ch. 8, or in Frisby 1980, ch. 3.

21.   Efferent control of retinal function is found in many species, and has been extensively studied in invertebrates. It surely exists in primates, but for technical reasons, little work on brain-to-retina control mechanisms has been done, although a fair amount is known about brain control of eye movements. For the invertebrate work, see Barlow, Chamberlain, and Kass 1984.

22.   See Jacobs 1981, 83–95, for a general discussion of cortical chromatic mechanisms in monkeys. Jacobs' entire survey in his ch. 3, "Mechanisms for color vision," is recommended.

23.   DeValois and DeValois 1975, 138. Cf. Zeki 1973 and 1980. Zeki's contention that area V4 has special significance for the perception of color has been contested in, for example, Krüger and Fischer 1983. The issue is debated in sec. V of Mollon and Sharpe 1983. As of this writing it has not been resolved to general satisfaction, though it now appears that chromatically responsive cells are much more numerous and widely distributed among the various regions of visual cortex than had been earlier supposed.

Notes to Chapter II

1. This use of 'objectivism' and 'subjectivism' comes from Campbell 1969. Some of the following criticism of objectivism is indebted to that excellent article.

2. For a discussion of "validity limits" and "established theories" and their pertinence to revolutions in physical theories, see Rohrlich and Hardin 1983.

3. Polarization of the light can, under special circumstances, have a small effect (the "Haidinger brush" phenomenon). Phase plays a role in interference effects, but only insofar as it governs the wavelength of light that reaches the eye.

4. For a discussion of the unique hues, see Ch I sec. 4.

5. In one sense it is not, because, at its best and at the right wavelengths, the eye is capable of distinguishing wavelengths which differ from one another by as little as one nanometer. But consider the ear, which is not only able to make fine frequency discriminations, but also able to identify very many of the components of a complex waveform. In this respect the eye is severely limited, and that is the root of metamerism.

6. Indeed, there are indefinitely many *metameric* matches for spectral unique yellow. For instance, if an observer's unique yellow were at 575 nm on the spectrum, an appropriate mixture of spectral 550 nm and 650 nm light would match it exactly.

7. There are hidden complications here, such as the observer's adaptive state, which are built into the specification of the opponent-response function. Opponent-response curves, such as those shown in figure I-14, are based on data taken under very restrictive circumstances.

8. This is the approach adopted in Averill 1985. Averill proceeds to suggest how color in the "anthropocentric" sense, i.e., color as we experience it, may be a function of color understood in this physical way. But, as we shall see in the present chapter, perceived color depends upon too many variables besides the properties of matter outside the body for there to be any functional dependence of perceived color on the latter alone.

9. This seems to be the position adopted in Smart 1975. This paper by Smart is ably criticized in Averill, *op cit.*

10. This view is held by a good many philosophers, though they are apt to be squeamish about being labeled "subjectivists." A representative example of the position is Bennett 1971. Cf. his discussion of Locke's "analytic thesis."

11. This fact should give philosophers pause. Cf. Sellars 1956, sec. III: "We thus see that

x is red iff *x* looks red to standard observers in standard conditions is a necessary truth *not* because the right-hand side is the definition of '*x* is red', but because 'standard conditions' means conditions in which things look what they are."

12. Hurvich 1981, 72. You can demonstrate the hue shift for yourself by putting an ordinary frosted lightbulb in front of a white wall, and looking at both the bulb and the wall through a piece of red celluloid. Since the wall is not spectrally selective, the only difference between the light reflected from the wall and that emitted by the bulb will be that the latter is more intense. But you will notice that the bulb seen through the celluloid is yellower than the wall seen through the same celluloid.

13. Hurvich 1981, 175–177. The explanation given here is Hurvich's. There are other interpretations of the effect. Probably it depends upon several factors. See Festinger, Coren and Rivers 1970. A brief review of the literature may be found in Beck 1972, 49–50.

14. "Subjective" colors are fascinating, indeed startling, phenomena. They have no generally accepted explanation, but there are some plausible theories which involve the assignment of different response times to the opponent mechanisms. See Jameson 1972 and Zrenner 1983.

15. Recall the discussion of stabilized images in Chapter I.

16. The spectral curves for these may be found in Wyszecki and Stiles 1967 or Judd and Wyszecki 1963. It is interesting to notice that neither source B nor source C has an equal-energy spectrum.

17. In any study of the psychophysics of color in which chromatic-response curves are derived, the curves for one observer will differ from those of another. The variation between observers will generally exceed the variations in performance of the same observer. It is interesting to notice that the chromatic-response curves for the C.I.E. average observer, which are derived in the same article from which figures II-5 A and B were taken, are different from *both* of those curves.

18. Published in Baltimore by Munsell Color, a division of the Macbeth Company, which is a division of the Kollmorgen Corporation. Post-1968 editions correspond to the current standards. For our guesstimates, the differences between editions are not important.

19. There are occasional cases in which otherwise normal observers have strikingly deviant loci for a unique hue other than green. Most observers have a unique-yellow locus quite close to 577 nm, but one normal trichromat proved to have her unique yellow at 536 nm! Most people would see this as a yellowish green. See Akit, Ejima, and Takahashi 1982.

20. This may seem to understate the case, given that color (including achromatic color) differences define visual shapes. But some people suffering from

neurological disorders do report that colors detach themselves from the surfaces of objects in various ways. See Critchley 1965.

21. For an extensive review of the literature on this subject, see Beck 1972.

22. The problems of color rendition for realist painters and photographers receive a nice discussion in chapters 19 and 20 of Evans 1948.

23. Evans 1948, 163. Evans's whole discussion of brightness perception in chapter 10 is warmly recommended.

24. Ibid. On the other hand, experience with the NCS color system suggests that with the proper conceptual scheme and a modicum of training, unsophisticated observers can attain surprising levels of reliability in color identification without the use of a material standard. However, reasonable control of the illumination is required. See Chapter III.

25. This term, so widely used by the general public, is usually avoided by color scientists because it has at least five distinct but easily confusable senses. "Shade is the most overworked of the colorant terms." (Judd and Wyszecki 1963)

26. The C.I.E. average observer was established to standardize color-mixture functions and metameric matches, not to serve as a standard for unique hues. But given the color-mixture functions, the chromatic response functions and their neutral points—the unique-hue loci—can be calculated. Hurvich and Jameson (1957) did just this. The unique-green locus for the Average Observer was different from that for either of their experimental subjects.

27. There is no single choice of aperture surround which is neutral for all colors; a light gray will interact with dark colors, and a dark gray will interact with light colors.

28. McCollough 1965. There is a very large literature on this phenomenon. A nice discussion is Harris 1980.

29. The investigation of these effects has been a major industry in perceptual psychology of the last decade. Discussions may be found in Harris (ed.) 1980, Blakemore 1973, Frisby 1980, and Levine and Shefner 1981, just to mention a few.

30. But notice that at the point at which she begins to report color, she will detect the stimulus 20 per cent of the time and, for almost all of these presentations she will still report no color.

31. See the superb discussion of optical mixture, the spreading effect, and "Les Poseuses" in Homer 1964, beginning on p. 164.

32. Festinger, Coren, and Rivers 1970. The data from this study suggest that Hurvich's explanation of the effect in terms of variation in receptive-field sizes (Hurvich 1981, 175–177) is not the whole story.

33. Sanford 1981 makes a very similar criticism of Jackson's sense-datum theory. The present argument was arrived at independently.

34. See Price's contribution to Schilpp 1959 along with Broad's response.

35. That is, they are neither reddish nor yellowish nor bluish nor greenish.

Notes to Chapter III

1. These are pairs of hue perceptions produced by light stimuli which, when mixed in appropriate proportions, will yield an achromatic response. See the discussion of the Hurvich-Jameson cancellation procedures in Chapter I.

2. A qualification is in order here. This is not a full-blooded vector space. For instance, there is no well-defined operation of vectoral addition.

3. Hård and Sivik 1981, 137. This level of average accuracy is quite remarkable, considering that the comparison standard is a mental one. These results do not compromise our earlier insistence on the variability among normal observers, for this variability falls within the limits found in the NCS studies. As we previously observed, the disagreements among normal observers that arise as a result of their perceptual differences are too small to show up in most of the color-naming tasks in everyday life.

4. The exception is elementary red. We recall that unique red is to be found in the spectrum only at low light levels. At moderate levels, all spectral reds are slightly yellowish.

5. But the unit sizes of the Hue, Value, and Chroma steps in the Munsell system are not equal from one dimension to the other. See Kuehni 1983, 61.

6. However, the number of distinguishable *hues* is about 160.

7. If the neural circuitry involved in sensuous imagining were at least in part the circuitry involved in perceiving, it would not be surprising that we should be unable to imagine that which we are unable through normal means to perceive. There is some evidence of such an overlap in the circuitry. For one thing, people can sometimes confuse sensings and imaginings. Subjects were instructed to imagine an apple being displayed on a screen. A real but dim picture was projected on the screen. The subjects did not detect it as real, even though it was plainly visible to bystanders (Perky 1910). Another experiment involved changes in electrical potentials at electrodes planted on the scalp near the visual cortex, the *visual evoked response*. Subjects were first asked to look at sequences of visual stimuli, in this case, circles and squares. The corresponding VERs were recorded and averaged. Circles yielded one characteristic response pattern, squares another. The same subjects were then asked to imagine circles and squares. The averaged VERs for the imagined circles had similar profiles to the averaged visual VERs for the perceived circles, and the averaged VERs for the imagined and perceived squares also resembled one another (Herrington and Schneider 1968).

8.   In the 1950s and 1960s there was a considerable literature on the problem of the incompatibility of color. Some examples are Putnam 1956 and 1957, Pap 1957, Remnant 1961, Radford 1965, and Kenner 1965. Of these, it was Radford 1965 which separated out the issues in the most satisfactory way (the standard for judging this is, of course, its agreement with the positions taken in the present discussion!). The incompatibility of colors was, apparently, what led Wittgenstein to abandon the doctrines of the *Tractatus* (see Austin 1980 and Hacker 1972). Wittgenstein continued to try to find the solution to the problems of the relationships among the colors in the use of color language (see, for instance, the *Remarks on Color*), but his analyses of these relationships and those of his followers were always short of the mark. This is because, as we shall see in our discussion of color language, our experience of color shapes the way we describe it; the structure of color space is not established by convention.

9.   There is no doubt that the reports are both reflective and sincere. In a personal communication, Plantanida writes:

Hew and I were about as amazed as you were by the results of our experiments. . . . When I participated as a subject in the experiment, I experienced three of the percepts commonly reported by our subjects. Most of the time the field appeared to be a single binary color composed of both red and green. Occasionally, I would see an island composed of a cluster of very tiny spots of one color, say red, superimposed upon a field of another color, in this case, green, that did not appear to have any punctate structure. Very rarely, I experienced a grainy mixture of red and green in which I was able to perceive just barely resolvable red dots and green dots. This latter percept was rather fleeting in nature and was always preceded by and dissolved into the non-textured binary color. Hew, on the other hand, reported the occurrence of the grainy mixture of red and green much more frequently than the uniform binary color. . . . In response to your question about the possibility of subjects misdescribing what they saw, I can state with certainty that when I saw the single binary color, it was just that: and when I saw the grainy array of red and green dots, it was perceptibly different from the binary color experience. Our subjects spontaneously reported the three major categories of color experience outlined in our article. When a subject reported a binary color, we questioned them about whether the color appeared to be composed of minute colored spots. Most often, subjects reported that they saw an array of tiny dots, but they also saw binary colors not composed of arrays of dots.

10.   For this reason, one ought not to appeal to such asymmetries in an attempt to argue that spectral inversion is impossible. This is what distinguishes the line of attack on the spectral inversion problem which will be taken in the present essay from those which were employed (in rather different ways) by Harrison 1973 and Clark 1985c. The issue of what is essential and what is accidental to the colors is vexing, however, and is not adequately resolved in these pages.

11.   The matter is very complicated. Sivik 1976 finds that excitement, as characterized by semantic scales, correlates with chromaticity rather than with hue. Wright and Rainwater 1962 concur on the importance of chromaticity, but other studies, along with a considerable tradition, stress hue differences. But the warm-cool distinction does seem to be strongly correlated with hue on every account.

12. The physiological evidence, summarized and criticized in Kaiser 1984, is equivocal, to some extent because the data are methodologically flawed, but on balance it suggests that the red-yellow group is more arousing than the blue-green group. There are undoubtedly many different variables which need careful separation, both because the dimensions of color themselves interact and because civilization's overlay of conventions and colored objects devoid of biological significance has dulled the potency of color as a biological signal. See Humphrey 1976.

13. " . . . it has been shown in electrophysiological experiments that neurons having an input from the fovea can be found in the monkey superior colliculus." (Jacobs 1981, 91) The superior colliculus has a pivotal role in the regulation of eye movement.

14. Here, as elsewhere, the term 'phenomenal' is not meant to carry all the epistemic burdens of 'appears'; in our sense, a phenomenal property is not to be understood as being a property something has just in case it appears to have it.

15. Similarities and connections between touch and hearing are explored in much of the work of Georg von Békésy. See, for instance, von Békésy 1959.

16. In a private communication, Levine suggests that the polarity could be separated from the experienced hue, leaving a "residue" of phenomenal green.

17. Fuld, Werner and Wooten 1983. Further investigations have made the case for brown's being an elementary color rather murky. See Hurvich 1985.

18. The reader may also wonder, since nothing we have said so far would suggest why color space is to be represented by a sphere rather than some other three-dimensional solid. And, indeed, as one might have expected from the general fact that differences in the particulars of a color system will reflect differences in the features of color experiences or colorants that one wishes to emphasize, the solid chosen has varied from one author to another. Ebbinghaus, for instance, adopted a double pyramid, with black at one apex, white at the other, and the unique hues along the diagonals of the base, in order to articulate the fundamental psychological role of these hues. Munsell, on the other hand, gave no pride of place to the unique hues, choosing instead to give more weight to such considerations as equalizing the number of equal perceptual hue steps from one hue category to another, and letting the artist's subtractive complements lie approximately across from one another. So he chose a hue circle. But both Munsell and Ebbinghaus wanted to represent the fact that as colors approach either black or white in lightness, the perceptual hue differences among them diminish. So in both cases, planes of equal lightness (which will be perpendicular to the achromatic axis) will be reduced in area as one approaches either the black or the white pole. If one chooses to describe the hue circuit at each brightness or lightness as a circle with the achromatic axis at its center (as in H-B-S space), the resulting solid will be a sphere.

19. Quoted in Berlin and Kay 1969, 159.

20. The wisdom of the 1950s seems to have persisted well past 1970. Witness these remarks from Quine 1973, 71:

We speak of sameness of color to mean matching and most red surfaces do not match. Sameness of color, ordinarily so called, is not sameness of color in the sense in which red is a color. The very notion of *a* color, in the latter sense, is unnatural. Whether some arbitrary interval in the spectrum is a color, in this sense, depends on the casual matter of their being a word for it; and this matter of vocabulary varies from culture to culture. The notion of a color, in this sense, is less basic than the notion of a color word.

Wittgenstein and his followers of course endorse a similar position. Here, for example, is Hacker (1972, 160) on Wittgenstein:

We have a colour system, as we have a number system. Do these systems reside in the nature of numbers and colours or in *our* nature? (*Zettel*, 357). *Not* in the nature of numbers or colours, is Wittgenstein's emphatic reply. We are continually tempted to take our grammar as a projection of reality, instead of taking our conception of the structure of reality to be a projection of our grammar. For we are driven to justify our grammar by reference to putative facts about the world, e.g. 'But there really are four primary colours'. So we think of our concepts of colour as justified, for they characterize the world as it is. For I *would* look in vain for a fifth primary colour; we put the four primary colours together because they are similar and we contrast colour with shapes and notes because they are different (*Zettel*, 331). It is against the conception of this sort of justification . . . that the claim that grammar is arbitrary is directed. The relevant sense in which grammar is arbitrary is the doctrine of the autonomy of grammar.

21. Quoted in Berlin and Kay 1969, 160.

22. Think of the stereotypical representation of the rainbow as consisting of colored bands. Though we recognized it as a stylization, we do not see it as a serious distortion of the truth; we object to it far less than to a representation in which the colors are out of order.

23. This linguistic confounding of blue and green occurs frequently (Berlin and Kay, Appendix II) and seems to be paralleled by a psychological difficulty many people have in agreeing on whether various objects are to be called "blue" or "green." More about this later.

24. Munsell 1946. There are discussions of the Munsell system in Kuehni 1983, 60–62, and Judd and Wyszecki 1963, 221–234. A more technical treatment is in Wyszecki and Stiles 1967.

25. 'Hue', 'Value' and 'Chroma' are technical terms in the Munsell system. They are capitalized to distinguish them from their non-Munsell counterparts.

26. "The dominant wavelength of a color indicates what part of the spectrum has to be mixed with some neutral standard to match the given color"

(Judd and Wyszecki 1963, 137). There has occasionally been a tendency on the part of some authors to confuse or to attempt to identify hue with dominant wavelength. This is, as we have already argued, a mistake. The relation between the two concepts is discussed by Judd and Wyszecki on pages 137, 337, and 352.

27. This is a crude estimate based on casual inspection of the published data in a variety of experiments in the course of which the subjects' unique hues were fixed.

28. The case for red's special status is well made in Humphrey 1976:

I shall list briefly some of the particular evidence which demonstrates how, in a variety of contexts, red seems to have a very special significance for man. (1) Large fields of red light induce physiological symptoms of emotional arousal—changes in heart rate, skin resistance and the electrical activity of the brain. (2) In patients suffering from certain pathological disorders, for instance cerebellar palsy, these physiological effects become exaggerated—in cerebellar patients red light may cause intolerable distress, exacerbating the disorders of posture and movement, lowering pain thresholds and causing a general disruption of thought and skilled behaviour. (3) When the affective value of colours is measured by a technique, the 'semantic differential', which is far subtler than a simple preference test, men rate red as a 'heavy', 'powerful', 'active', 'hot' colour. (4) When the 'apparent weight' of colours is measured directly by asking men to find the balance point between two discs of colour, red is consistently judged to be the heaviest. (5) In the evolution of languages, red is without exception the first colour word to enter the vocabulary. . . . (6) In the development of a child's language red again usually comes first, and when adults are asked simply to reel off colour words as fast as they can they show a very strong tendency to start with red. (7) When colour vision is impaired by central brain lesions, red vision is most resistant to loss and quickest to recover.

29. I.e., no more difficulty than other people do. Rosch 1973.

30. Wright 1975, 338–339. The issues Wright addresses here have inspired a spate of recent papers: Dummett 1975 and 1979; Peacocke 1981; Linsky 1984; Travis 1985. Of particular interest is Parikh 1983.

31. In a private communication, visual scientist Davida Teller disputes this claim. In her view, what happens is that small peripherally presented chromatic stimuli look more desaturated than foveally presented ones (red, it is generally agreed, is an exception), and so they can presumably be matched one to one to desaturated foveal stimuli. There are several comments to be made in reply. First, one can to some extent judge for oneself. The present writer finds the chromatic deliverances of his peripheral vision to be unequivocally "generic." Second, it is plain that peripheral visual shape does have this generic quality, and the philosophical freight could be delivered by this fact alone. Third, the number of distinguishable hue steps is reduced as a sample becomes progressively less saturated, so it would be true that *in foveal vision*, a given desaturated sample could equally well (or badly) match *in hue* several close, but distinct saturated samples. So, even if Teller is right, the problem of generic hues could be rooted in desaturation. But, finally, at least some of those who have done the experimental work on peripheral hue nam-

ing seem to think that there is a factor besides desaturation in peripheral color vision. Here are some quotations from Gordon and Abramov (1977): "At these eccentricities (50, 40, and 72 degrees), color-matching functions are grossly different from foveal ones, and lights, especially from the middle of the spectrum, appear desaturated and of uncertain hue" (p. 202). "Subjects often commented that, in the periphery, hues were often somewhat uncertain; the exception was red: whenever any red appeared in a stimulus, subjects had much more confidence in their judgements . . . in the periphery, the small (1.5 degree) target was generally achromatic and of uncertain hue" (p. 204). "It is worth noting that subjects generally used two of the four hues, together with the achromatic category, to describe any light. Virtually no light was seen as totally saturated or of unique hue; red and green were never seen simultaneously; very rarely (one subject) blue, green and yellow were used together" (p. 204).

32. Figure III-6 and its description are adapted from Barlow and Mollon 1982, 4–5.

33. The kind of situation being alluded to here is not metameric matching in general, but the circumstance in which the subject has to decide, given a series of randomly presented pairings of color samples (light spots, say) in which there are small differences between the dominant wavelengths of some of the samples, whether or not a particular pair match in color. This is the typical "difference threshold" experiment. In what follows, we apply to such experiments the kind of signal detection analysis which is more commonly applied to the determination of "absolute thresholds."

34. That is, having the form of a normal or "bell-shaped" curve.—CLH.

35. Signal-detection theory, on which the following discussion is based, was first advanced as an analysis of communication problems in electrical engineering in the early 1950s and was applied to psychophysics a few years later. An early collection of papers edited by one of the pioneers in psychophysical applications is Swets 1964. A more recent discussion of theoretical issues is Vickers 1979. Elementary expositions of signal detection theory are to be found in recent psychophysics texts such as Levine and Shefner 1981.

36. Fourier analysis tells us that the shorter the time of emission of a signal, the greater the range of frequencies it must contain. A wave packet of zero temporal width—one that exists only at an instant—must have infinitely many frequency components. The indeterminacy relations in quantum mechanics illustrate the same basic natural fact.

37. As a rough check on this conjecture, one may find the spectrum locus of the 75 per cent red, 25 per cent yellow phenomenal estimate in a color-naming experiment such as those described in Werner and Wooten 1979, and locate a Munsell Hue chip that has a dominant wavelength close to that spectral locus. The association of a dominant wavelength with a Munsell chip may be made by means of the Munsell-C.I.E. conversion charts in Wyszecki and Stiles 1967. In the present case, the locus is about 620 nm, and the

roughly corresponding Munsell Hue for a chip of high Chroma and middle Value is 7.5 Red. If we then consult the National Bureau of Standards color-designation system, we find that such a chip is described as "moderate reddish orange" and is immediately adjacent to the region specified as "moderate red". As a further check, it is interesting to look up the red and orange category boundaries that Berlin and Kay marked down for American English. Their informants included this same Munsell chip within the boundaries of both 'red' and 'orange' (Berlin and Kay 1969, 119).

38. The instrumental specification, such as the 1932 C.I.E. standard, will be useful for predicting color matching, but not color appearance. Level 6 is thus somewhat differently conceived than the other levels. The 1932 C.I.E. system is widely used for industrial and commercial purposes. It would not have served our purposes in the present work to explain the assumptions and applications of the system, except to observe that it is intended to capture in standard form the color matches made by an average observer. Interested readers may find satisfactory accounts in many general books on color such as Kuehni 1983, Hurvich 1981, Evans 1948, Judd and Wyszecki 1963, and Boynton 1979.

Notes to the Appendix

1. Newton 1730; 1952. Proposition X, Problem V. Quoted in Land 1985.

2. Certainly this supposition has been made by a considerable number of able philosophers, who have attempted to extract philosophical morals from Land's theory. Some representative examples are McGilvray 1983, Campbell 1982, and Churchland 1986. (Of these authors, Campbell is most aware of some of the problems with retinex theory, although he seems unaware that none of them arises with opponent theory.) Had their attention been directed to opponent theory instead, the present work might never have been written.

3. This view is ably advocated in the interpretation of the "Land effects" by Judd 1960. Such an approach to color phenomena is very like the interpretation of visual illusions to be found in Gregory 1973.

4. Such as Horn 1974. For a criticism of Horn's model and a retinex-based alternative to it, see Blake 1985.

5. The most recent manifestation of this is an unusually interesting feature section of the *Journal of the Optical Society of America A* dedicated to articles on the topic of computational approaches to color vision. See Krauskopf 1986.

6. McCann, McKee, and Taylor 1976. This paper is a particularly thorough and thoughtful defense of retinex theory.

7. Brainard and Wandell 1986. This effect occurs because the algorithm is normalized by reference to a mean value of the paper lightnesses. If the papers are selected so as to give a large variation in the mean value from one

Mondrian to the next, the estimate of the test papers will vary correspondingly. One would expect that the McCann-Land procedure could be defeated by a similar strategy.

8. There are, of course, those who would say this about Hurvich-Jameson opponent-process theory. The difference is that everyone is agreed that opponent mechanisms play a very important role in color vision, whereas the same cannot be said of the mechanisms posited by retinex theory.

9. Note by CLH: Actually, a place for opponency has been made in retinex theory, but only in a peripheral way. McCann, McKee, and Taylor (1976) propose that opponency functions as a transmission expedient from retina to visual cortex, with the three retinex channels reconstituted in the cortex. This now seems implausible. Alternatively, the nervous system can be taken to perform a transformation from retinex to opponent coordinates (Livingstone and Hubel 1984).

A Glossary of Some Technical Terms

Most of the entries in this glossary are definitions from the most recent edition of the *International Lighting Vocabulary* (International Commission on Illumination 1970), which is now being revised. These definitions are marked as 'CIE' followed by the standard reference number in the *Vocabulary*. Some other definitions are drawn from Levine and Shefner 1981, and credited accordingly, and a few are my own, based on various sources.

achromatic color (perceived)
Perceived color devoid of hue. (CIE 45-35-145)

achromatic color (psychophysical)
Psychophysical color of zero purity. (CIE 45-25-150) ('Purity' is a colorimetric term referring to a property of color stimuli—CLH)

adaptation
Change of sensitivity in response to different levels of stimulation.

anomalous trichromat
A trichromatic visual observer who makes some color matches that differ substantially from the matches of most trichromats.

aperture (perceived) colors
Color perceived as non-located in depth such as that perceived as filling a hole in a screen. (CIE 45-25-175)

average observer (colorimetric)
1. CIE 1931 standard colorimetric observer: Receptor of radiation whose colorimetric characteristics correspond to the spectral tristimulus values adopted by the International Commission on Illumination in 1931. (Uses observing field of angular subtense between 1 degree and 4 degrees.) (CIE 45-15-050)
2. CIE 1964 supplementary standard colorimetric observer: Receptor of radiation whose colorimetric characteristics correspond to the spectral tristimulus values adopted by the International Commission on Illumination in 1964. (Uses observing field of angular subtense greater than 4 degrees. (CIE 45-15-055)

Bezold-Brücke phenomenon
Change in the hue of the (perceived) color with change in luminance level within the range of photopic vision. (CIE 45-25-080) (Photopic vision is cone-mediated rather than rod-mediated (scotopic) vision—CLH)

brightness (British: luminosity)
Attribute of visual sensation according to which an area appears to emit more or less light. Note: This attribute is the psychosensorial correlate, or nearly so, of the photometric quantity *luminance*. (CIE 45-25-210)

chroma
Attribute of a visual sensation which permits a judgment to be made of the amount of pure chromatic color present, irrespective of the amount of achromatic color. Note: For colors of the same luminosity and hue, equal sensation intervals of saturation and chroma are identical. In a series of perceived colors of constant saturation, the *chroma* increases with the luminosity. This attribute is the psychosensorial correlate, or nearly so, of the colorimetric quantity *chrominance*. (CIE 45-25-235)

chromatic color (perceived)
Perceived color possessing a hue. Note: In everyday speech the word *color* is often used in this sense in contradistinction to white, black, or gray. The adjective *colored* usually refers to chromatic color. (CIE 45-25-135)

chromatic color (psychophysical)
Psychophysical color of greater than zero purity and hence possessing a dominant or complementary wavelength. (CIE 45-25-140)

CIE standard illuminants
The colorimetric illuminants A, B, C and D_{65}, defined by the C.I.E. in terms of relative spectral energy [power] distributions:
standard illuminant A, representing the full radiator at $T_{68} = 2,855.6$ degrees K(elvin);
standard illuminant B, representing direct sunlight with a correlated color temperature of $T_{68} = 4,874$ degrees K;
standard illuminant C, representing daylight with a correlated temperature of $T_{68} = 6,774$ degrees K;
standard illuminant D_{65}, representing daylight with a correlated color temperature of $T_{68} = 6,504$ degrees K. (CIE 45-15-145)

colorimetry
Measurement of colors, made possible by the properties of the eye and based on a set of conventions. (CIE 45-30-050)

colorimetry, visual
Colorimetry (photometry) in which the eye is used to make the comparisons. (CIE 45-30-055)

color (perceived)
Aspect of visual perception by which an observer may distinguish differences between two fields of view of the same size, shape and structure, such as may be caused by differences in the spectral composition of the radiation concerned in the observation. (CIE 45-25-130.1)

color (psychophysical)
Characteristic of a visible radiation by which an observer may distinguish differences between two fields of view of the same size, shape and structure, such as may be caused by differences in the spectral composition of the radiation concerned in the observation. (CIE 45-25-130.2)

complementary colors (additive)
Two color stimuli are complementary when it is possible to reproduce a specified achromatic stimulus by a suitable additive mixture of these two stimuli. (CIE 45-15-245)

complementary wavelength (of a color stimulus)
Wavelength of the monochromatic light stimulus that, when combined in suitable proportions with the color stimulus considered, yields a match with the specified achromatic light stimulus. (CIE 45-15-120)

cones
Special retinal receptor elements which are presumed to be primarily concerned with perception of light and color stimuli when the eye is adapted to light. (CIE 45-25-025)

contrast (subjective sense)
Subjective assessment of the difference in appearance of two parts of a field of view seen simultaneously or successively. (Hence: luminosity contrast, lightness contrast, color contrast, simultaneous contrast, successive contrast). (CIE 45-25-265) (The "objective sense" of 'contrast' is specified as a mathematical relationship between luminances—CLH)

criterion
In signal detection theory, an intensity sufficient to prompt a decision that a stimulus was present. (Levine and Shefner 1981)

d'
In signal detection theory, a measure of the discriminative capability of an observer.

dichromat
A color deficient perceiver for whom two colored lights suffice to produce a hue match with any arbitrary colored light.

diffraction
Deviation of the direction of propagation of a radiation, determined by the wave nature of radiation, and occurring when the radiation passes the edge of an obstacle. (CIE 45-05-100)

dominant wavelength (of a color stimulus, not purple)
Wavelength of the monochromatic light stimulus that, when combined in suitable proportions with the specified achromatic light stimulus, yields a

match with the color stimulus considered. Note: When the dominant wavelength cannot be given (this applies to purples) its place is taken by the complementary wavelength. (CIE 45-15-115)

fovea
Central part of the yellow spot, thinner and hence depressed, containing almost exclusively cones and forming the site of most distinct vision. It corresponds to a region of the external field 0.017 to 0.035 rad (1 to 2 degrees) in diameter. (CIE 45-25-040)

ganglion cells
Retinal cells that receive stimulation from other retinal cells and, in turn, stimulate cells in the lateral geniculate nucleus. The axons of ganglion cells form the optic nerve.

hue
Attribute of visual sensation which has given rise to color names, such as: blue, green, yellow, red, purple, etc. Note: This attribute is the psychosensorial correlate, or nearly so, of the colorimetric quantity *dominant wavelength*. (CIE 45-25-215)

illuminance; illumination (at a point of a surface)
Quotient of the luminous flux incident on an element of the surface containing the point, by the area of that element. (CIE 45-10-100)

interference
Attentuation or reinforcement of the amplitudes of the vibrations of a radiation, occurring where coherent wave-trains overlap. (CIE 45-05-095)

irradiance
Quotient of the radiant flux incident on an element of the surface containing the point, by the area of that element. (CIE 45-05-160)

lateral geniculate nucleus (LGN)
Portion of the thalamus that receives signals from ganglion cells and relays them to the visual cortex.

lateral inhibition
Condition in which responses from one area of a receptive field oppose the responses from another area. (Levine and Shefner 1981)

lightness
Attribute of visual sensation in accordance with which a body seems to transmit or reflect diffusely a greater or smaller fraction of the incident light. Note: This attribute is the psychosensorial correlate, or nearly so, of the photometric quantity *luminance factor*. (CIE 45-25-225)

luminance (in a given direction, at a point on the surface of a source or a receptor, or at a point on the path of a beam.)

Quotient of the luminous flux leaving, arriving at, or passing through an element of surface at this point and propagated in directions defined by an elementary cone containing the given direction, by the product of the solid angle of the cone and the area of the orthogonal projection of the element of surface on a plane perpendicular to the given direction. (CIE 45-10-080)

luminous flux
Quantity derived from radiant flux by evaluating the radiation according to its action upon a selective receptor, the spectral sensitivity of which is defined by the standard spectral luminance efficiencies. (CIE 45-10-020)

macula lutea; yellow spot
Central part of the retina, containing a yellow pigment. (CIE 45-25-035)

Maxwell spot
The image of the macula lutea, fleetingly seen with a change in the spectral character of the incident light.

metameric color simuli; metamers
Spectrally different radiations that produce the same color under the same viewing conditions. Note: The corresponding property is called *metamerism*. (CIE 45-15-250)

monochromatic radiation
Radiation characterized by a single frequency. By extension, radiation of a very small range of frequencies or wavelengths, which can be described by stating a single frequency or wavelength. (CIE 45-05-010)

nanometer
One billionth of a meter. Formerly the millimicron, the nanometer is the standard unit of wavelength measurement.

optic disk
Receptor-free portion of the retina where the optic nerve leaves the eyeball.

photometry
The measurement of light weighted according to its effectiveness in stimulating human visual response.

psychophysics
The measurement of an organism's sensory response capabilities.

radiance (in a given direction, at a point on the surface of a source or a receptor, or at a point on the path of a beam)
Quotient of the radiant flux leaving, arriving at, or passing through an element of surface at this point and propagated in directions defined by an elementary cone containing the given direction, by the product of the solid angle of the cone and the area of the orthogonal projection of the element of surface on a plane perpendicular to the given direction. (CIE 45-05-150)

radiant flux
Power emitted, transferred, or received in the form of radiation. (CIE 45-05-135)

receptive field (retinal)
Area of the retina which, when stimulated, causes a particular neuron to respond.

reflectance
Ratio of the reflected radiant or luminous flux to the incident flux. (CIE 45-20-040)

related (perceived) color
Color perceived to belong to an area or object in relation to other perceived colors in the visual field. (CIE 45-25-160)

retina
A thin light-sensitive layer of neural tissue on the inside rear portion of the eye.

rods
Special retinal receptor elements which are presumed to be primarily concerned with perception of light stimuli when the eye is adapted to darkness. (CIE 45-25-030)

saturation
Attribute of a visual sensation which permits a judgment to be made of the proportion of pure chromatic color in the total sensation. Note: This attribute is the psychosensorial correlate, or nearly so, of the colorimetric quantity *purity*. (CIE 45-25-225)

sensitivity
Inverse of the stimulus required for a criterion response. (Levine and Shefner 1981).

spectrum (of a radiation)
1. Spatial display of a complex radiation produced by separation of its monochromatic components.
2. Composition of a complex radiation. (CIE 45-05-040)

stabilized retinal images
Stimuli that do not move across the retina when the eye moves.

surface (perceived) color
Color perceived to belong to the surface of a non-self-luminous object. (Adapted from CIE 45-25-165)

signal detection theory
Psychophysical theory in which the detectability of a stimulus replaces the classical "threshold." (Levine and Shefner 1981)

threshold
Minimal perceptible quantity. (Levine and Shefner 1981)

transmittance
Ratio of the transmitted radiant or luminous flux to the incident flux. (CIE 45-20-085)

trichromat
A normal visual perceiver who requires three colored lights to provide a hue match for an arbitrary colored light.

tristimulus values (of a color stimulus)
Amounts of the three reference or matching stimuli required to give a match with the color stimulus considered, in a given trichromatic system. (CIE 45-15-060)

unrelated (perceived) color
Color perceived to belong to an area with completely dark surroundings. Note: The color appears self-luminous. (CIE 45-25-155)

Further Reading

The literature on the scientific aspects of color and color vision is staggeringly large, but there are surprisingly few books that are well-written, directed to the intelligent layperson, and accurate. Here are five books that I have read with profit and interest:

Leo M. Hurvich, *Color Vision*. Sunderland, Mass.: Sinauer Associates, 1981.
  A lucid introduction to the subject, with many excellent illustrations, written from the point of view of modern opponent-process theory by one of its co-founders. Begin your reading here.

Rolf Kuehni, *Color: Essence and Logic*. New York: Van Nostrand Rhinehold, 1983.
  An ideal introduction to various aspects of color for those who like their introductions to be concise without being shallow or inaccurate. Kuehni is a color technologist, and his treatment of color order systems is especially useful.

Ralph M. Evans, *An Introduction to Color*. New York: John Wiley and Sons, 1948.
  What Evans has to say about the visual system is of course dated, but there are many interesting discussions of the phenomena of (approximate) constancy and the plurality of factors that influence color appearance. With the current emphasis on algorithms for constancy, it is useful to have Evans remind us of the psychological and judgemental aspects of the bundle of phenomena that fall under this category. The book has numerous illustrations of various color phenomena.

Deane B. Judd and Günter Wyszecki, *Color in Business, Science and Industry*, 3rd edition. New York: John Wiley and Sons, 1975.
  This is a classic textbook and useful reference work. As its title suggests, the book's principal emphasis is on color technology. And what a complicated business that is! Unlike Evans' book, this is to be dipped into mainly for information. It does not go overly far in combining business (or science and industry) with pleasure.

Kurt Nassau, *The Physics and Chemistry of Color: The Fifteen Causes of Color*. New York: John Wiley and Sons, 1983.
  Everything you've always wanted to know about the physical basis of color stimuli, and much more. To the best of my knowledge, there is no other book like this one. Although it is not forbidding to the lay person, it will be read with profit mostly by those who have at least a passing acquaintance with modern physics or chemistry. It has virtually nothing useful to say about visual science, but that was not its purpose.

B I B L I O G R A P H Y

Akita, M., Ejima, Y., and Takahashi, S. 1982. Differences of unique yellow loci between individuals. *Color Research and Application*, v. 7 n. 2 pt. 2, 168–172.

Albers, J. 1963. *Interaction of color*. New Haven: Yale University Press.

American Society for Testing and Materials 1968. Standard method of specifying color by the Munsell system. Designation D 1535-68. Philadelphia: ASTM.

Anderson, Jr., R. M. 1974. The illusions of experience. In Cohen *et al.* (eds.) 1974, 549–561.

Armstrong, D. M. 1961. *Perception and the physical world*. London: Routledge and Kegan Paul.

Armstrong, D. M. 1968. *A materialist theory of the mind*. London: Routledge and Kegan Paul.

Armstrong, D. M. 1969. Colour-realism and the argument from microscopes. In Brown and Rollins (eds.) 1969, 119–131.

Armstrong, D. M. 1978. *A theory of universals*. Vol. II of *Universals and scientific realism*. Cambridge: Cambridge University Press.

Armstrong, D. M. 1979. Perception, sense data and causality. Ch. 4 of Mac-Donald (ed.) 1979.

Arnheim, R. 1974. *Art and visual perception*. Berkeley and Los Angeles: University of California Press.

Austin, J. 1980. Wittgenstein's solution to the color exclusion problem. *Philosophy and Phenomenological Research* 41, 142–149.

Austin, J. L. 1962. *Sense and sensibilia*. Oxford: Oxford University Press.

Autrum, H. (ed.) 1979. *Comparative physiology and evolution of vision in invertebrates. Handbook of sensory physiology*, vol. VII/6A. Berlin: Springer-Verlag.

Averill, Edward W. 1982. Color and the anthropocentric problem. *Journal of Philosophy* v. 82, n. 6, 281–303.

Barlow, H. B. 1986. Why have multiple cortical areas? *Vision Research* 26, 23–32.

Barlow, H. B., and Mollon, J. D. (eds.) 1982. *The Senses*. Cambridge: Cambridge University Press.

Barlow, R. B., Chamberlain, S. C., and Kass, L. 1984. Circadian rhythms in retinal function. In Hilfer and Sheffield (eds.) 1984, 31–53.

Bartleson, C. J. 1976. Brown. *Color Research and Application*, v. 1 n. 4, 181–191.

Beck, J. 1972. *Surface color perception*. Ithaca: Cornell University Press.

Békésy, G. von 1959. Similarities between hearing and skin sensations. *Psychological Review*, 66, 1–22.

Békésy, G. von 1970. Improved musical dynamics by variation of apparent size of sound source. *Journal of Music Theory*, v. 14 n. 2, 141–163.

Bennett, Jonathan 1971. *Locke, Berkeley, Hume: Central themes*. Oxford: Clarendon Press.

Berlin, B., and Kay, P. 1969. *Basic color terms*. Berkeley and Los Angeles: University of California Press.

Bidwell, S. 1901. On negative after-images and their relation to certain other visual phenomena. *Proceedings of the Royal Society of London* B 68, 262–289.

Billmeyer, F. W., and Wyszecki, G. (eds.) 1978. *Colour 77*. Bristol: Adam Hilger.

Birren, F. 1961. *Color psychology and color therapy*. Secaucus, N.J.: Citadel.

Blake, A. 1985. On lightness computation in the Mondrian world. In Ottoson and Zeki (eds.) 1985, 45–59.

Blakemore, C. 1973. The baffled brain. Ch. 1 of Gregory and Gombrich (eds.) 1973, 9–48.

Blanshard, B. 1962. *Reason and analysis*. La Salle, Ill.: Open Court.

Bornstein, M. H. 1973. Color vision and color naming: A psychological hypothesis of cultural difference. *Psychological Bulletin* 80, 257–285.

Bornstein, M. H., Kessen, W., and Weiskopf, S. 1976. Color vision and hue categorization in young human infants. *Journal of Experimental Psychology* 2, 115–129.

Bornstein, M. H., and Marks, L. 1982. Color revisionism. *Psychology Today*, Jan. 1982, 64–73.

Bouman, M. A., and Walraven, P. L. 1957. Some color naming experiments for red and green monochromatic lights. *Journal of the Optical Society of America* 47, 834–839.

Boynton, R. M. 1975. Color, hue and wavelength. Ch. 9 of Carterette and Friedman 1975.

Boynton, R. M. 1979. *Human color vision*. New York: Holt, Rinehart and Winston.

Brainard, D. H., and Wandell, B. A. 1986. An analysis of the retinex theory of color vision. *Journal of the Optical Society of America A* 3, 1651–1661.

Bradley, M. C. 1963. Sensations, brain-processes, and colours. *Australasian Journal of Philosophy* 41, 385–393.

Brill, M. H., and West, G. 1986. Chromatic adaptation and color constancy: A possible dichotomy. *Color Research and Application*, v. 11 n. 3, 196–204.

Brindley, G. 1960. *Physiology of the retina and visual pathways*. 1st ed. London: Edward Arnold.

Brindley, G. 1970. *Physiology of the retina and visual pathways*. 2nd ed. Baltimore: Williams and Wilkins.

Brown, J. L. 1965. Afterimages. Ch. 17 of Graham (ed.) 1965.

Brown, R. and Rollins, C. D. 1969. *Contemporary philosophy in Australia*. London: Allen and Unwin.

Bruner, J. S. 1957. Neural mechanisms in perception. *Psychological Review* 64, 340–358.

Buchsbaum, G. 1980. A spatial processor model for object color perception. *Journal of the Franklin Institute* 310, 1–26.

Butler, R. J. (ed.) 1968. *Analytical philosophy, Second series*. Oxford: Blackwell.

Butterfield, J. F. 1968. Subjective (induced) color television. *Society of Motion Picture and Television Engineers Journal* 77, 1025–1028.

Butterfield, J. F. 1970. Subjective color created by black-and-white animation. *Society of Motion Picture and Television Engineers Journal* 79, 523–526.

Campbell, K. 1969. Colours. In Brown and Rollins (eds.) 1969, 132–157.

Campbell, K. 1982. The implications of Land's theory of colour vision. In Cohen (ed.) 1982, 541–552.

Carterette, E. C., and Friedman, M. P. (eds.) 1975. *Handbook of perception*. Vol. V: *Seeing*. New York: Academic Press.

Chang, J. J., and Carroll, J. D. 1980. Three are not enough: An INDSCAL analysis suggesting that color space has seven (±1) dimensions. *Color Research and Application*, v. 5 n. 4, 193–206.

Chapanis, A. 1965. Color names for color space. *American Scientist* 53, 327–346.

Cheng, C-Y. (ed.) 1975. *Philosophical aspects of the mind-body problem.* Honolulu: University Press of Hawaii.

Chevreul, M. E. 1839; 1967. *The principles of harmony and contrast of colors.* New York: Van Nostrand Reinhold.

Churchland, Patricia 1986. *Neurophilosophy.* Cambridge, Mass.: MIT Press.

Churchland, Paul 1984. *Matter and consciousness.* Cambridge, Mass.: MIT Press.

Clark, A. 1985a. Qualia and the psychophysical explanation of color perception. *Synthese* 65, 377–405.

Clark, A. 1985b. A physicalist theory of qualia. *The Monist* 68, 491–506.

Clark, A. 1985c. Spectrum inversion and the color solid. *Southern Journal of Philosophy* 23, 431–443.

Clark, A. forthcoming. *Sensory qualities.*

Cohen, J., and Gordon, P. A. 1949. The Prevost-Fechner-Benham subjective colors. *Psychological Bulletin* 46, 97–136.

Cohen, L. J. (ed.) 1982. *Logic, methodology, and philosophy of science.* Amsterdam: North-Holland.

Cohen, R. S. *et al.* 1974. *PSA 1974.* Dordrecht: Reidel.

Cohen, R. S., and Wartofsky, M. W. (eds.) 1983. *Language, logic and method.* Dordrecht: Reidel.

Commission International de L'Éclairage 1970. See International Commission on Illumination 1970.

Conklin, H. C. 1973. Color categorization. *American Anthropologist* 75, 931–942.

Cornman, J. 1974. Can Eddington's 'two' tables be identical? *Australasian Journal of Philosophy* 52, 22–38.

Cornman, J. 1975. *Perception, common sense and science.* New Haven: Yale University Press.

Cowey, A. 1979. Cortical maps and visual perception. *Quarterly Journal of Experimental Psychology* 31, 1–17.

Crane, H., and Piantanida, T. P. 1983. On seeing reddish green and yellowish blue. *Science* 221, 1078–1080.

Critchley, M. 1965. Acquired anomalies of colour perception of central origin. *Brain* 88, 711–724.

Day, R. H. 1972. Visual spatial illusions: A general explanation. *Science* 175, 1335–1340.

Derrington, A. M., Krauskopf, J., and Lennie, P. 1984. Chromatic mechanisms in lateral geniculate nucleus of macaque. *Journal of Physiology* 357, 241–265.

DeValois, R. L., and DeValois, K. K. 1975. Neural coding of color. Ch. 5 of Carterette and Friedman (eds.) 1975.

Dijksterhuis, E. J. 1961. *The mechanization of the world picture.* Oxford: Oxford University Press.

Dobelle, W. H., Mladejovsky, M. G., and Girvin, J. P. 1974. Artificial vision for the blind: Electrical stimulation of visual cortex offers hope for a functional prosthesis. *Science* 183, 440–444.

Dobelle, W. H., Mladejovsky, M. G., Evans, J. R., Roberts, T. S., and Girvin, J. P. 1976. "Braille" reading by a blind volunteer by visual cortex stimulation. *Nature* 259, 111–112.

Dummett, M. 1975. Wang's paradox. *Synthese* 30, 301–324.

Dummett, M. 1979. Common sense and physics. Ch. 1 of MacDonald (ed.) 1979.

Ekman, G. 1954. Dimensions of color vision. *Journal of Psychology* 38, 467–474.

Estévez, O., and Spekreuse, H. 1982. The "silent substitution" method in visual research. *Vision Research* 22, 681–691.

Evans, R. M. 1948. *An introduction to color.* New York: Wiley.

Evans, R. M. 1974. *The perception of color.* New York: Wiley.

Feigl, H., and Scriven, M. 1956. *Minnesota Studies in the Philosophy of Science.* Vol. 1. Minneapolis: University of Minnesota Press.

Festinger, L., Coren, S., and Rivers, G. 1970. The effect of attention on brightness contrast and assimilation. *American Journal of Psychology* 83, 189–207.

Fieandt, K. von, and Moustgaard, I. K. 1977. *The perceptual world*. London: Academic Press.

French, P., et al. (eds.), 1981. *Foundations of analytic philosophy. Midwest Studies in Philosophy v. 6.* Minneapolis: University of Minnesota Press.

Frisby, J. P. 1980. *Seeing: Illusion, brain and mind*. New York: Oxford University Press.

Fuld, K., Werner, J. S., and Wooten, B. R. 1983. The possible elemental nature of brown. *Vision Research* 23, 631–637.

Gerard, R. M. 1958. *Differential effects of colored lights*. Unpublished Ph.D. dissertation, University of California/Los Angeles.

Gilchrist, A. L. 1977. Perceived lightness depends on perceived spatial arrangement. *Science* 195, 185–187.

Gilchrist, A. L. n.d. Lightness contrast and failures of constancy: a common explanation. In ms.

Gleason, H. A. 1961. *An introduction to descriptive linguistics*. New York: Holt, Rinehart and Winston.

Goethe, J. W. 1840; 1970. *Theory of colors*. Trans. by Eastlake. Cambridge, Mass.: MIT Press.

Goldstein, E. B. 1980. *Sensation and perception*. Belmont, Cal.: Wadsworth.

Gordon, J., and Abramov, I. 1977. Color vision in the peripheral retina. II. Hue and saturation. *Journal of the Optical Society of America* 67, 202–207.

Gouras, P. 1985. Colour coding in the primate retinogeniculate system. In Ottoson and Zeki (eds.) 1985, 183–198.

Gouras, P., and Zrenner, E. 1982. The neural organization of primate color vision. *Color Research and Application*, v. 7 n. 2 pt. 2, 205–208.

Graham, C. H. (ed.) 1965. *Vision and visual perception*. New York: Wiley.

Grassman, H. G. 1853. Theory of compound colors. In MacAdam 1970, 53–60.

Gregory, R. L. 1973. *Eye and brain*. 2nd edition. New York: McGraw-Hill.

Gregory, R. L., and Gombrich, E. H. (eds.) 1973. *Illusion in nature and art*. New York: Scribners.

Haber, R. N., and Hershenson, M. 1980. *The psychology of visual perception*. 2nd edition. New York: Holt, Rinehart and Winston.

Hacker, P. M. S. 1972. *Insight and Illusion*. Oxford: Clarendon Press.

Hård, A, 1976. The Natural Colour System and its universal application in the study of environmental design. In Porter and Mikellides (eds.) 1976, 109–119.

Hård, A., and Sivik, L. 1981. NCS-Natural Color System: A Swedish standard for color notation. *Color Research and Application*, v. 6 n. 3, 129–138.

Hardin, C. L. 1983. Colors, normal observers, and standard conditions. *Journal of Philosophy*, v. 80, n, 12, 806–813.

Hardin, C. L. 1984a. A new look at color. *American Philosophical Quarterly* 21, 125–133.

Hardin, C. L. 1984b. Are scientific objects coloured? *Mind* 93, 491–500.

Hardin, C. L. 1985a. The resemblances of colors. *Philosophical Studies* 48, 35–47.

Hardin, C. L. 1985b. Frank talk about the colours of sense data. *Australasian Journal of Philosophy* 63, 485–493.

Harris, C. S. 1980. Insight or out of sight?: Two examples of perceptual plasticity in the human adult. In Harris (ed.) 1980, 95–150.

Harris, C. S. (ed.) 1980. *Visual coding and adaptability*. Hillsdale, N.J.: Erlbaum.

Harrison, B. 1973. *Form and content*. Oxford: Blackwell.

Harrison, B. 1986. Identity, predication and color. *American Philosophical Quarterly* 23, 105–114.

Harth, E. 1982. *Windows on the mind: Reflections on the physical basis of consciousness*. New York: Morrow.

Heider, E. R. 1972. Universals in color naming and memory. *Journal of Experimental Psychology* 93, 10–20.

Helmholtz, H. von 1911; 1924. *Physiological optics*. 3rd ed. Southall (ed.). New York: Dover.

Helson, H. 1938. Fundamental principles in color vision. I. The principles governing changes in hue, saturation, and lightness of non-selective samples in chromatic illumination. *Journal of Experimental Psychology* 23, 439–471.

Hering, E. 1920; 1964. *Outlines of a theory of the light sense*. Trans. by Hurvich and Jameson. Cambridge, Mass.: Harvard University Press.

Herrington, R. W., and Schneider, P. 1968. The effect of imagery on the waveshape of the visual evoked response. *Experientia* 24/II, 1136–1137.

Hilfer, S. R., and Sheffield, J. B. (eds.) 1984. *Molecular and cellular basis of visual acuity: Cell and developmental biology of the eye.* New York: Springer-Verlag.

Holman, E. L. 1979. Is the physical world colourless? *Australasian Journal of Philosophy* 57, 295–304.

Holman, E. L. 1981. Intension, identity and the colourless physical world: a revision and further discussion. *Australasian Journal of Philosophy* 59, 203–205.

Homer, W. I. 1964. *Seurat and the science of painting.* Cambridge, Mass.: MIT Press.

Horgan, T. 1984. Functionalism, qualia, and the inverted spectrum. *Philosophy and Phenomenological Research* 44, 453–469.

Horn, B. K. P. 1974. Determining lightness from an image. *Computer Graphics and Image Processing* 3, 277–299.

Hood, D. C., and Finkelstein, M. A. 1983. A case for the revision of textbook models of color vision: The detection and appearance of small brief lights. In Mollon and Sharpe (eds.) 1983, 385–398.

Hume, D. 1739;1955. *Treatise of human nature.* Ed. by Selby-Bigge. Oxford: Oxford University Press.

Humphrey, N. K. 1971. Colour and brightness preferences in monkeys. *Nature* 229, 615–617.

Humphrey, N. K. 1976. The colour currency of nature. In Porter and Mikellides (eds.) 1976, 95–98.

Humphrey, N. K. 1972. "Interest" and "pleasure": Two determinants of a monkey's visual preferences. *Perception* 1, 395–416.

Hunt, R. W. G. 1982. A model of colour vision for predicting colour appearance. *Color Research and Application,* v. 7 n. 2 pt. 1, 95–112.

Hurvich, L. M. 1972. Color vision deficiencies. Ch. 23 of Hurvich and Jameson (eds.) 1972.

Hurvich, L. M. 1978. Two decades of opponent process. In Billmeyer and Wyszecki (eds.) 1978, 33–61.

Hurvich, L. M. 1981. *Color vision.* Sunderland, Mass.: Sinauer.

Hurvich, L. M. 1981. Colour vision and its deficiencies. *Impact of Science on Society,* v. 31 n. 2, 151–164.

Hurvich, L. M. 1985. Opponent-colours theory. In Ottoson and Zeki (eds.) 1985, 61–82.

Hurvich, L. M., and Jameson, D. 1955. Some quantitative aspects of an opponent-colors theory: II. Brightness, saturation and hue in normal and dichromatic vision. *Journal of the Optical Society of America* 45, 602–612.

Hurvich, L. M., and Jameson, D. 1956. Some quantitative aspects of an opponent colors theory: IV. A psychological color specification system. *Journal of the Optical Society of America* 46, 416–421.

Hurvich, L. M., and Jameson, D. 1957. An opponent-process theory of color vision. *Psychological Review* 64, 384–108.

Hurvich, L. M., and Jameson, D. 1969. Human color perception: An essay review. *American Scientist* 57, 143–166.

Hurvich, L. M., Jameson, D., and Cohen, J. D. 1968. The experimental determination of unique green in the spectrum. *Perceptual Psychophysics 4*, 65–68.

Ingling, C. 1977. The spectral sensitivity of the opponent-color channels. *Vision Research* 17, 1083–1089.

International Commission on Illumination 1970. *International Lighting Vocabulary*, 3rd edition. Paris: Bureau Centrale de la CIE.

Jackson, F. 1977. *Perception.* Cambridge: Cambridge University Press.

Jacobs, G. H. 1981. *Comparative color vision.* New York: Academic Press.

Jameson, D. 1972. Theoretical issues of color vision. In Jameson and Hurvich (eds.) 1972, 381–412.

Jameson , D. 1985. Opponent-colors theory in the light of physiological findings. In Ottoson and Zeki (eds.) 1985, 83–102.

Jameson, D., and Hurvich, L. M. 1955. Some quantitative aspects of an opponent-colors theory: I. Chromatic responses and spectral saturation. *Journal of the Optical Society of America* 45, 546–552.

Jameson, D., and Hurvich, L. M. 1956. Some quantitative aspects of an opponent-colors theory: III. Changes in brightness, saturation and hue with chromatic adaptation. *Journal of the Optical Society of America* 46, 405–415.

Jameson, D., and Hurvich, L. M. 1961. Complexities of perceived brightness. *Science* 133, 174–179.

Jameson, D. and Hurvich, L. M. (eds.) 1972. *Visual psychophysics.* Vol. VII/4 of *Handbook of sensory physiology.* Berlin: Springer-Verlag.

Jameson, D., and Hurvich, L.M. 1972. Color adaptation: Sensitivity, contrast, afterimages. Ch. 22 of Jameson and Hurvich (eds.) 1972.

Jameson, D., and Hurvich, L. M. 1975. From contrast to assimilation: In art and in the eye. *Leonardo* 8, 125–131.

Jameson, D., and Hurvich, L. M. 1978. Dichromatic color language: "Reds" and "greens" don't look alike but their colors do. *Sensory Processes* 2, 146–155.

Jameson, D., Hurvich, L. M., and Varner, F. D. 1979. Receptoral and postreceptoral visual processes in recovery from chromatic adaptation. *Proceedings of the National Academy of Sciences U.S.A.* 76, 3034–3038.

Judd, D. B. 1940. Hue, saturation and lightness of surface colors with chromatic illumination. *Journal of the Optical Society of America* 30, 2–32.

Judd, D. B. 1960. Appraisal of Land's work in two-primary color projections. *Journal of the Optical Society of America* 50, 254–268.

Judd, D. B., and Wyszecki, G. 1963. *Color in business, science and industry.* 2nd edition. New York: Wiley.

Kaiser, P. 1984. Physiological response to color: A critical review. *Color Research and Application,* v. 9 n. 1, 29–36.

Keating, E. G. 1979. Rudimentary color vision in the monkey after removal of striate and preoccipital cortex. *Brain Research* 179, 379–384.

Kelly, K. L., and Judd, D. B. 1976. *Color: Universal language and dictionary of names.* National Bureau of Standards Special Publication 440. Washington: U.S. Government Printing Office.

Kenner, L. 1965. The triviality of the red-green problem. *Analysis* 25, 147–153.

Krauss, R. N. 1968. Language as a symbolic process in communication. *American Scientist* 56, 265–278.

Krauskopf, J. (ed.) 1986. *Computational approaches to color vision.* Feature section of *Journal of the Optical Society of America A,* v. 3 n. 10, 1648–1757.

Krüger, J., and Fischer, B. 1983. Colour columns and colour areas. In Mollon and Sharpe (eds.) 1983, 291–296.

Kuehni, R. G. 1983. *Color: Essence and logic.* New York: Van Nostrand.

Lamb, T. D. 1985. Properties of cone photoreceptors in relation to colour vision. In Ottoson and Zeki (eds.) 1985, 151–164.

Land, E. H. 1959. Experiments in color vision. *Scientific American,* v. 200 n. 5, 84–99.

Land, E. H. 1977. The retinex theory of color vision. *Scientific American,* v. 237 n. 6, 108–128.

Land, E. H. 1983. Recent advances in retinex theory and some implications for cortical computations: Color vision and the natural image. *Proceedings of the National Academy of Sciences* 80, 5163–5169.

Land, E. H. 1985. Recent advances in retinex theory. In Ottoson and Zeki (eds.) 1985, 5–18.

Land, E. H., Hubel, D. H., Livingstone, M. S., Perry, S. H., and Burns, M. M. 1983. Colour-generating interactions across the corpus callosum. *Nature* 303, 616–618.

Land, E. H., and McCann, J. J. 1971. Lightness and retinex theory. *Journal of the Optical Society of America* 61, 1–11.

Lennie, P. 1984. Recent developments in the physiology of color vision. *Trends in Neurosciences*, v. 7 n. 7, 243–248.

Levine, J. 1983. Materialism and qualia: The explanatory gap. *Pacific Philosophical Quarterly* 64, 354–361.

Levine, M., and Shefner, J. M. 1981. *Fundamentals of sensation and perception.* Reading, Mass.: Addison-Wesley.

Linksz, A. 1964. *An Essay on color vision.* New York: Grune and Stratton.

Linsky, B. 1984. The identity of indistinguishables. *Synthese* 59, 363–380.

Livingstone, M. S., and Hubel, D. H. 1984. Anatomy and physiology of a color system in the primate visual cortex. *Journal of Neuroscience* 4, 309–356.

MacAdam, D. L. (ed.) 1970. *Sources of color science.* Cambridge, Mass: MIT Press.

Mach, E. 1897; 1959. *Contributions to the analysis of the sensations.* Trans. by Williams. La Salle, Ill.: Open Court.

MacLeod, D. I. A. 1985. Receptoral constraints on colour appearance. In Ottoson and Zeki (eds.) 1985, 103–116.

MacDonald, G. F. (ed.) 1979. *Perception and identity: Essays presented to A. J. Ayer with his replies.* Ithaca, N.Y.: Cornell University Press.

Maloney, L. T., and Wandell, B. A. 1986. Color constancy: A method for recovering surface spectral reflectance. *Journal of the Optical Society of America A* 3, 29–33.

Marks, L. E. 1978. *The unity of the senses.* New York: Academic Press.

Marmor, G. S. 1978. Age at onset of blindness and the development of the semantics of color names. *Journal of Experimental Child Psychology* 25, 267–278.

Marr, D. 1982. *Vision.* New York: Freeman.

Mazokhin-Porshnyakov, G. 1969. *Insect vision.* Trans. by Masironi and Masironi. New York: Plenum.

McCann, J. J., and Benton, J. L. 1969. Interaction of the long-wave cones and the rods to produce color sensations. *Journal of the Optical Society of America* 59, 103–107.

McCann, J. J., McKee, S. P., and Taylor, T. H. 1976. Quantitative studies in retinex theory. A comparison between theoretical predictions and observer responses to the "color Mondrian" experiments. *Vision Research* 16, 445–458.

McCollough, C. 1965. Color adaptation of edge-detectors in the human visual system. *Science* 149, 1115–1116.

McGilvray, J. A. 1983. To color. *Synthese* 54, 37–70.

McNeill, N. B. 1972. Colour and colour terminology. *Journal of Linguistics* 8, 21–33.

Menzel, R. 1979. Spectral sensitivity and colour vision in invertebrates. Ch. 9 of Autrum (ed.) 1979.

Menzel, R. 1985. Colour pathways and colour vision in the honeybee. In Ottoson and Zeki (eds.) 1985, 211–234.

Michael, C. R. 1985. Non-oriented double opponent colour cells are concentrated in two subdivisions of cortical layer IV. In Ottoson and Zeki (eds.) 1985, 199–210.

Mollon, J. D., and Sharpe, L. T. (eds.) 1983. *Colour Vision.* New York: Academic Press.

Moreland, J. D. 1972. Peripheral color vision. Ch. 20 of Jameson and Hurvich (eds.) 1972, 517–536.

Mountcastle, V. B. 1967. The problem of sensing and the neural coding of sensory events. In Quarton *et al.* (eds.) 1967.

Mundle, C. W. K. 1971. *Perception: Facts and theories.* New York: Oxford University Press.

Munsell, A. H. 1946. *A color notation.* 14th ed. Baltimore: Munsell Color.

Munsell Color Company 1976. *Munsell book of color.* Baltimore: Munsell Color.

Nassau, K. 1980. The causes of color. *Scientific American* v. 242 n. 10, 124–154.

Nassau, K. 1983. *The physics and chemistry of color: The fifteen causes of color.* New York: Wiley.

Newton, I. 1730;1952. *Opticks,* 4th ed. New York: Dover.

Noorlander, C., Koenderink, J. J., den Ouden, R. J., and Edens, B. W. 1983. Sensitivity to spatiotemporal colour contrast in the peripheral visual field. *Vision Research* 23, 1–11.

Ottoson, D., and Zeki, S. (eds.) 1985. *Central and peripheral mechanisms of colour vision.* London: Macmillan.

Pap, A. 1957. Once more: Colors and the synthetic a priori. *Philosophical Review* 66, 94–99.

Parikh, R. 1983. The problem of vague predicates. In Cohen and Wartofsky (eds.) 1983, 241–261.

Peacocke, C. 1981. Are vague predicates incoherent? *Synthese* 46, 121–141.

Perkins, M. 1983. *Sensing the world.* Indianapolis: Hackett.

Perky, C. 1910. An experimental study of imagination. *American Journal of Psychology* 21, 422–452.

Pickford, R. W. 1951. *Individual differences in colour vision.* London: Routledge and Kegan Paul.

Porter, T. 1973. An investigation into colour preferences. *Designer*

Porter, T., and Mikellides, B. (eds.) 1976. *Color for Architecture.* New York: Van Nostrand.

Putnam, H. 1956. Reds, greens and logical analysis. *Philosophical Review* 65, 206–217.

Putnam, H. 1957. Red and green all over again: A rejoinder to Pap. *Philosophical Review* 66, 100–103.

Quarton, G. C., Melnechuck, T., and Schmitt, F. O. (eds.) 1967. *The Neurosciences.* New York: Rockefeller University Press.

Quine, W. V. O. 1973. *The roots of reference.* La Salle, Ill.: Open Court.

Radford, C. 1965. Incompatibilities of Colours. *Philosophical Quarterly* 15 207–219.

Ratliff, F. 1965. *Mach bands: Quantitative studies on neural networks in the retina.* San Francisco: Holden-Day.

Ratliff, F. 1972. Contour and contrast. *Scientific American* 236, 91–101.

Ratliff, F. 1976. On the psychophysical bases of universal color terms. *Proceedings of the American Philosophical Society,* v. 120 n. 5, 311–330.

Remnant, P. 1961. Red and green all over again. *Analysis* 21, 93–95.

Rhees, R. 1954. Can there be a private language? *Proceedings of the Aristotelian Society.* Supplementary volume 28, 77–94.

Rohrlich, F., and Hardin, L. 1983. Established theories. *Philosophy of Science* 50, 603–617.

Rosch, E. H. 1973. Natural categories. *Cognitive Psychology* 4, 328–350.

Rossotti, H. 1983. *Colour: Why the world isn't grey.* Princeton: Princeton University Press.

Rozeboom, W. W. 1958. The logic of color words. *Philosophical Review* 67, 353–366.

Salapatek, P, and Cohen, L. B. (eds.) in press. *Handbook of Infant Perception.* New York: Academic Press.

Sanford, D. H. 1981. Illusions and sense-data. In French *et al.* (eds.) 1981, 371–385.

Savage, C. W. 1970. *The measurement of sensation.* Berkeley: University of California Press.

Schein, S. J., Marrocco, R. T., and de Monasterio, F. M. 1982. Is there a high concentration of color-selective cells in area V4 of monkey visual cortex? *Journal of Neurophysiology* 47, 193–213.

Schilpp, P. A. (ed.) 1959. *The philosophy of C. D. Broad.* New York: Tudor.

Schrödinger, E. 1926; 1970. Thresholds of color differences. In MacAdam (ed.) 1970.

Schwartz, E. 1983. Cortical mapping and perceptual invariance. *Vision Research* 23, 831–835.

Sellars, W. 1956. Empiricism and the philosophy of mind. In Feigl and Scriven (eds.) 1956.

Shapley, R. 1986. The importance of contrast for the activity of single neurons, the VEP and perception. *Vision Research* 26, 45–61.

Shepard, R. N. 1962. The analysis of proximities: Multidimensional scaling with an unknown distance function II. *Psychometrika* 27, 219–245.

Shoemaker, S. 1975. Functionalism and qualia. *Philosophical Studies.* 27. 291–315. Also in Shoemaker 1984a, 184–205.

Shoemaker, S. 1984a. *Identity, cause and mind: Philosophical essays.* Cambridge: Cambridge University Press.

Shoemaker, S. 1984b. The inverted spectrum. In Shoemaker 1984a, 325-357.

Sivik, L. 1976. The language of colour: Colour connotations. In Porter and Mikellides (eds.) 1976, 123-139.

Smart, J. J. C. 1961. Colours. *Philosophy* 36, 128-142.

Smart, J. J. C. 1975. On some criticisms of a physicalist theory of colors. In Cheng (ed.) 1975, 54-63.

Svaetichin, G. and MacNichol, E. F., Jr. 1958. Retinal mechanisms for chromatic and achromatic vision. *Annals of the New York Academy of Sciences* 74, 385-404.

Swartz, R. J. (ed.) 1965. *Perceiving, sensing and knowing.* Berkeley: University of California Press.

Swets, J. A. (ed.) 1964. *Signal detection and recognition by human observers.* New York: Wiley.

Teller, D. Y. 1980. Locus questions in visual science. In Harris (ed.) 1980, 151-176.

Teller, D. Y. 1984. Linking propositions. *Vision Research* 24, 1233-1246.

Teller, D. Y., and Bornstein, M. H. in press. Infant color vision and color perception. In Salapatek and Cohen (eds.) in press.

Teller, D. Y., and Pugh Jr., E. N. 1983. Linking propositions in color vision. In Mollon and Sharpe (eds.) 1983, 577-596.

Terstiege, H. 1983. The C.I.E. coding system. In Mollon and Sharpe (eds.) 1983, 563-567.

Thomas, J. P. 1970. Model of the function of receptive fields in human vision. *Psychological Review* 77, 121-134.

Thornton, J. E., and Pugh Jr., E. N. 1983. Red/green color opponency at detection threshold. *Science* 219, 191-193.

Travis, C. 1985. Vagueness, observation and sorites. *Mind* v. 94, n. 375, 345-366.

Uttal, W. R. 1981. *A taxonomy of visual processes.* Hillsdale, N.J.: Erlbaum.

Van Esch, J. A., Koldenhof, E. E., Van Doorn, A. J., and Koenderink, J. J. 1984. Spectral sensitivity and wavelength discrimination of the human peripheral visual field. *Journal of the Optical Society of America A*, 1, 443-450.

Vickers, D. 1979. *Decision processes in visual perception.* New York: Academic Press.

Vision, G. 1983. Primary and secondary qualities: An essay in epistemology. *Erkenntnis* 17, 135–169.

Vos, J. J. 1986. Are unique and invariant hues coupled? *Vision Research* 26, 337–342.

Walls, G. L. 1960. "Land! Land!" *Psychological Bulletin* 57, 27–48.

Wasserman, G. S. 1978. *Color vision: An historical introduction.* New York: Wiley.

Werner, J. S., and Wooten, B. R. 1979. Opponent chromatic mechanisms: Relation to photopigments and hue naming. *Journal of the Optical Society of America* 69, 422–434.

Westheimer, G. 1972. Visual acuity and spatial modulation thresholds. Ch. 7 of Jameson and Hurvich (eds.) 1972.

Westphal, J. 1982. Brown: Remarks on colour. *Inquiry* 25, 417–433.

Westphal, J. 1984. The complexity of quality. *Philosophy* 59, 457–472.

Wilson, G. D. 1966. Arousal properties of red versus green. *Perceptual and Motor Skills* 23, 947–949.

Wilson, M. H., and Brocklebank, R. W. 1955. Complementary hues of after-images. *Journal of the Optical Society of America* 45, 293–299.

Wilson, M. H., and Brocklebank, R. W. 1961. Colour and perception: The work of Edwin Land in the light of current concepts. *Contemporary Physics* 3, 91–111.

Wittgenstein, L. 1977. *Remarks on color.* Ed. by Anscombe, Berkeley: University of California Press.

Worthey, J. A. 1985. Limitations of color constancy. *Journal of the Optical Society of America A* 2, 1014–1026.

Wright, A. A., and Cummings, W. W. 1971. Color-naming functions for the pigeon. *Journal of the Experimental Analysis of Behavior* 15, 7–17.

Wright, B., and Rainwater, L. 1962. The meaning of color. *The Journal of General Psychology* 67, 89–99.

Wright, C. 1975. On the coherence of vague predicates. *Synthese* 30, 325–365.

Wright, W. D. 1967. *The rays are not coloured.* Bristol, U. K.: Adam Hilger.

Wyszecki, G., and Stiles, W. S. 1967. *Color science.* New York: Wiley.

Yarbus, A. L. 1967. *Eye movements and vision.* Trans. Haigh. New York: Plenum.

Yolton, J. 1984. *Perceptual acquaintance from Descartes to Reid.* Minneapolis: University of Minnesota Press.

Zeki, S. 1973. Colour coding in rhesus monkey prestriate cortex. *Brain Research* 53, 422–427.

Zeki, S. 1980. The representation of colours in the cerebral cortex. *Nature* 284, 412–418.

Zeki, S. 1985. Colour pathways and hierarchies in the cerebral cortex. In Ottoson and Zeki (eds.) 1985, 19–44.

Zrenner, E. 1983. Neurophysiological aspects of colour vision mechanisms in the primate retina. In Mollon and Sharpe (eds.) 1983, 195–210.

Zrenner, E. 1985. A new concept for the contribution of retinal colour-opponent ganglion cells to hue discrimination and colour constancy: The zero signal detector. In Ottoson and Zeki (eds.) 1985, 165–182.

Acknowledgments

Figure I-1 from page 32 of *The Physics of Chemistry and Color* by Kurt Nassau. Copyright © 1983 by John Wiley & Sons. Reproduced by permission of the publisher.

Figure I-2 from page 32 of *Vision and the Eye* (second edition) by M. H. Pirenne. Copyright © 1967 by Methuen & Co. Reproduced by permission.

Figure I-3 from "Organization of the primate retina" by J. E. Dowling and B. B. Boycott, *Proceedings of the Royal Society of London*, B 166. Reproduced by permission of the authors and publisher.

Figures I-4 and I-9 from *Illusion in Nature and Art*, edited by R. L. Gregory and E. H. Gombrich. Copyright © 1973 by Colin Blakemore, Jan B. Deregowski, E. H. Gombrich, R. L. Gregory, H. E. Hinton, and Roland Penrose. Reproduced with the permission of Charles Scribner's Sons.

Figures I-6, I-7A and I-7B from *The Pyschology of Visual Perception* (second edition) by R. N. Haber and M. Hershenson. Copyright © 1980 by Holt, Rinehart and Winston. Reproduced by permission of the publisher.

Figure I-11 from "Neural coding of color" by R. L. DeValois and K. K. DeValois, in *Seeing*, volume V of *Handbook of Perception* edited by E. C. Carterette and M. P. Friedman. Copyright © 1975 by Academic Press. Reproduced by permission of the publisher and authors.

Figure I-12 and I-18 from *Comparative Color Vision* by G. H. Jacobs. Copyright © 1981 by Academic Press. Reproduced by permission of the publisher.

Figure I-15 from "The analysis of proximities: multidimensional scaling with an unknown distance function, II" by R. N. Shepard, in *Psychometrika 27*, 1962, p. 236. Reproduced by permission of *Psychometrika*.

Figure I-16 from "Opponent chromatic mechanisms" by J. S. Werner and B. R. Wooten, in *Journal of the Optical Society of America*, 69, number 3, p. 428. Reproduced by permission of the authors and the Optical Society of America.

Figure I-17 from *The Measurement of Colour* (4th edition) by W. D. Wright. Copyright © 1969 by Adam Hilger, IOP Publishing Ltd., Redcliffe Way, Bristol. Reproduced by permission of the author and publisher.

Figures II-1, III-1, and III-5 from *Color Vision* by Leo M. Hurvich. Copyright © 1981 by Sinauer Associates. Reproduced by permission of the author.

Figure II–4 from *Color in Business, Science and Industry* (2nd edition) by D. Judd and G. Wyszecki. Copyright © 1963 by John Wiley & Sons. Reproduced by permission of the publisher.

Figures II–5A and II–5B from "An opponent-process theory of color vision" by L. M. Hurvich and D. Jameson in *Psychological Review*, 64, 1957, p. 389. Reproduced by permission of the authors.

Figure II–9 from Rosenblith, *Sensory Communication*. Reproduced courtesy of MIT Press.

Figure III–2 from "NCS-Natural Color System: A Swedish standard for color notation" from A. Hard and L. Sivik, in *Color Research and Application*, vol. 6, no. 3. Copyright © 1981 by John Wiley & Sons. Reproduced by permission of the publisher.

Figure III–3 from "Color-naming functions for the pigeon" by A. A. Wright and W. W. Cummings, in *Journal of the Experimental Analysis of Behavior* 15, 1971, p. 12. Reproduced by permission of the *Journal*.

Figure III–4 adapted from *Basic Color Terms* by B. Berlin and P. Kay. Copyright © 1969 by the University of California Press and the Regents of the University of California. Used by permission of the publisher.

Figure III–6 from *The Senses* edited by H. B. Barlow and J. D. Mollon. Copyright © 1982 by Cambridge University Press. Reprinted by permission of the publisher and authors.

Plate 1: "Spectrum Graph Paper," reprinted courtesy of the Technical and Education Center of the Graphic Arts, College of Graphic Arts and Photography, Rochester Institute of Technology, Rochester, New York.

Plate 3: Catalogue 1970.253, *Haystack in Winter* by Oscar Claude Monet (French 1840–1926), oil on canvas, 65.4 × 92.3 cm. (25 3/4 × 36 3/8 in.). Gift of the Misses Aimee and Rosamond Lamb in memory of Mr. and Mrs. Horatio A. Lamb. Courtesy, Museum of Fine Arts, Boston.

Plate 4: from Plate VIII–8 of *Interaction of Color* by Josef Albers. Copyright © 1963 by Yale University Press. Reprinted courtesy of the publisher.

Plate 6: from Plate XI of *An Introduction to Color* by Ralph M. Evans. Copyright © 1948 by John Wiley & Sons. Reproduced by permission of the publisher.

I N D E X E S

INDEX OF NAMES

Abramov, I., 206
Akita, M., 199
Armstrong, D. M., 60, 113, 114, 123, 128, 179
Austin, J., 202
Austin J. L., 69
Averill, E. W., 198

Barlow, H. B., 25, 206
Barlow, R. B., 197
Beck, J., 86, 199, 200
Békésy, G. von, 168, 203
Bennett, J., 198
Benton, J. L., 10
Berkeley, G., 71
Berlin, B., 140, 156, 204, 207
Bezold, W. von, 72, 102, 103
Bidwell, S., 93
Blake, A., 190
Blakemore, C., 200
Blanshard, B., 121, 122
Bornstein, M. H., 156, 163, 167, 196
Bouman, M. A., 100
Boynton, R. M., 42, 146, 207
Brindley, G., 40
Broad, C. D., 108, 201
Brocklebank, R. W., 92, 188
Brown, J. L., 93
Buchsbaum, G., 190
Butterfield, J. F., 72

Campbell, K., 198
Chamberlain, S. C., 197
Chang, J. J., 120
Chomsky, N., 169

Churchland, P., 144
Clark, A., 202
Cohen, J., 79
Conklin, H. C., 156
Coren, S., 199, 200
Cornman, J., 60
Cowey, A., 112
Crane, H., 124, 125
Critchley, M., 200
Cummings, W. W., 152

Delacroix, E., 49
Democritus, 59
Derrington, A. M., 197
DeValois, K. K., and R. R., 52, 57, 197
Dijksterhuis, E. J., 156
Dummett, M., 205

Ebbinghaus, H., 203
Ejima, Y., 199
Ekman, G., 42
Evans, R. M., 25, 51, 86, 87, 88, 89, 106, 182, 183, 188, 200, 207

Festinger, L., 199, 200
Fieandt, K. von, 10
Finkelstein, M. A., 180
Fischer, B., 197
Frisby, J. P., 197, 200

Gerard, R. M., 166
Gleason, H. A., 155
Goethe, J. W., 50, 188
Gordon, J., 206

Graham, C. H., 53
Grassman, H. G., 29, 196

Haber, R. N., 10, 25
Hacker, P. M. S., 202, 204
Hård, A., 116, 201
Hardin, C. L., 198
Harris, C. S., 53, 200
Harrison, B., 142–145, 202
Heider, E. R., 41
Helmholtz, H. von, 30, 83, 189, 196
Helson, H., 192
Hering, E., 29, 30, 37, 40, 53, 83, 189, 196, 197
Herrington, R. W., 201
Hershenson, M., 10, 11, 25
Homer, W. I., 200
Hood, D. C., 180
Hubel, D. H., 54, 197
Hume, D., 42, 81, 96, 97, 108, 128, 140
Humphrey, N. K., 203, 205
Hunt, R. W. G., 35, 196
Hurvich, L. M., 30, 39, 40, 49, 51, 52, 78, 79, 83, 94, 110, 114, 162, 188, 189, 196, 197, 199, 200, 201, 203, 207

Ingling, C., 34, 38

Jackson, F., 96, 97, 105, 201
Jacobs, G. H., 152, 154, 181, 197, 203
Jameson, D., 30, 39, 40, 49, 79, 83, 114, 162, 192, 197, 199, 200, 201
Judd, D. B., 11, 67, 69, 73, 95, 120, 141, 182, 183, 184, 188, 192, 199, 200, 204, 205, 207

Kaiser, P., 166, 203
Kass, L., 197
Kay, P., 140, 156, 204, 207
Keating, E. G., 149–150
Kelly, K. L., 67, 141, 183, 184
Kessen, W., 196
Krauskopf, J., 197
Kries, J. von, 49
Krüger, J., 197
Kuehni, R. G., 120, 142, 201, 204, 207

Lamb, T. D., 49
Land, E. H., 50, 87, 187, 197
Leibniz, G. W., 134–135
Lennie, P., 33, 197, 192
Levine, J., 135, 203
Levine, M., 53, 131, 197, 200, 206
Linsky, B., 205
Livingstone, M. S., 197
Locke, J., 71, 132, 198

MacAdam, D. L., 178
Mach, E., 16, 53, 104, 197
MacLeod, D. I., 197
MacNichol, E. F., 30
Marks, L. E., 131, 132, 133, 163
Marr, D., 190, 192
Mazokhin-Porshnyakov, G., 152
McCann, J. J., 10, 191
McCollough, C., 200
Menzel, R., 131, 148, 151
Mollon, J. D., 25, 197, 206
Monet, C., 51, 86, 87
Moore, G. E., 42
Moreland, J. D., 101
Moses, Grandma, 86, 87
Moustgaard, I. K., 10
Munsell, A. H., 159, 203, 204

Nassau, K., 2, 4, 195
Newton, I., 187

Ottoson, D., 197

Pap, A., 202
Parikh, R., 205
Peacocke, C., 205
Perky, C., 201
Piantanida, T., 124, 125, 202
Pickford, R. W., 163, 164
Price, H. H., 108, 201
Pugh, Jr., E. N., 40
Putnam, H., 202

Quine, W. V. O., 204

Radford, C., 202
Rainwater, L., 202
Ratliff, F., 156, 162, 168
Remnant, P., 202
Rhees, R., 155
Rivers, G., 199, 200
Robson, J. G., 53
Rohrlich, F., 198
Rosch, E., 41, 117, 168, 205
Rumford, Count (B. Thompson), 188
Russell, B., 90
Ryff, W., 155

Sanford, D. H., 201
Schilpp, P. A., 201
Schneider, P., 201
Schrödinger, E., 175
Sellars, W., 198
Seurat, G. P., 71, 102

Shapley, R., 189, 192, 197
Sharpe, L. T., 197
Sheffner, J. M., 53, 131, 197, 200, 206
Shepard, R. N., 42
Shoemaker, S., 142–143
Sivik, L., 116, 201, 202
Smart, J. J. C., 81, 198
Stiles, W. S., 67, 160, 178, 195, 199, 204, 206
Svaetichin, G., 30
Swets, J. A., 206

Takahashi, S., 199
Teller, D. Y., 16, 35, 40, 112, 163, 196, 205
Terstiege, H., 89
Travis, C., 205

Uttal, W. A., 112, 197

van Esch, J. A., 173
Vickers, D., 180, 206

Walls, G. L., 51, 188, 189
Walraven, P. L., 100
Washington, G., 102
Wasserman, G. S., 105, 196
Weiskopf, S., 196
Weiskrantz, L., 150
Weisstein, N., 53
Werner, J. S., 35, 42, 174, 203, 206
Wiesel, T., 54
Wilson, M. H., 92, 188
Wittgenstein L., 202, 204
Wooten, B. R., 35, 42, 174, 203, 206

Worthey, J. A., 191, 197
Wright, A. A., 152
Wright, B., 202
Wright, C., 170, 178, 182, 205
Wyszecki, G., 11, 67, 69, 70, 73,
    95, 120, 160, 178, 182, 195,
    199, 200, 204, 205, 206, 207

Yarbus, A. L., 22
Yolton, J., 8
Young, T., 189, 196

Zeki, S., 192, 197
Zrenner, E., 199

INDEX OF SUBJECTS

achromatic colors, 25
adaptation, 25, 48, 83, 93
"advancing" and "receding"
    colors, 129
afterimages, 51, 92, 140
algorithmic models of lightness
    and color constancy, 190,
    207
alien colors, 145
analysis of proximities, 41
anomalous trichromats, 78
anthropocentric properties, 65,
    198
aperture colors, 46, 114
aperture mode, 84
average observer (C.I.E.), 28,
    89, 159, 162, 182, 199, 200
    and 10-degree viewing field,
    70
    and 2-degree viewing field,
    70

base rate, 13
basic color terms, 156
    evolution of, 164
Benham disk, 72, 91
Bezold-Brücke hue shift, 45, 70,
    142
binary hues, 39
"blind sight," 150

blind spot, 8
brain gray, 23, 95, 174
brightness, 26
Brunswik ratio scale, 86
Bureau of Standards and the
    Inter-Society Color Council,
    182, 184
Butterfield encoder, 72

C.I.E. (Commission Interna-
    tionale de l'Éclairage), 70,
    73, 207
    see also 'average observer'
    and 'standard light
    sources'
Chroma (Munsell), 80, 159, 201
chromatic adaptation, 48, 83
chromatic cancellation proce-
    dure, 39
chromatic colors, 26
chromatic response, 36, 76,
    117, 160
chromatically opponent cells,
    52
chromaticness (NCS), 119
"class A" and "class B" exper-
    iments, 40
cognitive states and sensory
    states, 87

color categories in everyday
life, 88, 90, 183
color category boundaries, 157,
166, 169, 179, 183, 184
color category foci, 157
color constancy, 46, 83, 191
color deficiency, 10, 78, 145
color memory, 49, 89, 183
color naming, 42, 117, 122, 141,
174, 206
color order systems and
spaces:
H-S, 116, 139
H-B-S, 127, 203
Munsell, 159, 184, 201, 203,
204
NCS, 116, 127, 140, 200
OSA-UCS, 119
limitations on, 120, 126, 146
color qualities, essential properties of, 66, 126, 202
color television, 33, 71
color vision of other species,
148
colored shadows, 50, 188
complements, 39
complex cells, 56
cone-excitation ratios, 27
cones, 10, 26
connections across sensory modalities, 131
"cool" hues, 129, 131, 137
correct rejection (signal detection theory), 177
cortical blindness, 150
cortical chromatic mechanisms,
56, 192
criterion (signal detection theory), 177

Dani people of New Guinea,
41, 117, 168
dichroic materials, 6, 69

dichromats, 78, 145, 150
distributed representation, 53
dominant wavelength, 28, 160,
204
double-opponent cells, 52

eigengrau 23. See 'brain gray'
elementary colors (NCS), 116,
128, 140, 183
elevation words, 168
emotional response to color,
163, 166, 205
externality of colors, illusion of,
82
eye-tracker, 125

false alarm (signal detection
theory), 177
"feature detectors," 56, 94,
110, 181
filling-in, 22, 92, 124
filters, 69
fovea, 8, 11
functionalists, 144

ganglion cells, 12
ganzfeld, 22
gerrymandered physical properties, 65, 81
Grassman's laws, 151

Haidinger brush, 198
Hermann grid illusion, 17
hit (signal detection theory),
177
Hue-Brightness-Saturation
space, 127
hues, 25, 159, 201
binary, 39, 116, 185
novel, 144
unique, 37
hue coding, 130

hue-cancellation, 52
Hue-Saturation space, 116, 139

Impressionist painters, 50
indeterminacy, 97, 108, 180
    of colors, 81, 101, 170, 180,
    205
    of color-term boundaries, 170
individual differences, 79, 163,
    182
infant color vision, 41
Inter-Society Color Council-
    National Bureau of Stan-
    dards, 141, 182
irradiance, 63
isomeric color matches, 28, 73

just-noticeable differences, 178

lateral geniculate nucleus, 54
lateral inhibition, 15
    Hering-type, 53, 197
light and dark colors, 129
lightness, 26
lightness constancy, 25, 86
luminance, 33

Mach bands, 16, 17, 53
Mach card, 88, 104
machine vision, 190
macula lutea, 11, 22
macular pigment, 71, 167
mathematical opponent the-
    ory, 34
Maxwell spot, 11
McCullough aftereffect, 93
memory color, 105
metameric color matches, 28,
    46, 64, 73, 78, 191, 206
miss (signal detection theory),
    177
Mondrian image, 190

monochromats, 78
Munsell Book of Color, 68, 80,
    119, 159, 185
Munsell color chips, 182, 191
Munsell Color Company, 157,
    199
Munsell color system, 119, 141,
    159, 184, 201
Munsell-C.I.E. conversion
    charts, 160, 206
Müller-Lyer illusion, 87, 106

Natural Color System (NCS),
    116, 127, 140, 200
Necker cube, 88, 106, 112
neural code, 34, 171
neural unit, 12, 52
normal conditions, 183
normal observers, 67, 76, 80, 89
novel colors, 144

objectivism, 59, 65
on-center, off-surround unit,
    13
opponent pair, 26
opponent theory, 30, 52
optic chiasma, 53
optic disk, 8, 22
optical fusion, 71, 102
Optical Society of America, 159
Optical Society of America—
    Uniform Color Space, 119

peripheral vision, 101, 205
phosphenes, 94
photopigment absorption, 31
polarity, 130
polarized light, 198
primaries:
    light-mixing (additive), 28,
    42

colorant-mixing (subtractive), 42, 196
principle of univariance, 26

radiance, 63
receptive field, 12
reddish green, 29, 124
reduction screen, 24, 49, 83
related colors, 116
relative reflectance of opaque bodies, 63, 80
relative spectral energy of light sources, 63, 80
relative transmittance of transparent or translucent bodies, 63
resemblance route, 114
retinal image, 8
Retinex (retina-cortex) Theory, 188
rods, 10

saturation, 26, 35, 119, 140
sense data, 95
sensitivity, 177
sensory states and cognitive states, 87
"shade" of color, 89, 200
signal-detection theory, 206
signal/noise ratio, 173
simple cells, 56
simple, unanlyzable qualities, 42
simultaneous contrast, 24, 49, 53, 84, 87, 92, 141, 151, 189
source A (incandescent lamp), 73
source B (near sunlight), 73
source C (near daylight), 73
spatial opponency, 52
spectral inversion, 138, 142
spreading effect, 72, 102, 110
stability of colors, 82

stabilized images, 22, 124
standard conditions, 67, 80, 183
standard light sources (C.I.E.):
source A (incandescent), 73
source B (near sunlight), 73
source C (near daylight), 73
standard observer, 62
see also 'average observer' and 'normal observer'
"subjective" colors, 72, 92
subjectivism, 59, 65, 67, 81, 198
successive contrast (afterimaging), 51, 92, 140
surface colors, 46

tetrachromat, 146
threshold of detection, 98
threshold of discrimination, 174, 206
translucent materials, 69
trichromats, 78
tristimulus values, 76

unique hues, 37
unique-hue axis, 54
unrelated colors, 114

Value (Munsell), 80, 159, 201
variations among normal subjects, 163
viewing tube, 24, 70
visual colorimetry, 69
visual cortex, 54
visual evoked response, 201
visual periphery, 173
visual shape, 82, 111, 199
von Kries-type shift, 189

"warm" and "cool" colors, 129, 131, 137

yellowish blue, 29, 124